MOTHERS & DAUGHTERS

Funded by the Government of Canada
Financé par la gouvernement du Canada | Canada

Demeter Press
140 Holland Street West
P. O. Box 13022
Bradford, ON L3Z 2Y5
Tel: (905) 775-9089
Email: info@demeterpress.org
Website: www.demeterpress.org

Demeter Press logo based on the sculpture "Demeter" by Maria-Luise Bodirsky
www.keramik-atelier.bodirsky.de

Printed and Bound in Canada

Library and Archives Canada Cataloguing in Publication

Mothers and daughters (Bradford, Ont.)
Mothers and daughters / edited by Dannabang Kuwabong, Janet MacLennan, and Dorsía Smith Silva.

Includes bibliographical references.
ISBN 978-1-77258-133-1 (softcover)

1. Mothers and daughters — Literary collections.
I. Kuwabong, Dannabang, 1955–, editor II. Smith Silva, Dorsía, editor
III. MacLennan, Janet, 1975–, editor IV. Title.

PN6071.M7M62 2017 808.8'035252 C2017-906718-4

MIX
Paper from responsible sources
FSC® C004071

MOTHERS & DAUGHTERS

EDITED BY
DANNABANG KUWABONG, JANET MACLENNAN,
AND DORSÍA SMITH SILVA

DEMETER

DEMETER PRESS, BRADFORD, ONTARIO

To the mothers that love their daughters
fiercely, boldly, and very proudly.

Table of Contents

III. Mothers and Daughters in Literature

Acknowledgments

We are deeply indebted to our friends and family for their words of understanding and ecnouragement. We give you a million thanks.

Introduction

Facets of Mothers and Daughters

DANNABANG KUWABONG, JANET MACLENNAN AND
DORSÍA SMITH SILVA

> *Each facet catches the light in its own way. It glints and sparkles and flashes uniquely. It would almost be possible to believe that the facet was the jewel; not just a tiny part of it. But, then, as we move the jewel another facet catches the light.* —Neil Gaiman, *The Kindly Ones*

Mothers and Daughters explores facets of the relationships between mothers and daughters, daughters and mothers. This unique dyad represents a complexity that calls for significant attention and attracts profound inquiry. In this vein, reading *Mothers and Daughters* will be a rewarding addition to the literature on mothering and motherhood and a worthwhile read.

The multiplicity of themes presented by the authors on mothers and daughters, the vast array of writing styles, and the intellectual enrichment derived from reading the material for this text are invaluable. In particular, the collection examines such themes as the following: connection and separation; joy and grief; what we remember and what we forget; what we find and what we lose; what we treasure and what we discard; what we learn and what we need to unlearn; who we are, who we can be, who we become, and who we have been; empowerment and disempowerment; home and homecoming; motherland and afar; what to hold of the old and embrace of the new; when to push away, when to push back, when to pull in with all our might; agency and weakness; advocacy and voicelessness; pain and healing; and independence and dependence.

Expanding on the mother-daughter dyad, Adrienne Rich says the following: "Probably there is nothing in human nature more resonant with charges than the flow of energy between two biologically alike bodies, one of which has lain in amniotic bliss inside the other, one of which has labored to give birth to the other. The materials are here for the deepest mutuality and the most painful estrangement" (218). Although we begin with Rich's powerful words about mothers and daughters, our intent is actually positioned as a critical response to Rich's work. In "Matroreform: Feminist Mothers and Their Daughters Creating Feminist Motherlines," Fiona Green, drawing on Gina Wong-Wylie's works, critiques the notion of matrophobia articulated in Adrienne Rich's *Of Woman Born: Motherhood as Experience and Institution* for failing to consider the complicated variety of relational issues between mothers and daughters. *Mothers and Daughters* is a collection intended to be an expansion of *matroreform*; it details in a variety of ways the voices of mothers and daughters as they fashion new openings for a poetics of matroreform relations.

To that end, *Mothers and Daughters* is a welcomed and awaited addition; it is nuanced with an inspirational and stimulating transdisciplinary, multi-format gathering of creative work, literary and reflective essays, and narratives. It also marks and celebrates the twentieth anniversary of the Motherhood Initiative for Research and Community Involvement (MIRCI). *Mothers and Daughters* is the third such collection of high scholarship, excellent creative work, deep reflections, semi-(auto) biographies, heartrending memoires, and other writings that explore and examine the complications of mother-daughter relationships, following *Mothers and Daughters Connection, Empowerment, Transformation* edited by Andrea O'Reilly and Sharon Abbey in 2000 and *Mothers and Daughters*, a special issue of the *Journal for Motherhood Initiative* from 2008.

Rich's evocative words quoted above have generated an awareness of the irrevocable bonds between biological mothers and daughters. By establishing the biological likeness between mothers and daughters, she tied womanhood/femaleness to the biological (pre) determinism, which argues that every mother was a daughter and every daughter is a potential mother in the future. Thus, Rich calls for a recognition of this "deepest mutuality and the most painful estrangement" (218), and if possible to prioritize the mother-daughter relationship as a centrepiece of feminist discourses and to move it away from the analytical control of male psychologists. Rich's style and format in the book—a gallimaufry including diary entries, social anthropology, history, and literary analysis—gave feminist discourse on motherhood a new format with which to operate. *Mothers and Daughters* incorporates all of these formats to generate an exciting read. It follows late twentieth and twenty-first century reassessments of the mother-daughter relationship, moving it away from the control of psychoanalyses, and liberating it by situating the discourses in cross/multi/inter/disciplinary facets that "enhance and encourage the continuum of women.... that links us back over the years to our mothers and their mothers before them" (Walters 9).

From the 1980s through 2002, there was a flurry of individually authored and edited collections of critical studies and creative anthologies focusing on the mother-daughter relationship from different academic and cultural disciplines too numerous to annotate here. These anthologies of essays, studies, and creative texts have reexamined mother-daughter issues from greater compassionate, understanding, and positive positions, without brushing off the troubling and negative aspects of the relationship. This explosion of book-length studies has also explored how historical, cultural, racial, economic, and locational situations impact and define the mother-daughter relationship in different communities (Friday; Chodorow; Hirsh; Collins; Bell-Scott; Brown-Guillory; Kamel; Nice; Kearns; Waters; Malin; Kendell; Caplan; Giorgio; Bloom).

However, the most significant response to Rich's call, we argue, came in the form of the first international conference on mothers and daughters, which was hosted at Atkinson College, York University, Toronto, and was coordinated by Andrea O'Reilly. This conference brought together a global community of transdisciplinary feminist scholars and cultural activists to discuss and take back the issues relating to mothers and daughters in feminist scholarship and action. Subsequently, 2008 saw the birth of the Motherhood Initiative for Research and Community Involvement (MIRCI), and the *Journal of the Motherhood Initiative for Research and Community Involvement* (*JMI*). This journal created a transnational forum for research and publications on motherhood.

In this current treatment of mothers and daughters in relation to each other, several of the essays draw heavily on the motherhood theories developed by feminists from the 1980s to the present in order to develop their central narrative representations of their relationships with their mothers or as mothers with their daughters. To read these texts, whether creative or biographical meditations on motherhood, it is helpful then to recognize the influences of these theoretical foremothers on the subject. Their studies explain women's ambivalence toward their desires to be mothers and/or to play the roles of dutiful daughters while they observe the subservient positions of their own mothers in relation to their fathers in the homeplace. The complications of motherhood/mothering ambivalence caused by personal anxieties and compulsory motherhood immobilize women already suffering from psychological disturbance from even minimally mothering their daughters.

For instance, art theory examines the role of art in healing and restoring positive memories of bonding between mothers and daughters. Such art as painting or writing recreates controllable images of the relationship, which no longer threaten the individuals who must have suffered the trauma of a turbulent relationship (Pennebaker and Evans). Art therapy for grieving mothers or daughters who have lost their loved one—either because the loved one is dead or left home for good—is also a tempting proposition because art can validate the argument that most mothers and daughters never want to let go even if the relationship is problematic. By holding onto the image of the daughter or mother through art, the mother may seek individuation through holding on to daughters. Art, such as the art of hair styling, aesthetically becomes the mother's way of constructing static and idealized images of the absent daughter. Through art, a mother may control the daughter as her object of emotional security.

Based on mothering/motherhood theories extrapolated from women's (auto)biographies, Jo Malin argues that within women's (auto)biographies, whether collaboratively or individually narrated, especially when it is the daughter writing the (auto)biography of the self or of the mother, the narrative becomes a vehicle invoking the maternal presence to vindicate the daughterly position of bonding with the mother (Chodorow). Nancy Chodorow's idea that women's self-identifications are embedded in mother-daughter relationships is thus proved in some of the texts in Malin's book. It should be noted that most of the early theories fail to recognize motherhood by adoption. Yet in contemporary mothering and motherhood theories, the adoptive mother's relationship with the adopted daughter can be equally as affirming of or as disruptive to each other. Thus, it is necessary to look for theories of adoptive parenting to fill in some of the gaps in the principal theories on the mother-daughter relationship. Similarly, the contemporary challenge to mothering/motherhood, which practice developed principally from heterosexual two-parent family situations (father and mother figures), is that of the prevalence of single parenting and same-sex couples parenting. Of course, a reading of ethnic mothering—including pan-African, Latin American, pan-Asian, pan-European, pan-Middle eastern, Australasia, and pan-Caribbean mothering practices, and the addition of issues dealing with female-headed households, lesbian mother-daughter and lesbian daughter-mother relations among others—show how these areas have become centre stage in contemporary third-wave feminist scholarship on mothering (Walker; Kamel; Bell-Scott; Nice; Brown-Guillory; Nice; Kearns; Waters; Malin; Kendell 2000; Caplan; Giorgio; Bloom; Smith Silva; Smith Silva and Alexander).

Mothers and Daughters also testifies to the achievements of third-wave feminist scholarship on mother-daughter relations. Essentially, the book signals the inception of a potential fourth wave of research and scholarship on mother-daughter relations, already hinted at in *Twenty-First Century Motherhood: Experience, Identity, Policy, Agency*, edited by Andrea O'Reilly, which shows an increase of texts being written about the topic in the last decade. However, most of the texts on mothers and daughters presently in circulation are motivational books on how to repair damaged mother-daughter relationships. Nonetheless, it is exciting to note the amount of creative work being done on the subject, thus projecting mother-daughter issues into mainstream culture and academe.

Interestingly, though many voices advocate the depathologization of mother-daughter relations in the fields of psychotherapy and genetics, a few of the chapters in the book explore motherhood narratives through psychology theories to explain the psycho-emotional effects of trauma, mourning, and melancholia that the illness and death of a mother can impact daughters. Trauma narratives—as expressive writing related as memoirs, testimonials, art, poetry, flash fiction, and reflexive contemplation, done by both mothers and daughters—are therapeutic. Yet various interpretations of maternal trauma narratives still linger in the peripheries of academia. Thus, this book includes chapters dealing with this peripheralized yet fundamental issue in mother-daughter relationship discourse. Mother-daughter narratives of melancholia do not solely represent separation blues, as was often theorized; rather, in their roles as mourning narratives, they also function as healing texts for the authors (Henke; Pennebaker and Evans).

Some chapters explore the narratives that question the political and religious feminization of nations—a feminization that equates nationhood with motherhood and citizenship with sonship or daughterhood—, such as those texts set in Latin America, Canada, and Ireland. Using historical theories, the essays erect better foundations to develop clearer perspectives on how mother-daughter narratives subvert the state as well as religious and cultural institutions that frustrate female development as individuals. In addition, diaspora and postcolonial feminist theories as engaged in South Asian studies are used to read the transnational multicultural texts written by daughters of the South Asian diaspora that reveal complicated mother-daughter relations.

Mothers and Daughters evokes intellectual curiosity through the variety of social, cultural, and personal perspectives from which the authors approach and comment on their topics. Each of the fourteen chapters and eight poems exhibits profound differences in content, form, genre, and radiates its own particularity of theme and presentational mode to effectively constitute a thread to weave the quilt of voices that give *Mothers and Daughters* a richness not found in books that focus solely on theoretical explorations and explications of mother-daughter relationships. Each discovery herein is a bridge that links interconnected themes to capture the essence of mother-daughter relationships. The variations of commonalities and the similarities of differences enable us to catch glimpses of literatures from different nationalities, ethnicities, and personalities. It is the hope that in another five to ten years, more texts of this nature will be released to further expand and consolidate the study of mothers and daughters.

FACETS OF MOTHER-DAUGHTER EXPERIENCES

Mothers and Daughters comprises so many themes—all facets of mother-daughter experiences—that we did not want to privilege some themes over others. Instead, we organized the collection around three sections—"Mothers and Daughters in a Creative Space," "Mothers and Daughters in Our Memory," and "Mothers and Daughters in Literature"—with the intent of letting the themes of individual pieces emerge and shine on their own. In doing so, we build on the opening quotation: the idea that each facet of mother-daughter discovery may be so captivating as to make the reader believe for a moment that the one facet is the whole. Until, at least, another equally captivating facet appears. Yet, these facets are indeed all part of a greater whole.

In Section I of *Mothers and Daughters*, "Mothers and Daughters in a Creative Space," writers look at the changing dimensions of mothers in the sphere of their multiple connections to their daughters. By exploring this multifaceted relationship, writers explore and expand this dyad and lay the groundwork for engaging in a dialogue between mothers and daughters. Drawing from personal experiences, the art of poetry and painting, and the medium of fiction, these contributors illustrate the important arena of complex dimensions that emerge between mothers and daughters.

The collection begins with two poems by Dorsía Smith Silva. Exploring the relationship between African and African-American mothers and daughters, Smith Silva shares a tender portrait of a mother, grandmother, and daughter taking care of their hair in "Embroidery." The first stanza illustrates how the mother oils her daughter's scalp and sections it in a "field of fours" before she starts the braiding process. The second stanza shifts to the daughter who is now a mother responsible for braiding her own daughter's hair. Like she learned from her mother, she rubs coconut oil into her daughter's scalp and watches the spirals "spring back into place."

In the last stanza, the circle is now complete as the mother figure from the second stanza helps her mother with her hair. After she uses the hot comb to press her mother's hair straight, she lightly applies oil to the ends of her mother's hair. These personal moments strike the truth of memory and display the deep strands of love at the core of these mother-daughter relationships.

The following poem "Directions" examines the harried life of a busy mother while she raises her daughters named Eloise and Jane. In an attempt to have some time for herself and perhaps achieve recognition for her hard work taking care of the children, she ponders leaving her children and daily responsibilities for a brief amount of time. Yet she feels tied to her parental responsibilities and wonders if she can leave without feeling guilt or remorse. Smith Silva raises the poignant question of how mothers can place their wellness first in such demanding contemporary times, and articulates the challenges and doubts to finding viable solutions at the end of the poem. There are no easy answers here. The poem ends with the mother unable to resolve her situation, as she searches for guidance without a definitive plan of action.

Laurie Kruk's short story titled "The Wedding Collection" focuses on the strained relationship between an academic daughter named Lenore and her ill mother. When she decides to examine her mother's sewing career of making wedding dresses from the time she was in the "fourth grade until she left for university" for her dissertation project, Lenore rekindles some unflattering and amicable memories of her mother. Kruk uses realistic, taut, and humorous dialogue and description to juxtapose the connections and disconnections between Lenore and her mother, especially as they are separated by Lenore's world of academe and her mother's fading life in a hospital bed hooked up to pain medication. As she refuses to physically and emotionally let go of her mother, Lenore holds tightly to their shared experiences and concrete recollections in her dissertation. Kruk's story speaks for the many mothers and daughters that experience challenges, empowerment, and ultimately healing through the networks of the mother-daughter relationship.

Priya Parrotta Natarajan describes her relationship with her mother who is called "Amma" (the South Indian word for "mother") in "Costas, (or, If You Prefer, a Tale of Two Cafés)." With an engaging framework, the story confronts memories of childhood with fragments of environmental issues, such as diminishing coastlines. These significant details engage in the spirit of the mother-daughter bond that has shared yet varied experiences and of the threats to humanity as posed by eroding Mediterranean, Caribbean, and South Asian coastlines. Parrotta Natarajan shows how the ability to remember is the greatness of feeling. By recounting these fresh images, she reveals the essay's unique capacity to resonate beyond the literal word and tangible page.

Renee Norman's poetry captures multiple images of mothers and daughters in her poems titled "Gardens" and "My Mother's Linens." In "Gardens," Norman recalls planting seeds with her daughter and links the imagery of nurturing to her relationship with her students. In this sense, professors "mother" their students by nourishing their academic capabilities, mental and personal growth, and emotional maturity. As she works in the soil, Norman also revisits the memory of her mother's garden and father's graveyard. By the end of the poem, Norman returns to focusing on her daughter and on her own interest in exploring new possibilities. The lasting symbolic message is one of helping others grow and developing self-fulfillment.

"My Mother's Linens" further extends Norman's memory of her mother. This time she is bonded to her mother through the crystallized markers of family linens. As she touches the folds of the linens, Norman recreates the physical closeness with her mother and preserves this powerful recollection intact. As she explores the longing and loving for her mother, Norman reminds readers that we are all vulnerable to our memories and emotions, especially when they concern deceased family members.

In "Painting through Ruptured Maternal Identity," Batya Weinbaum writes of a painful loss of motherhood after her daughter decides to cease communication with her upon turning eighteen. As Weinbaum states, this distant relationship with her daughter is difficult to accept—especially when considering that the two had "almost a symbiotic relationship." By trying to recreate memories of her daughter and their mother-daughter dyad, Weinbaum attempts to reconcile her journey of exploring feminist mothering, single motherhood, and eventually isolated motherhood. Although she eventually finds solace through painting, she hopes to mend the contentious connection with her daughter. She also hopes to show her daughter her artwork, which reflects moments of her daughter's life and their time together. In this vein, art has become a refuge and site of healing and (self-) revealing for Weinbaum.

Charlotte Henay's "Sitting with My Mother's Bones" emerges from a complication of words, memories, and experiences, which explore identity, indigeneity, heritage, and narrative in a transnational context. Throughout her story, Henay addresses the various intersectionalities within personal spheres and maternal narratives. These conversations recreate meanings of women's voices and matrilineal heritage as constructions of agency, emancipation, resistance, and transformation. This awareness of the intersecting use of form converges with Henay's confrontation of the struggles and conflicts of mothers and daughters and the different stages of their relationship. Yet, it is her insight into this relationship that highlights the advocacy and knowledge of these women.

"Daughters of the Dust," a poem by Dorsía Smith Silva, adopts its title from the movie written, directed, and produced by Julie Dash in 1991. Set in 1902, the film explores the Great Migration of African Americans; the central family lives on one of the Sea Islands, off the coast of Georgia. According to George Nelson in his article titled "Daughters of the Dust," the matriarch of the family represents "the collective African past" and "links to the days of slavery" (110). Likewise Sanja Škifić and Rajko Petković in "Intertextual Symbolism, Gullah and Language Conflict in *Daughters of the Dust*" state that the film engages in "an immersion in the postcolonial exploration of the importance of communal memories and the cultural heritage of the ancestors" (108). Building upon this memory of Africans and African Americans, Smith Silva's concluding poem intertwines African and African American daughters, ancestors, and future generations through the common bonds of shared journeys and created bridges. As they come from the "same womb" of motherland Africa, they share the complex experiences of slavery, and identity as Queenie and Nanny, and Ashanti, Yoruba, Guinea women. Like the film, the poem movingly traces the daughters' journey—particularly as they express lamentation from the suffering during slavery to their feelings of hope, celebration, and empowerment as they remember their historical strength and gain healing and transformation through the African drum.

Section II of *Mothers and Daughters*, "Mothers and Daughters in Our Memory," explores different manifestations of memory about mothers and daughters. In the myriad relationships of mothers and daughters and daughters and mothers, memory swirls and twirls, rests, and remains. It can be enduring and unforgettable, haunting and painful, uplifting, and joyful. And in our memory, we can paint in broad brush strokes the many colours of experience, reach across time and distance, contemplate an interweaving of experiences, wash through waves of the past to crystallize meaning, see ourselves in reflections within reflections, and capture feelings in a moment in time to make them tangible for future generations. The section begins with Andrea O'Reilly's chapter "Across the Divide: Contemporary Anglo American Feminist Theory on the Mother-DaughterRelationship," which builds discussions on what mothers and daughters need in their relationships and how past and present theory can give new agency to the dyad. The section then continues with Dorsía Smith Silva's poem "Glow," which captures memories of the unparalleled experience of giving birth through the use of rich and powerful images of nature. Memory of the beginning of the mother-child connection is cast forward into dreams as Smith Silva's poetic wisdom shines.

"Isthmus" by Donna Sharkey also searches for memories of motherhood. Sharkey becomes a mother upon the adoption of a daughter, suffers with the spectre of losing her daughter to mental illness, and ultimately becomes a mother of a daughter lost. Although earlier in the narrative the reader is privy to the thoughts and feelings of both mother and daughter, the story is later disconnected from this unity, much as the living bond between mother and daughter becomes uncoupled. Still, Sharkey tells of memorable moments of reaching out across great distances, however tentative and fleeting these connections.

Cheryl Chaffin's "Grandma's Husband: Parenting with My Mother" reflects upon interpretations of whom can or should parent, and probes (and pushes back against) a sense of boundaries of the role of mother. In so doing, Chaffin is prompted to examine her own relationship as a daughter to her mother as she becomes a mother who shares mothering with her mother.

Memory can at once be painful and hopeful. Smith Silva's "For the Child" explores the thoughts of a woman—caught in a world of oppressive patriarchal norms that usually places blame on unwed mothers and their children—who decides to abort her child in an attempt to have her child be reborn in different circumstances. Here we see the power of memory of the past to possibly yield to a better future.

Alma Simounet-Bey never had the chance to become a mother to a (living) daughter, a loss that is palpably mourned in "The Worst Is Not the Worst: Memories of Motherhood and Multiple Miscarriages." Through the construction of her narrative, she allows wave after wave of long-ago grief and bewilderment to wash into clarity from the perspective of the present. In this way, she can pass on a maternal understanding to future mothers (of future daughters), even while unable to do so in her own life as a mother.

Mary Bronstein's piece—"The Facsimile of Existence: Mothers and Daughters in Perpetual Reproduction of Identity and Image"—peers at the reflections within reflections inherent in the mother-daughter dyad. Poetry is paired with psychoanalytic thought as a way of querying the very simultaneous and interconnected existence of mothers to daughters.

Sometimes, memory is lost to us even as we are living. Then our loved ones remain to remember. In "Researching Death," Norman confronts the painful reality of preparing for her mother's death as her mother battles dementia at the age of eighty-nine. The poetic piece speaks of the all too common reality of grieving for loved ones as we lose them to illnesses of the mind. In "Exploring Pantsuit Nation: A Message for Our Daughters," Dorsía Smith Silva adds her voice to the flow of collective memory. Imagining what our future daughters will need to hear and heed, she shares a message of a painful past and present, but also of an always promising future.

Section III of *Mothers and Daughters*, "Mothers and Daughters in Literature" begins with Cristina Herrera's essay "Daughter of the Disappeared or *Hija de La República*: Maternal Imagery, Daughterly Identity, and Argentina's 'Dirty War' in Carolina De

Robertis's *Perla.*" Her essays takes the reader through the labyrinths of a mother's and granddaughter's pain caused by the ghosts of memories of a disappeared pregnant daughter and the uncertainty of the existence of a granddaughter rumored to have been born to the daughter. Herrera incisively traces the relationship fault lines that create tensional relations between Perla, the daughter of the disappeared biological mother victim of the political regime supported by her adoptive mother and her group labelled as Mothers of the Republic in the novel. Perla, argues Herrera, is thus placed at the intersections of opposing psycho-emotional pulls, which are further complicated by the appeals of her distant grandmother for a filial bonding with her and her group, Las Madres de la Plaza de Mayo. In her reading of the novel, Herrera advances the position that De Robertis appropriately represents the consequences for Argentinian women as the military junta conflated patriarchal sociocultural and politicized Catholic Christian moral injunctions on female roles in the country, with an oppressive nationalist narrative that equated nationhood with womanhood/motherhood. Consequently, the collapse of the Argentine nation was blamed on a perceived collapse of Argentinian women's moral purity. Thus, for Perla, argues Herrera, the political arena into which she is born is saturated with contradicting images of motherhood and daughterhood in which the good mother is a supporter of the methods of repression, whereas the bad mother is symbolized by the mother who speaks out for justice. Herrera draws on theories of trauma and feminist readings of madness as a subversive narrative trope. Of course, Herrera also argues that the trope of madness as a mask of deception worn by those bad mothers resisting the system. Perla must accept all her histories: the past cannot be erased, the present must be negotiated, and the future must be ensured for Perla's yet to be born daughter. To underscore her argument, Herrera engages theories of reconstructive psychology that accept ambivalences in identity formation as a healthy practice, and through which memories are sifted to generate individual agency. *Perla*, concludes Herrera, should be read as a narrative of healing—a healing that creates a psycho-emotional clearing for a new period in which motherhood is not dictated by a conflation of a masculinist ideal of nationhood and biological motherhood.

Dannabang Kuwabong's essay, "*Her Mother's Ashes*: South Asian Daughters Reimagining the Mother to Reimagine the Self in Diasporic Locations" draws upon multiple North American diasporic South Asian daughters' narrative representations of their mothers as reconstructive journeys into their own attempts to understand themselves as daughters through their mothers. Traversing different countries from South Africa, Canada, the United States of America, India, Pakistan, and Sri Lanka, the stories are read as memory retrievals that problematize different types of mother-daughter relationships. Through his careful and insightful reading of these stories, Kuwabong addresses how these narratives insinuate cultural, geopolitical, social, gender, and transnational uniformities and cohesions, but which, nonetheless, also simultaneously exhibit centrifugal cultural forces that expose vast differences. In engaging theories of gender performance, diaspora studies, transitional/transnational relations, and generational continuities and contiguities toward comparative readings of selected stories, Kuwabong develops a coherent and persuasive argument that these daughterly narratives demonstrate areas of both conjunctions and disjunction that undermine a singular perspective reading of the multiplex of cultural cartographies denoting South Asian mother-daughter relationships. He concludes convincingly that through these diverse affiliative narratives, South Asian daughters reimagine their matrilineage inheritances as terrains for self-imaging. Thus, Kuwabong asserts, that these stories act as unfinished testimonials of South Asian daughters' search of meaning of their relationships with their biological and cultural mothers through reflexive examinations of daughter-mother dyads in Canada, the United States of America, South Africa, and India.

Corollary to Herrera's perception of a dawn of hope for a future mothering praxes in *Perla*, Lidiane Cunha's essay, "Lives of Mothers and Daughters in Brazil and Canada: The Mother's Artistic Influence as Seen by Four Women Writers," examines how maternal agency is either stifled or encouraged in two different cultural locations, though influenced by the same ethics of Catholic Christianity. Generally, one is aware that the conditions in Brazil, though significantly different from Argentina, impose similar controls over women, perceptually tied to motherhood.

Thus, in reading the narratives from Brazil, Cunha examines the conditions that invalidate women's desire to rise above the social limitations imposed on them, and hence cannot effectively transfer any maternal agency to their daughters. This, argues Cunha, creates tensional intergenerational relationships that subsequently generate a distancing between mothers and daughters. Cunha's position does not focus on the problems of psycho-emotional bonding alone, but expands to discuss the restrictive conditions curtailing any attempts by artistically gifted mothers from developing their creative potential or even transferring their dreams unto their daughters. But, states Cunha, the novel projects these acts of female insubordinations as harbingers of a new Brazilian womanhood, without diminishing the relevance of the social expectations of the woman's role as a mother.

Cunha's essay moves on to consider alternative narratives, though not from the same cultural setting. In her reading of the short fiction set in Québec, another Catholic Christian dominated society, Cunha reveals different value systems that encourage women's self-growth and participation in public roles acting as teachers, nurses, factory workers, etc. The comparative reading of stories by four writers, revelatory as it is, nonetheless, is problematic as Cunha may be misinterpreted as setting up a north-south dichotomy that often privileges the north over the south in matters of cultural politics. Such a position fails to see Cunha's balanced reading that does not gloss over the ambivalences towards motherhood and daughterhood in both cultures. Cunha shows that in both places, the image of the strong maternal figure guarantees the development of an independent minded daughter.

In "'Their Mother Was Waiting For Her': Mother-Daughter Relations and Irish Identity in Deirdre Madden's *One by One in the Darkness*," Charlotte Beyer insightfully examines the complicated relationships among three Northern Irish sisters with their mother, complicated by the background of religious-ethnic strife and the traumatic memory of their father's murder in this conflict. Beyer's project seeks to disturb the predominantly phallocratic Irish literary canon to create reading spaces for the inclusion of female-authored texts. Thus, by focusing on this women-centred text, Beyer shows how Madden's narrative challenges the construction of Ireland as an ideal maternal figure who must sacrifice personal desires and needs for the sake of Ireland. Showing an in-depth understanding of the historical and contemporary conflicts that have dogged Ireland, Beyer teases out Madden's subtlety of questioning these limitations to Irish Catholic female agency while creating strategic openings in the Madonna-whore dichotomy.

By exploring the three sections of *Mothers and Daughters*, readers will examine how the organizing topics intertwine. Memory may inspire creativity, literature calls on memory, creative spaces make literature possible, and so on. Collected together, each facet leads to its own discovery. Through the intermingling of poetry, reflective essays, literary essays, narratives, short fiction, and artwork, *Mothers and Daughters* generates a paradigm of contemplative and exegetical readings.

In addition, the collection serves as personal, collaborative, and academic discoveries for readers. Ultimately, *Mothers and Daughters* informs us of the diverse ways of approaching, reading, listening to, and understanding mother-daughter relationships through a global gathering of styles of representation—a multifaceted exploration of a compelling relational, social, and cultural dynamic.

WORKS CITED

Bell-Scott, Patricia, editor. *Double Stitch: Black Women Write about Mothers and Daughters*. Beacon, 1991.

Bloom, Harold, editor. *The Joy Luck Club, Blooms Modern Critical Interpretations*. Infobase Publishing, 2009.

Brown-Guillory, editor. *Women of Color Mother-Daughter Relationships in 20th-Century Literature*. University of Texas Press, 1996.

Caplan, Paula J. *The New Don't Blame Mother: Mending the Mother-Daughter Relationship*.Routledge, 2000.

Chodorow, Nancy. *Reproduction of Mothering: Psychoanalysis and the Sociology of Gender*. Universityof California Press, 1978.

Collins, Patricia Hill. *Black Feminist Thought: Knowledge, Consciousness and the Politics of Empowerment*. Routledge, 1990.

Friday, Nancy. *My Mother My Self*. Delta, 1977.

Gaiman, Neil. *The Sandman Vol. 9: The Kindly Ones*. Vertigo, 2012.

Giorgio, Adalgisa. *Writing Mothers and Daughters: Renegotiating the Mother in Western European Narratives by Women.* Berghahn Books, 2002.

Green, Fiona J. "Matroreform: Feminist Mothers and Their Daughters Creating Feminist Motherlines." *Mothers and Daughters, Journal of the Association for Research on Mothering*, vol. 10, no.2, Fall/Winter 2008, pp. 11-21.

Henke, Suzette A. *Shattered Subjects: Trauma and Testimony in Life Writing.* Palgrave Macmillan, 2000.

Hirsch, Marianne. *Mother/Daughter Plot: Narrative, Psychoanalysis, Feminism.* Indiana University Press, 1989.

Kamel, Rose Yalow. *Aggravating the Conscience: Jewish-American Literary Mothers in the Promised Land.* Lang, 1988.

Kearns, Caledonia. *Motherland: Writings by Irish American Women About Mothers and Daughters.* W. Morrow, 1999.

Kendall, Elizabeth. *American Daughter: Discovering My Mother.* Random House, 2000.

Malin, Jo. *The Voice of the Mother: Embedded Maternal Narratives in Twentieth-Century Women's Autobiographies.* Southern Illinois University Press, 2000.

Nelson, George. "Daughters of the Dust." *Ebony*, vol. 66, no. 12, 2011, pp. 108-111.

Nice, Vivian E. *Mothers and Daughters: The Distortion of a Relationship.* Palgrave, 1992.

O'Reilly, Andrea, editor. *Maternal Theory: Essential Readings.* Demeter Press, 2007.

O'Reilly, Andrea, editor. *Mothers and Daughters, Journal of the Association for Research on Mothering*, vol. 10, no.2, Fall/Winter 2008.

O'Reilly, Andrea. *Twenty-first Century Motherhood: Experience, Identity, Policy, Agency.* Demeter Press, 2010.

Pennebaker, James W., and John F. Evans. *Expressive Writing: Words That Heal Idyll.* Arbor, 2014.

Rich, Adrienne. *Of Woman Born: Motherhood as Experience and Institution.* Virago, 1976.

Škifić, Sanja, and Rajko Petković. "Intertextual Symbolism, Gullah and Language Conflict in *Daughters of the Dust.*" *Acta Linguistia*, vol. 9, no. 2, 2015, pp. 106-125.

Smith Silva, Dorsía, editor. *Latina/Chicana Mothering*. Demeter Press, 2011.

Smith Silva, Dorsía, and Simone A. James Alexander, editors. *Feminist and Critical Perspectives on Caribbean Mothering*. Africa World Press, 2013.

Walker, Alice. *In Search of Our Mothers' Gardens: Womanist Prose*. Harcourt, 1983.

Walters, Suzanna Danuta. *Lives Together/Worlds Apart: Mothers and Daughters in Popular Culture*. University of California Press, 1992.

I.
MOTHERS AND DAUGHTERS IN A CREATIVE SPACE

1.
Embroidery

DORSÍA SMITH SILVA

I sit between my mother's legs.
She takes the needle of the comb
to separate my hair
into a field of fours.
With her right index finger,
she scoops a wave of white coconut oil
to weave into my hair.
Her fingers cross the rows,
go deep into my scalp,
and then braid the sections smooth.

My daughter kneels before me,
I unbraid her hair to find
brown cascading waves unfolding.
I rub the coconut oil
along the edges of the ripples.
The spirals dance downward,
then spring back into place.

Hunched over my mother in the kitchen,
I pull a comb through white and black strands,
press the wires straight,
amid ringlets of smoke.
I tap her ends with oil,
watch the tiny clouds glitter
like black glass.

2.
Directions

DORSÍA SMITH SILVA

She pauses at each shelf's edge
wondering what will happen
if she falls off forever

Just to teach them a lesson
she should go for just a day
past confetti scribbles
past cupped Cheerio faces
past candy-coated jackets
marked Eloise and Jane

She is looking for her feet
She is looking for her tongue
She is looking for her eyes

She searches on the shelf's edge
with no answers

3.
The Wedding Collection

LAURIE KRUK

1. *Initial Advising:*

I have never loved the sight of my mother feeding her old Singer, pins bandoleering her sleeve, hands guiding the cloth of another wedding dress to its desired joining. From grade four till I left for university, I found her hunched over her sewing table most weekends and some week nights. This continued until she got sick, just two years ago. So I was surprised when my advisor, Dr. Howard Carruthers ("Carrie"), suggested I consider making Mom's wedding dress obsession the topic of my dissertation. Handicrafts and "marginal" cottage industries were hot in the sociology of work subdiscipline, which had become my specialty. Still, I suppose I'd never seen it as my mother *working* so much as finding a way to piss off Dad.

Because practically every time that she slipped downstairs after supper, Dad would make this gargling sound, low in his throat, pop open another beer, then turn up the TV volume on the game to drown out the whining of the motor as she pressed on the pedal, faster and faster. Sometime after his third beer, Dad would open the basement door to yell, "Hey! Could you see about this button on my good shirt," or "The workpants could use a new zipper, too" while "she had the monster fired up." Or he would wonder aloud about the waste of time and money being spent on a dress some "sillygoose girl" would only wear once—if "he didn't leave her in the lurch." Sitting with my homework at the dining room table, I couldn't help but marvel at my mother eloping with the

Polish baseball star, my Dad, Henrick "Hank" Brozowski, despite her father's Irish prejudices against DPs, "displaced persons." Was she reliving dreams of star-crossed romance as she spread tulle, lace, and cotton eyelet across her cutting tables?

Mom's dresses never made her much money. After all the fittings, tea, sharing of stories, photos and plans, it seemed she didn't have the heart to charge her friends and neighbours much more than the price of her material, a few clocked hours of furious sewing. Lack of profit probably allowed her to justify her work as a kind of "community service." Yet she really took pride in her dresses, requesting one wedding photo from each bride to stick on the bulletin board above her Singer. There she grew a garden of smiling couples, glossy pictures gradually curling with winter's furnace blasts, to be replaced by shiny new pairs by summer's end.

All this ran through my head as I sat in Carrie's office at end of term. He scratched his chin, made a note on a yellow legal pad. "What was it called? Your mother's business?"

So much paper to fill made me tongue-tied. "It didn't have a name." Shit, that sounded weird. This was the first time Carrie had actually found the occasion to talk to me, alone, outside of the gang of awed grad students passing through his classes. Youngish, single (Straight? Gay? There were bets either way), an Oxford scholarship student still trailing a hint of acrossthepond crispness, Carrie was the "hot" prof in my department. He looked disappointed now at my nonanswer. Then he brightened and scribbled something down.

"Unauthorized, of course. Underground. Perfectly understandable. But how did she advertise, solicit customers?" He tapped his teeth with the pen, leaning forward. Prickling with perspiration, I sat up straighter. Having Carrie as my supervisor would be a real boost to my academic career.

"Well I guess she went by her own name, if she advertised at all—it was probably mostly through neighbours, word of mouth."

His pen was hovering. "Her name? Age? Ethnicity?"

"Her married name, which she went by, was Marian Brozowski. She's sixty now, retired." It felt funny discussing my mother during what was supposed to be prethesis advising. "Now, she's Marian Kelly again. First generation Irish. My parents divorced, six years ago." *Divorced*, a bitter spice. "But my father's dead." As if that undid it. "He died last spring."

Carrie kept scribbling. "Ummf, that's too bad. Your loss, I mean." A raised eyebrow, another note. "Hmm. A feminist rebel, second-wave domestic entrepreneur—that could be your angle. Rejected patriarchal marriage after raising her family—post-sixties, am I right?" I nodded. In class, "the sixties" was always invoked as a cultural watershed akin to the parting of the Red Sea. "Look, why not consider making this your dissertation topic: women's unauthorized work, coming out of the home. You could start by interviewing your mother—properly contextualized, of course. Qualitative research, with a difference." He swung his pen like a conductor's baton, grinning boyishly. "It's ground breaking."

I twisted my empty coffee cup between my hands. "You think so?"

"I do." (God, what I'd give for that certainty, like the neat crease in his crossed trouser leg.) He tossed the pad onto the pile of papers heaping his desk. "Just remember, your topic must be approved by Grad Committee by the end of May. And then I'm away for most of the summer—the big Fabrications of Fashion conference in Buenos Aires, then my residency. But I'm sure we can hammer out your proposal by email, or Skype."

Skyping with Carrie? "I guess I have to decide pretty soon," I said, standing up as he looked over my shoulder, smiling at the next wannabee who was nervously flipping back her hair.

"Next Tuesday, same time, then?" He leaned into my shoulder, almost touching me. "A pleasure, Louise." And the girl moved in, before I could say that Louise was my aunt's name. A victim of childhood leukemia, Louise died long before I, Lenore, was born.

2. *Context*

It wasn't that Dad was the proverbial oldcountry patriarch, that he didn't believe women should work. Plenty of our friends' mothers did have degrees, or went back to school later, did part-time work as secretaries, nurses, or supply teachers. But Mom didn't get beyond grade-eleven vocational; she missed her last two years when her mother had her "little collapse" and she had to help look after Louise. Dad encouraged me to study hard to win a scholarship so

I could afford to go to university and get a good job. Our family income didn't stretch to putting me through school. "There are no free lunches, Lennie." He was proud of my A-average. He just wasn't so sure about my mother working, right in our home.

Whenever a "lady" (including even my nineteen-year-old cousin, Lucy) came over for a fitting, she and the lady would descend, whispering, to the basement. There my mother had rigged up a little changing corner with a couple of pink velour curtains strung on clotheslines, a full-length mirror, and a painted wicker chair. She would leave her "lady" in it to try on the latest dress "in-progress" while she went upstairs to make tea. When she first started, I wanted to share in the tea, chocolate biscuits, and gossip, but I was barred from the basement during her appointments. "I'm working now, Lennie. You go play." Or later, "You need to study." I would hear their laughter drift up through the furnace ducts, until the "lady" left, and Mom would slip out on the porch for a smoke. She would rock on the porch swing, smoke, and sigh. I wondered what those sighs were about. Was she disappointed with her life? Revisiting her girlhood as she smoked: before Louise died and she rushed into marriage to a man she met at the baseball field, a man who now picked up lost mittens and shovelled the school walk, "Uncle Hank" to the gradeschoolers? (The older kids called him "Ski Pole.") Now she had two misfit kids: klutzy Brad, who was never picked for schoolyard baseball, and Lennie the Learner, who loved books and hated home economics. Did she ever wonder if there was a "white wedding" in her own children's future?

3. *Exploratory Contact*

"Hi Mom."

"Lennie? Well this is a surprise." Her voice rose at the extravagance, my second long-distance call to Winnipeg in a week. The cough I dreaded almost began, but she cleared her throat thickly instead.

"I need to ask you a favour." I picked up a pen and doodled a stick-girl on the back of a pizza flyer. "It's for my dissertation." That magic word again.

"Oh, are you starting it now with professor—what is his name?"

"Carrie—Doctor Carruthers, I mean. He's quite a star, you know. I had a meeting with him, and I was telling him about your wedding dress work, and he thought it might be a good possibility—"

"My dresses? You told your professor about that?" Her embarrassment was palpable. "Lenore, you know I haven't sewn a dress for ... almost three years now. Simply haven't got the energy. The emphysema..."

"Dr. Carruthers says there's a lot of interest now in women and work. He thinks it could really help me get noticed, your sewing ... thing. Help me get a job, even." I doodled in a big skirt and veil for my stick bride.

"You never liked sewing anyway, Lennie. You remember how you almost failed Mrs. Moodie's class?"

She'd never forget. "But I wouldn't—wasn't—talking about actually sewing anything. God, no. Or you either, Mother." Be polite, Lennie: careful stepping is necessary. She barked a hoarse cough in relief. "What I need is to do an interview with you—just like my other interviews, remember, with the Mexican fruit pickers—Juan, Mariah—for my master's." Silence. "Dr. Carruthers was suggesting I focus on your workshop as a case study of Canadian women's working history." More silence. "Dr. Carruthers says you were a, a, a pioneer." I scored in long waves of hair for the stick bride, tearing through the paper.

She coughed. "Pioneer, hey? I'll have to think about it, Lennie. Maybe...." Metal clattered on metal. 5:40 p.m. there. She is probably standing at the western-facing window, getting ready to start her supper dishes. "Ah, a robin! It must be spring," she said. "Despite the six inches of snow today."

I said I'd talk to her as usual on Saturday and hung up, sweating. Round one to Mom.

4. *Transcript: August, Winnipeg. Lenore Brozowski interviews Marian Kelly*

Brozowski: Let's begin at the beginning. When did you first, um, start sewing wedding dresses? And why?

Kelly: Because of my sister-in-law. She was "in the family way," as we said then, and didn't want to go to a bridal store and deal with the snooty St. Boniface clerks, you know? [coughing, takes sip of water] And I felt sorry for her because she couldn't be married in her church, so I said I'd make her a dress—something modest but in the best satin, yes, and WHITE. [laughs]. Twenty years ago now. She was a Catholic girl; the boy was her high school sweetheart. And Wanda—can I say her name?—she liked my dress so much, she told her friends, and … I got good at it. You—my kids, Lenore and Bradley—were in school then, and my husband didn't really want me to work, he was, well, "old school." And I wasn't educated enough. [cough and laughs] Not that I ever made much money, but the sewing, it was mine. Had everything I needed, right in my basement. A sewing machine, some tables for cutting, a mirror. You know, I think Wanda became a teacher too, like you, Lennie.

B: Uh huh. Did you charge on an hourly basis? Or just for the final product?

K: Oh, not on an hourly basis. That would have been silly. Who kept track? I enjoyed doing it, you know. [lights a cigarette, coughs] I met the lady; I talked with her about her dress, and the kind of look she wanted—her day. I knew by then how much she could afford, so I worked from there. Costs, plus something extra. A flat rate, that's what it was.

B: Did you ever feel exploited in any way?

K: No, of course not! I enjoyed helping the lady, finding out about her plans. I loved seeing them in my gowns. And, of course, I looked forward to making my daughter a dress … someday. [pause] Those were the days, eh? I guess I chose to do wedding dresses like I chose to smoke [waves cigarette, coughs] and now, well, you don't have to say it—I'm paying for it. I've got emphysema. That's the truth. But I'm sixty and independent. I can smoke in my own home. No man to boss me. So I'm carrying on—until I have to stop. [END OF TRANSMISSION]

And she got up, butted her cigarette, went muttering into the bathroom. I stopped recording on my phone, put down my notes, felt my armpits prickle with damp. How long had it been since we'd really talked, for more than twenty minute weekly phone calls? Since before I left for my master's in Toronto. The emphysema—she was diagnosed last spring, but already she's on steroids to relieve breathlessness. Swollen ankles and wrists, stiff fingers. And still smoking.

I took a gulp of coffee, now cold. The certainty of those sociology 101 "isms": Marxism, socialism, feminism, capitalism. The place reeked, and I had to remind myself that this had been our deal: "Okay, Lennie I'll do it. But in my apartment, where I can smoke. And If I don't want to answer something, I don't."

Now the toilet flushed. I checked my notes. We'd gotten to question four, but there was still one sticking point: the ownership of her labour. I adjusted my (imported) scarf: I had dressed with care today in my black pantsuit with boxy gold-accented jacket, very Toronto, but it, too, was labelled "Made in Hong Kong." Well, at least it was washable.

Mom went into her bedroom. When she came out, her face was pink and shiny, like a child's balloon. "Here. I don't know if you remember these." She placed a thick envelope in my lap. I opened it, drew out photos, some brownish and curled, some still bright and shiny, everything from wallet to portrait sized. They revealed an army of brides, all sizes, all ages, St. Boniface neighbours or near neighbours. Family too. She sank back down into her armchair, rubbing her eyes. "Don't know if that can go in your, your—what do you call it again? Diss—?"

"DissERTATION. The photos? Not likely—strictly qualitative." (That's what Dr. Carruthers would say.) Some couples I knew; some I didn't. I spotted Cousin Lucy, beaming with her six-month belly tightly satin shining. And the stepdaughter of a former teacher, with appliquéd roses along the sleeves. Headless brides and grooms peeked from beneath the pile.

"They go back over twenty years now. I like to look at them, sometimes, and wonder how it all turned out. Husbands, children, work." She coughed. "Excuse me." Leaning over, she sorted through the shiny pieces of paper quickly, expertly, and handed me one. "This one reminds me of you. I would have made you a dress just like it, with a sweetheart neckline. And lisle cotton gloves, ah, Lesley Caron, Deborah Kerr."

"She's not a bit like me," I started to argue. The bride was freckle-faced with a big goofy smile. The groom stood a step back, as if in awe of her bridal aura. The bride is the Queen, Mom used to say—the groom is just her satellite, moon to the sun. But necessary, of course.

"It's her smile—see, she looks so happy. One of the happiest. And her hair—thick, copper coloured. Louise had a mane like that. You get it from her." She picked up her coffee cup. Frowned into it, then set it down with a decisive clunk.

"I think I'm ready for more questions, if you want to turn your phone back on."

"Thanks for showing me your collection. Sorry I'm not in it." And trying not to be rough, I pushed the photos back into the envelope, put it in Mom's lap. I began recording again. As she leaned forward, the envelope slid off her knees, and burst open. Brides spilled all over the floor. She choked a bit as I crouched down to recapture them, brushing off flecks of fallen ash. Caught my wrist, and said, hoarsely, "Okay, my turn: Are you happy, Lennie?"

5. *Post Interview*

My brother's apartment was empty when I got back, but "OPENING!" was scribbled on the kitchen whiteboard. (I had seen the artist's pictures in the paper Brad wrote for: paintings of flowers formed out of Crest and Colgate, a palette of pink, white and bluegreen streaks, manipulated with toothbrushes instead of paintbrushes.) Then in smaller script: "Won't need to brush TONIGHT!"

I found a frozen dinner that didn't look too old, popped it into the microwave, and then slid my phone into my valise: I'd listen to the interview later. On the plane, maybe. Edit it heavily. "Are you happy?" Jealous, obviously, of the university, of my ambitions, of Carrie. This was day number five out of a week-long research trip. Days one to four had been taken up with some things Mom had insisted we do first, like pick out new drapes for her apartment, go downtown to have lunch with the church ladies ("I've told them so much about you") and get our hair done. Remembering Carrie's lecture on standpoint theory, I consented to get my down-the-back mane cut and styled, just to please Mom. Would Carrie be impressed? What I saw as prep Mom called "catching up" after missing out on "your Toronto life." But tonight I had two more pages of research-board-approved questions, and she was still insisting on brunch with Brad and Phil at The Golden Samovar. Plus, there was Granny Brozowski, ninety-one, waiting in her nursing home. "She asks about you all the time, Lennie ... won't live forever" (cough.cough).

Channel surfing while I wolfed down chicken fettucine, I came across a show where affluent young women of America modelled variations of The Big White Dress in salons for their flocks of friends and supporters, including, usually, their mothers. The point of the exercise seemed to be to get the bride to "commit" to this expenditure—often paid for by someone else—just as she had earlier committed to her groom. Once I heard the prices were in the tens of thousands of dollars I switched it off, wondering what Marian Kelly would make of our latest capitalist romance.

Soaking in the tub later, I considered my own lack of romance and my singular grad school entanglement with Erik the Red, a manic Marxist. A brilliant, boyish monologist, he was entertaining for a while, and we shared a common interest in socialist politics and disdain for those "selling out." But when I failed to get my fellowship renewed, he moved on to a younger, still hopeful, PhD candidate. Wrapped in my brother's only available bath towel, I flopped down on the futon with an article on women and textiles. Vincent the cat tried to curl up at my feet. I pushed her off, let the pages of dense historical analysis loosen and slip away, drifting off into a dream. In it, I was getting ready for my own wedding in Winnipeg. Dad was alive, and Brad was married to Erik the Red's new flame. I was caught up in prewedding primping—pinning up my hair, putting on my face. And of course, The Big White Dress. We were all sitting in the family Chevy, on our way to a chapel, which was somewhere on campus, but when I got there, I suddenly realized I had forgotten to arrange for the groom. I was standing at the end of the aisle, wondering if I could make my vows just to myself, when Vincent knocked over my water glass. Sitting up, wet, I could hear Brad snoring lightly in the bedroom next door. I must remember to tell him; he'd find it funny, now that he and Phil had taken advantage of the new same-sex marriage legislation. Our family newlyweds introduced each other as "my legal wedded spice," respectively. As I rolled over in the duvet, I pulled Vincent to me, but she shook herself free, walked away.

6. *Second Interview: December, Winnipeg*

We actually didn't get to the interview until the day before I flew out—then we went from two in the afternoon till midnight, with spring rolls and chicken balls ordered in, taken with cups and cups of green tea. Her smoking almost killed me, but it was too cold to stand on the balcony for more than a frosty Winterpeg minute, sucking in air. Mom warmed to the task this time—her friends had insisted this was as good as going on *Oprah*—and she began by reminding me of how she had first tried to teach me to machine sew, with memorable results.

You were twelve. You ran the needle through your fingernail. The blood! You dripped all over Cherry Williamson's satin lining. And she needed it the next day, of course, for the studio pictures. Your father took you to emergency—they could only give you painkillers after they pushed out the needle—while I took a cab to Sears to buy more satin. Just as they were closing.

(Red as blood, white as satin.) *I remember. Dad stopped for jelly donuts, at Country Style, to cheer us both up.*

So stubborn. Hey? Too good for sewing. You liked a typewriter better.

Computer, you mean. Never typed. I wasn't good enough to sew with a machine. Besides, I wasn't remotely interested in weddings. Or the idea of marriage. A keener, a scholarship girl—that's what Dad encouraged me to be.

Not just Dad. Remember your graduation dress?

The blue one, with the big white collar?

No—green stripes, with a gored skirt. Buttons all down it. Little silver ones, remember? [Moving her hand slowly from throat to waist.]

You made that?

All of this didn't go into the transcript, of course. But what I planned to talk about, Mom didn't seem as interested in. I got what I could. (Capitalism? She let Dad manage the money, but thanks to an aunt who remembered her and "the cancer time," an inheritance arrived which meant she was free to live her own life after she turned fifty. Divorces cost money, and weren't usually done by "poor housewives." "Not that I ever hated your father;

we just got tired of each other. Poor Hank.") Then she began coughing, couldn't stop. Her lungs heaved, her face went pink, purple, then faded to almost grey. I jumped up to pat her back, get her water, then her pills. She couldn't get oxygen therapy until she quit smoking, the doctors said.

"Why do you have to do this to yourself?" I demanded as she gulped water, then air.

"What can't be mended..." she croaked, hand shaking, spilling water. "Sorry. Shall we take a break?"

Socialism. Being next door to the province of Tommy Douglas, we had a good argument about that one. *Was a society without wealth possible? Where did it exist? We all want a chance to rule. Even the bride is queen, she noted, the groom the king. Until, with luck, it's our turn.*

To rule?

Or, to serve somebody else. She shrugged. *Once you have a family, you'll understand—the power of making someone else happy.*

So the wedding dress work made you happy?

After my family, yes. I really wanted to make you, and your brother, happy, but once you were teenagers your lives got—complicated.

Freud had a famous question: "'What do women want?' What do you think?"

Why is it so difficult? What men want. She laughed, coughing again a little, making my own chest tense.

Love and work? That's what he said we needed, to be healthy, whole.

But love is work—or should be. She cough-laughed, reached for my hand. *Look at us, Lennie—how hard we're working!*

7. *Review of "Penelope's Sisters: Twentieth Century Women's Textile Art," by Brad Brozowski (Winnipeg Arts Scene)*

In 1979, Judy Chicago's "The Dinner Party" put the spotlight on women's creativity in a bold recreation of The Last Supper, using feminine sexual iconography in ceramic and textile art to offer a revisionist view of "herstory." *Penelope's Sisters* is a worthy 'daughter' of Chicago's project. Over a year ago, five researchers at the University of Toronto, under the leadership of Dr. Howard

Carruthers, sought out equally-silenced women's art. Carruthers says, "This show takes ten women who are hardly famous—some emerging artists, some skilled craftswomen, some the proverbial 'traditional housewife'—and presents work that might not be given such attention. Textile art, because it is wearable, usable, and so, disposable, is always the most invisible." The show uses a variety of media—computer technology, audiotape, photography, and three-dimensional displays—to demonstrate the many ways women engage with fabric. The quilts made for African victims of female genital mutilation by the Winnipeg Women's Collective, for instance, following on the AIDS quilt project, hang around the room. And the work of Marian Kelly (see artist photo) allows us to revisit the ostensibly repressive ritual of the white wedding, complete with formal gown. The hand-sewn original, donated by Mrs. Lucy Bachelder, formerly of St. Boniface, shows the incredible detail, including embroidery,that went into this dress, circa 1989, and the value it increasingly has for its original wearer. The PowerPoint display of brides wearing Ms. Kelly's dresses represents several generations of women who expressed their personal aesthetic through a nurturing relationship with a woman who was more than just a seamstress. Or as Ms. Kelly says, on the sound clips played at periodic intervals, "Feminist? I don't know. But I was a woman who worked hard to make other women happy—women who also had the dream of loving men."

8. *Afterword. "Finishing the Edges"*

The nurses were so nice, everybody kept saying, as the flowers were brought in, pillows fluffed and extra chairs found for visiting hours. Why had I never noticed this before, how the rituals of death and birth—including the birth of marriages—were secretly managed by women? On the first visit, I got off at the wrong floor—obstetrics—and watched a tiny black nurse, chanting in a Jamaican lilt, "You're doing fine, doing fine Dearie," walking with a hugely pregnant white woman, before the labouring woman stopped, bent over and bellowed, "She's coming, she's coming, holy shit!" I scurried back to the safety of the elevator.

I had just finished drafting my first two chapters, after sending

Carrie the edited interview, when I got the call from Brad. It was the day before Mom's birthday, 25 September, and I had written a note on my calendar to call her—underlined. The show had really been an unexpected gift; I got to work with Carrie for two solid weeks, plus two brilliant women's studies students who fell in love with Mom, and Mario, a postdoc in cultural studies from Manchester who organized us all by Skype, flying in the night before the opening. I attended two openings, plus the one in Winnipeg, wrote the page for "Marian Kelly" in the catalogue and was myself interviewed by a Toronto journalism student, who was more nervous than I was, blurting "wow" and "awesome" to my every answer. And Mom loved it. She kept saying, "What would your father think?" We could only afford tea, coffee and cookies at the Winnipeg opening, but I swear Mom was drunk by the time we drove her home, singing "I am Woman"—just the chorus, over and over. "I am strong/I am invincible."

"Hey, Lenn. How's it going?" Brad suddenly interrupted his own familiar opening. "Sorry, but it's the Queen."

"I know, I know, it's her birthday tomorrow. You planning something special this year?" Reluctantly, I turned from my computer screen.

"Lennie." Coughstammer. "Don't worry about her birthday. She's sick, sicker than we thought. She's in Winnipeg General—checked in yesterday."

"God, what for? I thought the drugs were working."

"You know she never did stop smoking, and last week she started spitting up blood. Very weak. At the least, it's pneumonia. Maybe worse, with COPD. When can you come?"

I phoned Carrie, left him a message, booked my flight. Two days later, Brad and I met with the doctors. A bad case but a tough pair of lungs, they said, to go this long. In a week, Mom rallied, stopped smoking, and recovered enough to go home. Then more homecare visits, help from Brad and Phil, oxygen delivered twice a week like huge bottles of formula. She had to sign a serious-looking form promising she wouldn't smoke and this time I believed her. Because Mom now had a new job: making sure I finished my dissertation. She proudly sent me "home, to your professor."

That fall, she phoned me twice, three times a week—damn Bell

Canada, she said—and asked how many pages I'd done. I'm not a machine, I said, half-scolding, so many stitches a minute. Then she wanted to see our interview. With some trepidation, I sent it. She said, "You clever girl. You didn't make me sound stupid." And she also asked for copies of the reviews of our show, which Carrie sent to me, my name highlighted in orange. I highlighted Mom's.

In early December, I heard from Brad that Mom was back in hospital and may not "be home for Christmas." I took my end-of-term marking with me and reclaimed Brad and Phil's futon, although reading crude undergraduate axioms about the rule of patriarchs seemed more meaningless than usual. There was already a few inches of snow on the ground by 6 December. Across the country, there would be vigils for the victims of the 1989 Montreal Massacre, when fourteen female engineering students—who hadn't known that their desire for work would be seen by one angry man as so offensive—were gunned down at École Polytechnique.

As we made our way into the hospital on this ominous day, I realized I was getting used to its smell of Lysol, urine, and wet wool. But I still wasn't used to the sight of Mom, looking so much older, grayer, shrinking under the sheets. Luckily, her senile roommate was asleep, snoring behind the privacy curtain. However, there was another lady, sitting beside Mom, when the three of us came in. She stood up, smiling.

"This is your daughter, isn't it?" she said, with a swoop in her voice, as if I were Angelina Jolie. "Lenore." She ignored Brad and Phil, who stood behind me, Phil whispering something to Brad.

"Yes, this's Lennie. She's working on—what d'you call it again?" Mom croaked.

"My dissertation. In sociology." I shook the woman's hand, wondering where I knew her from. She was wearing a cherry red winter coat, and held leather gloves trimmed with fur. Her soft brown eyes twinkled behind thick-lensed glasses.

"It's about me," Mom said. Brad, Phil, and I laughed.

I couldn't tell if she was offended but the other lady said. "Oh—I know—your mother's famous. She was in a show, just last spring."

"Did you see it?" That was it—the opening. For a while, there was a little crowd of St. Boniface women around Mom, making her eyes gleam and her colour rise alarmingly.

"Of course I did—my daughter is one of her brides! Amelia Watson, now Dupuis. I heard her picture was in it, so I went. Amelia was in Florida at the time so she missed out, but I sent her the article with your mama's picture."

"Sit down, everybody," said Mom. "You're making me tired."

Phil left to get more chairs. Brad shed his coat, kissed Mom on the cheek. I came next. Her breath lacked the warm earth smell I knew, smelled instead of rusty metal. "How are you doing today, Mom?"

"Can't complain. You make your bed ... you lie—" she struggled to sit up higher, groaning—"in it." Amelia's mother crossed her legs, sighed, nodded.

Brad and I tried to help Mom, but she pushed our hands away. "Don't fuss, for goodness' sake."

There was an awkward silence, covered by Phil's dragging in of two heavy chairs. The roommate moaned but didn't wake up.

Mrs. Watson soon left, saying she had to go to a funeral. The mood in the room seemed to darken, like the fading winter day beyond the window. I knew this time I would be here as long as she needed me. The doctor had already told us she was unlikely to last a month, but then, they had thought that before. After all, she had always been a hard worker. Brad was holding Mom's hand, and I took note of his new gold ring, still shiny. Now Phil was stroking Brad's back, as Brad stroked Mom's hand, in a kind of chain of comfort.

Mom reached up for me with her other, IV-taped hand. Said abruptly, "At least it's not cancer, Louise. I'm lucky, eh?" The blur outside must have been falling snow.

A nurse poked her head in and asked if we needed anything. Mom's eyes were closed, her breathing painfully loud. "Not now," she gasped. "I'm happy." I couldn't speak, so I squeezed her hand, gently, to avoid putting pressure on the needle piercing her skin. But didn't let go.

4.
My Mother's Linens

RENEE NORMAN

I fold tablecloths & napkins
a family dinner
it's a soothing motion
matching linen corners
women's hands over hands
always smoothing things over

there is satisfaction
in these movements
a contentment
in the rhythms
the connections between
one dinner & another
one generation & another

I love these linens
the way they fill my drawers
my mother
my heart
in the ones I choose
to lay out
busy hands
caressing lives
still folding
folding

the cloths in my mother's hands
no longer hers
the motions cradle her
like I cannot
over & over
smoothing

5.
Costas (Or, If You Prefer, A Tale of Two Cafés)

PRIYA PARROTTA NATARAJAN

I call my mother Amma. These days, most people in the West associate the name "Amma" with the famous, contemporary hugging saint who travels the world giving people magical hugs. Yes, my mother's hugs are magical, but no, my Amma and that Amma are not the same person. "Amma" is simply the South Indian word for "mother." Sometimes, I call Amma by another name: Profe. "Profe" is commonly used in our Spanish-speaking milieu as a short version of "professor," which she is by profession, although it is not an altogether inappropriate word for me to use to describe my mother, specifically. After all, she has been the greatest teacher life has given me.

Amma/Profe and I chose the name "Costas" for our two cafés. We were inspired in small measure by the popular café franchise in the UK with a similar name—Costa. But we were drawn to this name in greater measure by the landscapes that formed the foundation for our lives.

My mother and I both grew up in those places where land, sea, and sky meet, she in India and I in Puerto Rico. Neither one of us can locate our origins as one neat point or trace our journeys through straight lines, but more in the shapes of the meandering coastlines that formed our origins. Our lives have been global, defined more by encounter than by the consistencies that specific nations, cultures, communities, and families often claim as their own. We have discovered ourselves in those moments when borders dissolve and when the overlaps between languages, aesthetics, customs and values suddenly seem obvious and self-evident. And, perhaps most importantly, we have learned about ourselves and the world around us through our relationship with coastlines.

I was born in San Juan, Puerto Rico, in a hospital two blocks away from the ocean. I grew up near the sea. In the ocean, differences dissolved. The same water that reached the shores of Puerto Rico one day might, in some time, lap against the coast of Brazil. Or the coast of England. I sometimes wonder if all people who grew up by oceans have a special understanding of this interconnectedness. If all of us are, at some level, keenly aware that the materials that keep us alive—water and air, for instance—travel freely. That they circulate among us and invite us to appreciate the interdependence of our lives. It was by living on the coast that I was able to develop the spiritual space to understand and embrace the tremendous cultural diversities that my mother and father brought into our home.

Amma was born in Chennai, on the southeast coast of the Indian subcontinent. She was born into a family of classical musicians. The women in her family had all received training in Carnatic music, and at every family gathering voices and veenas would be brought out, and the beauty of this music would fill the moist, airy spaces of my great-grandparents' home. Some of these sessions were recorded, and when I listen to them, I always experience a particular sort of awe that is unlike the awe I experience when listening to music from other parts of the world. Perhaps it is the feeling of raw connection that one feels when meeting, in all its honesty and clarity, the sounds of their own, inherited spirit.

Appropriately enough, we first sat down to plan our cafés at an airport coffee shop in the international terminal in London Heathrow—a crossroads of the highest order. On napkins over mugs of chai, we sketched out our ideas. Our cafés would be global. Of this there was no doubt. We would never sacrifice the truth that comes with diversity for the validation that can come from cultural homogeneity. At every turn, we would affirm the common threads between seemingly disparate cultures and people. Any clear patterns in our décor and our food and drinks and music would not be the result of adherence to particular cultural models. On the contrary, they would reflect practices and sensibilities shared by people who may very well never meet each other.

This conviction radiated into our choice of music. The songs we'd play would be, for lack of a better way to describe it, "world music." Amma preferred Indian music, being from the subcontinent, born and raised. For me, music had always been a sublime form of dialogue, and as a result, my interests spanned multiple continents, and I enjoyed mixing and matching tracks in ways that people might not expect.

Easy flow from one cultural universe to another has been an important part of both of our lives. We do not treat the spaces in between diverse social worlds as entertaining places to visit from time to time. No, we live the majority of our lives in these spaces. They are our comfort zones, the resting place we require in order to continue our daily work of distilling from various situations those aspects resonating with people outside those spheres. It is exhausting at times. And it is for that reason that we found the idea of having a physical resting place, designed into existence by two like minds, so compelling and reassuring.

We chose to open one of these cafés in Washington, DC, and the other in San Juan, Puerto Rico. We relished the process of simultaneously setting up cafés in two radically different places because it forced us to consider the ways in which the two places can interact with and complement each other. We were going to manage the cafés separately, so in a way, acknowledging the common ground within the two cities was essential if we were to keep our close relationship going strong.

We had long discussions, and learned in the process that these two cities are equally vibrant, pulsating with life and possibilities for collaboration and celebration. San Juan has become this way through centuries of unlikely interactions between people from multiple continents and cultural persuasions. West Africa, Europe, South Asia, and the Indigenous Caribbean have met here, often in a spirit of violence, but equally in a spirit of cooperation and creative resistance. This is the tradition, and many among the latest wave of expats—including my parents—have embraced it and brought it into the future. Washington, DC, meanwhile, is home to people from quite literally the entire world. Culture is highly regulated in Washington, being as it the capital of the United States with an image of absolute authority to maintain. Absolute authority, I have learned, is one of diversity's most common and formidable challenges. Luckily, DC's cultural activists are ferocious and full of heart. Day by day, they are transforming the city into the kind of place that people from all over the world will feel comfortable living in.

"Fusion" was the word or label we used to manoeuvre our way around the fixed categories that existed only in people's imaginations. Conceding to this label opened up a universe of possibilities. Fusion has been a part of my life since I was a baby. Amma understood the secret to successfully transporting a culture across two oceans: find the resonances between her original South Indian Hindu culture and the new Hispanic Caribbean Judeo-Christian cultural surroundings.

In my earliest years, she and my grandmother created a powerful spiritual presence in my life, in the form of the artwork and stories and wise words that are part and parcel of the Hindu tradition in which both were raised. In my grandparents' house, and in our own, a colorful Pooja that was filled with flowers and incense and images of the divine made checking in with the universe an easy possibility. Amma gave me the foundation I needed to face the world with healthy amounts of confidence, sensitivity, and creativity. She showed me how each of the Hindu goddesses—Saraswati, Lakshmi and Durga—spoke to different aspects of our human existence and that although we may share more with one goddess than another, we must honour all three. After all, they are manifestations of the divine, and the divine can come in many forms.

In our house, spiritual truths like these very easily became cultural truths as well. The diversity of approaches to human existence, and the diversity of human existence itself became fundamentally linked in my mind. Coupled also with frequent travel, I learned firsthand that the best way to intuit humanity's unity was to experience its variety as much as possible. My mother's open interest in all people set a positive example for me.

Spirituality was implied in our cafés. We agreed that there was, therefore, no need to refer to religion overtly. We would not actively encourage faith-based events, nor would we adorn these spaces with representations of the divine. Instead, we decided to communicate what we understood to be the core of spirituality—the conscious practice of respecting and, ultimately, loving others—through the way we acted, and the sorts of social, political and cultural ideas and movements that we affirmed. And it goes without saying that storytelling was another crucial element of our purpose and process.

When I was in elementary school, Amma acted out chapters from the Ramayana and Mahabharata and cast my Beanie Babies in the lead roles. It was through these plays that our childhoods met. I grew up with more material abundance than my mother. Whereas my mother spent her early childhood acting out games with small unpainted magnets, I was acting out similarly elaborate games using a collection of toys that never played a role in my mother's childhood. Imagination was the common ground—and this was no small thing.

As a child my mother immersed herself in the mythologies of other coastlines. Captivated by the epic tales of the Greeks, the Romans, the Celts, and others, she began thinking about the world in wide and sweeping ways at a young age. I did not discover mythology until later, when my high school literature teacher assigned origin myths from Indigenous cultures from different parts of the world.

As a child, my imagination tended to be less epic influenced and directed than Amma's. I preoccupied myself more intensely with life's details. I enjoyed imagining my way through the minutiae of other people's lives. I spent one summer pretending to run a pub. I spent another working as a secret agent with my cousins. And yet another living with a friend in seventeenth-century Pennsylvania. At one point or another, I ran a spa, worked as a filmmaker, and had my own radio show. My mother didn't always keep up with these games, but I was no doubt inspired by her eagerness to understand other worlds through the books she read.

The stories that defined my Amma's childhood, as well as her professional life, made their way into my life at an early age. From her choice of names for the characters in my stories—"name the two characters Naipaul and Brathwaite, and have the heroines travel to Tobago," she once suggested—to her frequent mention of Jane Austen's ability to satirize her time, the literary and scholarly figures in her life soon became a part of mine. Over time, our discussions about both satire and Caribbean studies intensified. Without intending it, I lived my life in such a way that my Amma the Profe could remain my advisor, my confidante, and (when she would allow it) my partner-in-crime.

Depending on the type of conversation, we pull from different areas of common ground. When we talk about the social realities of growing up, Austen is our closest companion. We both attended primary and secondary schools where the closely related phenomena of materialism and preoccupation with status defined the social landscape. Together, we celebrate the art of satire—or perhaps more fundamentally, the art of making peace with reality by describing it.

When we talk about academics, we dive into our now-shared repository of perspectives from Caribbean studies. We discuss theory and apply it to our knowledge of not only the Caribbean, but other parts of the world as well. Through these sorts of conversations, I've learned how to question categories while remaining fully aware of the ways in which different geographic spaces cannot be meaningfully compared. It is also through these conversations that I've been able to practise the craft of turning everything—including life's most banal dilemmas—into an academic question. We joke about how what defines an academic, more than anything else, is the ability to turn life's mysteries into research projects.

These days, I identify primarily as an environmentalist, and my conversations with my mother have shifted accordingly. Now, we explore our favourite topics as though, suddenly, a new actor (the environment) has come into the scene. After some time at Oxford, where the importance of taking account of the nonhuman was impressed upon me, I returned to San Juan and we did exactly that. We reconsidered work that I'd done earlier on the connection between environmental degradation and a lack of respect for women. We revisited my papers on fugitive settlements that provided sanctuaries for maroon communities and wondered how the analysis would have been different if the mountains and rainforests of the greater Caribbean—the places where fugitives settled—were considered characters in the story.

Above all, we talked about Indigenous peoples—or perhaps more accurately, "Indigeneities." We discussed the politics of development, neoliberalism, and environmental degradation that had such profound implications for all people with close, conscious connections to the Earth—self-defined Indigenous peoples in particular. At the same time, we agreed that, certainly, the simple distinction between Indigenous and non-Indigenous peoples is not always appropriate. We recalled to one another the various ways in which connection to the Earth had been significant in our own growing up stories. We see ourselves as Indigenous in a way, and we wonder if all people share these characteristics—it's just that many live within geographies and worldviews that make it extremely easy to forget this. We agreed that at some point, the conversation about who is Indigenous and who is not (in the Caribbean especially) needs to give way to a discussion about lifestyle—and a firmly-rooted conviction that living in a sustainable way is ultimately the most reliable indicator of belonging to a particular place.

For each of us, a sense of belonging to a particular place occurs along coastlines. Amma has shared with me some stories from both Chennai and Mumbai (where she lived for many years). And I've told her what she already knew. I've told her how much San Juan's coastline means to me. How joyful I feel every time I walk to the beach to watch the colours of the ocean change as the sun sets and makes a light show out of the tropical sky. How scared I become whenever I see a change in the shoreline due to sea level rise or the advancing of a bad storm. I've told her how essential it seems to me that people from the world's coastlines united to communicate to the rest of the world how precious their ecosystems are. I say that if we were to lose these coastlines, the loss to human heritage would be tragic, and one day the world would realize so. Sometimes I talk about this a lot, but other times, I cannot find the strength to talk about it at all.

These conversations almost inevitably turn into brainstorming sessions. I brainstorm out loud, and she patiently listens. We tossed around many ideas. A musical compilation of songs from the world's coasts—"the kind of thing that Smithsonian Folkways and UNESCO do," we say. A human geography project on the resonances between different coastal societies. A research initiative of those communities in Puerto Rico whose cultural practices still speak deeply to the power of the sea. An artistic initiative around protecting baby sea turtles. (We were heartened to realize that this is very close to being achieved.) A booth at a farmers' market where we could sell our jewelry and our paintings and answer any questions that people might have about coasts. We've begun to bring these ideas into the cafés. We've put up large corkboards and decorated them with photos and quotations that suggest the sorts of change we're so passionate about. We host discussion groups on climate change and creative writing clubs where people can bring in their memoirs of lives by the sea.

It has taken a few years, but the cafés have begun to live up to their name. "Costas" has now become a deeply accurate descriptor of not only the "superficialities" of the café—its décor, its drinks menu, etc.—but also of the sorts of people and conversations that take place there.

Amma and I never really argued about how to go about this process. We know when to take charge and when to defer to each other. My mother knows the art of adapting to a new place better than I ever could. She knows how to find what she loves about home in the ecologies of another place. I, meanwhile, know what it means to return home after seeing the world, committing to its challenges and possibilities. Her imagination and my loyalty make for a nice combination.

Amma and I are lucky to live and work so well together, different though we are. We are a dynamic duo, a team that stays together through the laughter and through the sadness of shared values. The problems that many diasporic mothers and daughters are besieged with—language differences, embarrassment and judgment about social customs and preferences, and a general resentment about not understanding the predicament of the other—these tend not to be problems for us. What we have learned in our twenty-five years as diasporic Amma and daughter—and diasporic women—is that shared ethics is much more important than any overblown differences. The rest would wash away with the rain—temperate, tropical, drizzle, hurricane. In the end, it is all part of the same universe.

"Give me a room and I will show you the universe." These are the words that are written, in large hand painted letters, on the wall behind the bar in both cafés. It is our hope that, more than anything else, our cafés give people the spaces to ask questions about their universe—about the divine, ecology, culture, physics, whatever comes up. We've met so many new people so far—and the more we talk to others, the more we expand our empathy. And the more we realize that our story might be unique on the surface, but in the most essential ways, it is simply human.

6.
Gardens

RENEE NORMAN

I am growing a garden again
my youngest daughter
helps me pick out seeds, seedlings
map what should go where
plant what doesn't need
overnight soaking
tells me to write it down

this return to the earth
follows years of nurturing children
my own, others in classrooms,
universities

the black soil pungent
smells like the beginning of being
soaks up water on a sweltering day
like the elephants at the Calgary Zoo
greedy for liquid
spray after spray on tough dry dust hide

the pumpkin plant droops like me
in the heat of searing sun
perks up as leaves
wet
turn in supplication

I plant the beans and peas
plump
after their overnighter in water
remember my daughter's advice
my mother's lush garden long ago
the handful of dirt I sprinkled
on my father's grave
daydream about plants so close
together they strangle one another
or a bountiful harvest
I pick armloads for daughters

here in black soil
this earth womb
I plunge my hands
feel dirt enter my pores
stain me
with old rhythms
new possibilities
growing another kind of garden

7. Painting through Ruptured Maternal Identity

BATYA WEINBAUM[1]

If you can express mangled feelings in a work of art, you can overpower them. —Lili Lakich

Beginning motherhood at forty, I thought feminists had fought and won basic battles. I had been active since the seventies. I had written and published feminist theory inspired by Shulamith Firestone, Kate Millet, and Sheila Rowbotham, in addition to fiction, journalism, and poetry. I had studied with writers like Alix Kate Shulman and Marguerite Young, been active in the Women's Salon and the Feminist Writers Guild, been involved in women's caucuses of radical and professional organizations, seen movement and feminist venues review my books, been invited to keynote conferences, organized and mounted my own one-woman art and photography shows, sold art, read palms and cards in foreign venues and at women's craft shows and music festivals, recorded music, earned a master's, entered a doctoral program, and taught at universities. I had been flown nationally and internationally to present on campuses and at institutes such as The Hague, and was interviewed for newspapers and radio.

Having already established a professional identity, I thought myself able to have and raise a child on my own. I soon saw, through the experience of a pregnancy and subsequent events, that not much had changed. Men became paternalistic and opened doors. Yet I also suffered pregnancy discrimination by a white male thesis advisor at the doctoral level who questioned why I needed a PhD, since motherhood made me so happy. I was part of the second wave that changed so many things for women (Love), yet that experiential immersion did not protect me once I moved out of the progressive feminist bubble and into the deeper levels of reality, which required me to restructure my view of the world. How else could I fathom any of the above?

This essay will explore how this jolt formed my life, my emerging mother research and activism, my struggles as a single mother, the loss I felt when my daughter eventually separated from me to go out on her own after years of an almost symbiotic relationship, and how I dealt with the yawning emotional gap through art. Painting through this trauma—as I have written about another trauma (Weinbaum, "Painting through Trauma")—helped me mourn ruptures to my maternal identity, which had become so formative in my life over the years.

For eighteen years while raising my daughter, I had continued the feminist fight and battled on many fronts. I spontaneously arranged childcare at conferences and for my students in adjacent classrooms, started caucuses and task forces to improve the situation of professional mothers, researched activism among mothers, published about motherhood as an ethnographic and oral history research topic, and wrote about birthing in my ethnography (Weinbaum, *Islands of Women*). My daughter and my motherhood were the spectacles through which I carved my emerging professional identity, further cementing our relationship. Nonetheless, I struggled to keep the two of us and our dog and cats in adequate rentals. I got a tenure-track job, moved to Cleveland Heights, Ohio, and bought a house. With other mothers, I initiated a home school co-op, took my daughter to my university where she studied with students of mine from the College of Education or the Department of English who tutored her at my office desk, lost my tenure track-job in part for doing this, and found other contingent academic employment. Uncommitted to academe, I searched for family-friendly intentional communities, and we visited several. I took her to see the Dali Lama, started a wearable arts business, and integrated her into whatever projects I embarked upon as we went along. Our relationship was close. We "world schooled" rather than homeschooled, and her horizons were considerably broadened beyond her years by the way we read full-length novels and books like *The Women's Room* and *Midnight's Children* before she turned thirteen. She helped me run our wearable arts business and wrote book and film reviews for the journal I edit, *Femspec.*

At eighteen, suddenly, she was gone. I have had little or no direct contact with her since. I don't know her reasons for leaving. She's never told me although I offered to listen. Perhaps most painful was that I did not know where she was for about a year. I have made countless overtures to her, emailing, calling and leaving phone messages, sending cards and presents, inviting her to wherever I am, driving to deliver her guitar and art. She has called me once in five years, to ask if I had submitted my taxes so she could apply for college assistance. Losing her presence in my life felt like a loss of motherhood.

When she left, I was back on Isla Mujeres, Mexico, an island off the shore from Cancun in the Caribbean, where I had conceived and birthed her during fieldwork. We had returned for a gala *diezyocho* (eighteenth) birthday feast. Half-Mexican, she should have had this event at fifteen, but we were in the States then. Her dad from the Yucatan came to give her a gold watch and to gallantly dance with her at sunset on the pier. Also present for the feast were her midwife and the midwife's family, the nurse who had attended my daughter's birth, this woman's son, children she had played with when young, a serenading guitarist with whom I had worked the streets, the many people on the island who had helped to raise her until she was about four and we left for the United States.

My daughter had asked me to buy her a new dress, so I did. Although she had wanted to have the party and to reunite with her father, her female lover came to the party and wore a tie. This gender performance—whether intended or not—might have seemed odd, at best, to the traditional crowd. In other ways than this, she seemed to have difficulty fitting into the culture from which she had come, even though the trip had been motivated by her express desire to get in touch with her roots. Less than a month after the party, after trying to set up house in a hostel and work in tourism themselves, the way I did, the two ran off. They only got as far as my mother's in Oaxaca, but I did not know where they went. They told me they were going to Tulum for a week, yet secretly they packed and, unbeknownst to me, left for good.

She had run away before, once when we were living in Southern California and I was coming to the end of a short-term adjunct job—the economic stress was wearing for both of us, as well as my inability to provide a solid home base—and another time from Cleveland Heights when she got the news that she had gotten almost a complete scholarship to a college at seventeen and seemed terrified to attend.

Those earlier situations had been resolved. This time, walking through the streets—the same streets in which I had laboured to bring her into the world eighteen years before—I felt like the emotional afterbirth was coming out, as physical afterbirth leaves the mother's body following parturition. For eighteen years, she had been enveloped in my energetic womblike cocoon; suddenly, with a burst, she was out.

To divert myself from the pain of this tumultuous experience, I threw my energy passionately into exploring projects I had put on hold. Back in the United States once more, I was intermittently in and out of the house in which I had raised her. Though not living a traditional June-Cleaver-type lifestyle that the image usually holds, I was avoiding my "empty nest" which Betty Friedan claims does not even exist. Although it is not politically correct to admit that the phenomenon exists, according to Friedan, I came to feel that we can never heal if we continue to repudiate the idea. Denying the reality of women's traumatic loss when a child leaves home is the equivalent of saying that menstrual cramps, post-partum depression, and PMS are only societal-psychological symptoms of life under the patriarchy. For some women, these issues are real and exist and can be healed once acknowledged and adequately explored. I wanted to add the empty nest syndrome to this list. I am not alone in taking on such a subjective project; other women have begun writing, exploring the hidden grief that comes from having to let go of children who once were the center of their lives, and the inevitable ensuing ungrounding and unhinged confusion (Darling; Kadane).[2]

Two years after my daughter left, I was painting from the art of Ganga Devi, preparing for a trip to India to visit women painters in villages in Madhubani. Suddenly I realized I was painting feet first, and then once firmly grounded, slowly moving up to the image of a woman holding her baby in both arms. This direct contact between baby and mother stunned me. As the mother held her baby tightly gripped in her arms, an intense gaze interlocked the two of them. A sari wrapped them into one energetically. Painting, I realized why I felt disoriented. For eighteen years, I too had held this rigidly locked gaze, mother to child and back again. As a single mother of a single daughter, I had existed in just this sort of cocoon of the riveting maternal gaze relating to its object and the child staring reflectively back. With my daughter's abrupt departure, the womblike envelope surrounding us like a sheer aura had been torn apart. I had lost the defining object at which I had been gazing, through which I had been defining myself in relation to, for so many years.

Thus, I entered into representations of maternal subjectivity which Eti Wade discusses in "Refracting the Maternal Gaze: Mirroring and Mothering in Contemporary Photographic Practices." She argues that patriarchal culture rarely presents maternal subjectivity and that representational idealization often obscures actual maternal experience. She explores how artist-mothers who photograph their children often make images depicting a maternal gaze, contradicting the culture's conventional ideals. Wade advocates for mothers to make art from and about their own children to reclaim maternal subjectivity, a process in which I engaged.

Most maternal gaze theory points to the infant's ability to gaze at the caregiver; like Wade, I choose a different position of the same paradigm.[3] I turn that theory on its head. My daughter had gazed at me long enough to discover who she was; individuating,[4] coming in to her own personality, healing herself from the traumas of her childhood with me,[5] she set about successfully finding other people to gaze at to cohere her self-definition. She no longer looked to me as her mirror. I stopped being held together by her need to lock my eyes.

Since my focus had not only been on her but on organizing as a professional mother in organizations, in research, in writing and in the workplace, without this intense intertwining that had defined me for a number of years, I no longer knew who I was. To make up from this rupture from her physical engagement with me on a day-to-day level, I substituted gazing at photos of her—

and myself with her as her mother—and made art from these. Identity boundaries became blurred when I lost my identity as mother; my external identity evaporated; my professional identity had subsumed her as part of my identity; even as a professor I was feeding off or formed along with my identity as a mother—moving to take new jobs with her, not negotiating long-distance moves and travels on my own. When there was a rupture with my mother identity by her sudden departure, this ruptured all my identity and put my sense of who I was on unstable ground. Who was I, if I wasn't the mother-professional and professionally-invested mother?

Heather Tuffery's article "Are You Looking at Me? The Reciprocal Gaze and Art Psychotherapy" was very helpful in conceptually piecing together these intuitive understandings, although admittedly after the fact. Tuffery used Jacques Lacan[6] and other psychoanalytic theory to make the link between the reciprocity of the maternal gaze and the relationship between art, object, and spectator. As I read more, I understood why gazing at these photos—and the making art from them—soothed me. I had found a new anchor at last.

As a feminist mother, I had raised my daughter differently from kids she tried to befriend. This may have had unintended consequences. I must admit there was tension that existed, as my daughter began to emerge as a decidedly separate person and began the inevitable protest that she and I were not one. As Claudia (the nurse who attended at her birth) said in the hotel room we were living in that winter in Mexico, the *dieziocho* party was as much for me as for my daughter. I remember looking at Claudia blankly, on the bed in the hotel room, literally not understanding what she meant. Claudia explained that the party was also for me to celebrate that I would be free again. I didn't feel that the party was marking any liberation for me, although within a month of my daughter's departure, I tried to anchor myself by doing many of the projects I had bucket-listed and could not do while my daughter was still living with me. This included the Madhubani research trip, wandering around Varanasi writing poetry following cows, going to Taxco to make silver necklaces out of goddess images I had painted or collected, and going to

Figure 1. Mother and Child, Khahajaro Temple, 2012

Argentina to interview palmists.

I kept myself busy, going from project to project completing things I had put on hold, and added even more items. The list also included going to Khahajaro, in India, where I wanted to paint from goddesses in the temples (Weinbaum "On Tour"). I hadn't been able to go there when travelling with my daughter when she was twelve because of the erotic poses. She hadn't wanted to go see those, making clear that the thought repulsed her. Now, with her gone, I would be going to these temples to get in touch with my sexuality, which I had also put on hold while raising her.

At the temples, I found I was painting images of mothers and children, such as the one I photographed in Figure 1 and painted from once home. This surprised me, since the temples are mostly known and visited for carvings of erotic posing of women. Yet instead of rekindling my sexuality, I was drawn to sketching the women's bodies that were covered with children clinging to them—only 12 percent of all the female bodies at the temples. But those are the ones that drew me in and inspired me to make art.

When I came home, I made acrylic enlargements on canvas working from small watercolors made in the field. The first painting I developed was of a mother and a child in which clashing discordant energy emanated from a Mother-Earth type holding a child. I thought the painting expressed my culture crash on landing back in the States. But then—driven by my unconscious bubbling up—I switched to making sketches and water colors directly of photos I found around my house of my daughter, having connected with this archetype in India. I painted from her baby pictures and from pictures of myself as a mother, holding her as tightly as the woman in the sari held the baby in the painting I had put on my wall in my bedroom before I left (Figure 2).

Figure 2. Painting of Myself with My Daughter, 2012.

Like Dorothy, I found there was no place like home to get in touch with what I needed to work through in my own psyche, although I had journeyed to India for this realization. Those baby pictures, and pictures of myself as a mother which others had taken, had been around the house ever since my daughter had left. Each time I came back to the house in Cleveland where I had raised her, I was confronted with those pictures, which I found were leaving me emotionally paralyzed, causing me to sink into depression every time I came home. Then I would plan a new trip, and be off.

I started to repair my psyche by painting from pictures of her, which became intense. I painted a child trying to stand up and holding on; through painting this, I realized what kind of insecurity my daughter had grown up in, as we were always moving around. I painted another one called "Patriot Act Bunker" as it showed how tightly we clung together with all blowing apart around us. I was opening an empathetic channel to my daughter, understanding her more each time I did one of these paintings, as well as healing a part of my psyche that was blocked, allowing myself to cry and to release huge pieces of energy that had been stuck. I began to move through the defensive denial that I was feeling to let in her point of view with-

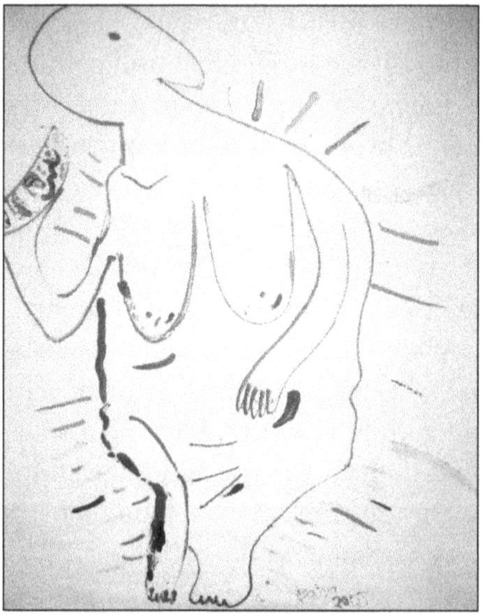

Figure 3. Red Earth Mother Goddess, 2005

out it engulfing me. I also felt connected on other levels, in other dimensions, in other moments in time—past, parallel universes, or future. Even though we had minimal to no contact, I could meditate on the feeling of being close to her and experience my own maternal presence by staring at a photograph, making a small water color, and then blowing up that painting to a medium-sized acrylic; sometimes I then collected objects and created a montage.

For years I had been painting from images of female divinity, including Earth mother goddesses (Figure 3), but these were always solitary goddesses, not goddesses with children, which I had never painted when my own child was actually still living with me. I had been painting from goddesses, having shows, giving workshops about the process of painting the divine feminine, and selling this work since the mid-1980s. But this was different. I was painting from my own photos of myself as a mother with my own child, and then also combining those with spiritual objects I had around the house or the studio, such as images of Meher Baba and a scarf from a Tibetan Buddhist ceremony, in an image called Mother of the Universe.

Figure 4. Sunrise Dispels Darkness, 2014

I painted a large canvas of my daughter that looks like she is rising out of the sea (Figure 4). The original photograph was actually taken by a professional photographer that I hired to cover her eighteenth birthday party. The way I painted her, she looks like a Mayan goddess rising out of the sea, an image I have painted and made jewelry from as well. This did not happen intentionally. But the process made me realize, as I painted, that she is just another wave of the sea. And it is natural that each wave comes in, and goes out. I was just a shore for a while, and it is natural that the wave went out. I became the mother, the earth, the shore, and experienced her as a wave, or a particle that the wave washed out, healing as the wave was leaving me. Thus, I truly experienced the healing power of art. After this shift, I added mixed media materials, specifically including strips of the art of women from Madhubani,[7] because I felt so very connected to the female-centred tradition of women's art.

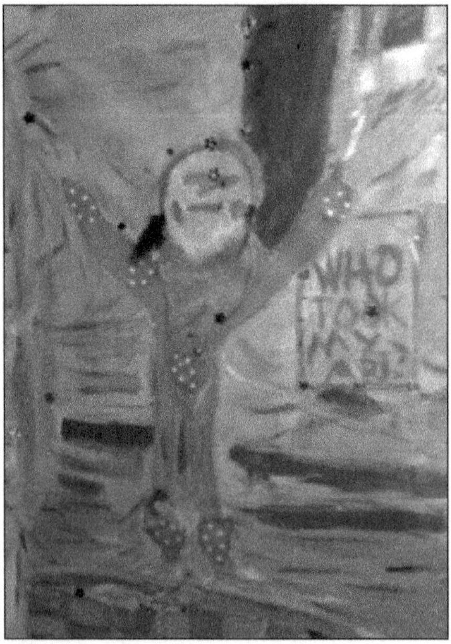

Figure 5. "Who Took My Art?" 2014.

The next painting I made was of a photograph taken by another professional photographer (Figure 5). In the last house, we had lived together she had asked to have a family portrait. I hired somebody, and he came to the house. He took photos of the two of us, and of her alone. I created this painting from one of the photographs depicting her jumping up on the porch, throwing leaves in the air, in front of a sign saying, "Who Took My Art?" (Someone in this college community had taken one of my paintings off the porch that I had left there one night when unpacking from a show.)

When I did this painting, I was struck by how frozen my psyche still was, stuck in the wrenching moment of the time that my daughter had left. My time was put on hold. I experienced myself as frozen, unable to move, to get beyond. I realized that I kept holding on, painting the images, hoping to release enough so that I can move on or to create a powerful channel of love, to magically draw her back. For several years, even when I travelled, I brought more photographs to work from and continued to paint.

Figure 6 represents the sudden break or fissure, the shadow side of mothering. I painted this after I read Alison Bechdel's *Are You My Mother?* and realized that my daughter was trying to destroy me, to prove that it was all right to leave me, and that the best

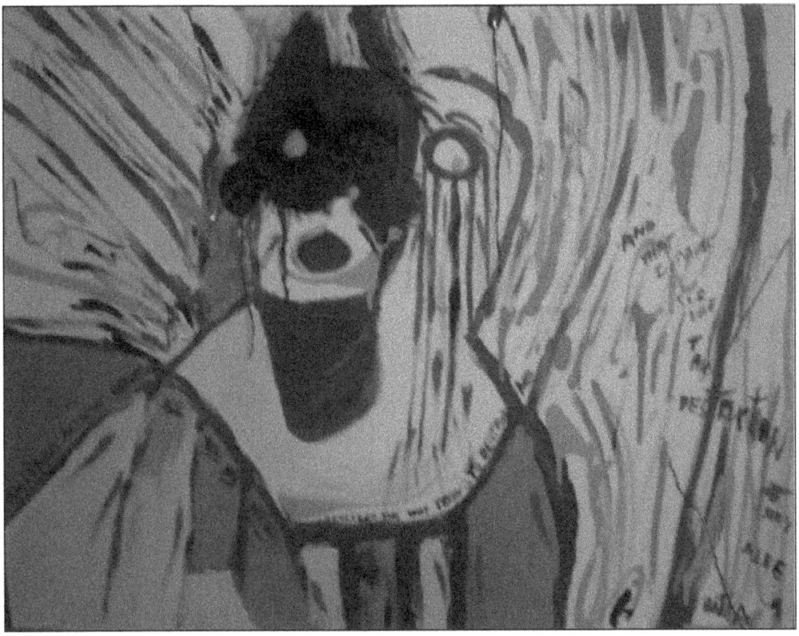

Figure 6. And Then I Read Alison Bechdel, 2012.

Figure 7. My Daughter and I Were Very Close, 2014

thing I could do was survive and live well, proving I could not be ruined. So art became a vehicle for my catharsis; art was a channel for deep emotion. Through art making, I facilitated a way to contain and integrate meaning that I had suppressed understanding of while still spinning in the posttraumatic stress of our prolonged separation and her sudden departure. Through art, I reconnected with my personal values. I used art as a space capable of holding conscious and unconscious material. The space the art holds became an alchemical vessel for processing multivalent experience that is not well understood and thus becomes sacred space. The artful imagery I created in the process of mourning the loss of my child and of my own motherhood is a kind of heartache, a swirling of grief-stricken poetry making its way to the shores of consciousness for all to see.

I hope that others can consider what the images reveal and look at the art in the context of awakening insights for themselves. Figure 7, with which I close, presents daughter and mother, perceived as "very close," but perhaps this is illusory, and cannot for a variety of reasons beyond a mother's control be sustained under patriarchy. I know that there is much more to heal, and much more to gouge out, in terms of honouring and reclaiming lost motherliness, lost powers as mothers, and reconnecting maternal identity with the forces of mother goddesses throughout time.[8] I still continue this process, and hope others might try also, for the benefit of more deeply understanding the impact of daughters' individuation on the mothers who raise them.

ENDNOTES

[1]I would like to acknowledge and appreciate the support, interest, and input of Susan Perlmutter, Janet Sharpe, Robin Toler, Rebekah Wray, Riki Perlman and various Demeter Press editors, each of whom has helped me along this arduous way.

[2]For evidence of the reason for rejection and denial of the syndrome, see Season Six of *The Good Wife* where Alicia Florrick, now a lead partner in a law firm and obviously kept very busy with more pressing issues, is asked by nearly everyone how she is dealing with empty nest as her son is about to go off to college. See also, for

feminist discourse analysis of postmaternal experience in popular media (Sheriff and Weatherall). Nonetheless, to allow for some women's experience, we need to emotionally fathom our own experience of this severing reality, rather than unilaterally reject that what is colloquially and pejoratively called empty nest exists just because it is sometimes used against women by mainstream media.

[3]See Freedman for the increasing difficulty of placing oneself within a framework; the difficulty (or revelation) compounded here is that I had come of age in the period of daughters' feminism, yet now I was in the position of the mother.

[4]See Jung on the individuation process.

[5]For further theoretical work offering insight to better comprehend the relationship between feminist mothers and their daughters consult Flax, Lawler.

[6]See Frois on psychoanalysis and Lacan to pursue the viability of psychoanalysis for understanding the development of the subject in aesthetic, cognitive, and social dimensions.

[7]For more about this women's art, which I import, see Weinbaum, "Madhubani Art."

[8]For more on how I am trying to do this now, see Weinbaum, "Feminist Spirituality" and "*Feminina Sube.*"

WORKS CITED

Bechdel, Alison. *Are You My Mother? A Comic Drama.* Houghton Mifflin, 2012.

Darling, Lynn. *Out of the Woods: A Memoir of Wayfinding.* Harper, 2014.

Flax, Jane. "The Conflict Between Nurturance and Autonomy in Mother-Daughter Relationships and within Feminism." *Feminist Studies*, vol. 4, no. 2, 1978, pp. 171-89.

Freedman, Barbara. "Frame-up: Feminism, Psychoanalysis, Theatre." *Theatre Journal: Perspectives in Theatre History*, vol. 40, no. 3, 1988, pp. 375-97.

Friedan, Betty. *The Fountain of Age*. Simon and Schuster, 2006.

Fróis, Joao Pedro. "Lacan in Art Education." *Visual Arts Research*, vol. 36, no. 2, 2010, pp. 1-14.

Jung, Carl. *Memories, Dreams, Reflections.* Translated by C.

Winston and R. Winston, Random House, 1989.
Jung, Carl. *Psychology and Religion: West and East.* Translated by R.F.C. Hull, Princeton University Press, 1989.
Jung, Carl. *Symbols of Transformation: An Analysis of the Prelude to a Case of Schizophrenia.* Trans. by R. F. C. Hull, Harper, 1962.
Kadane, J.M. *The Empty Nest: A Mother's Hidden Grief.* Kindle Edition, 2012.
Lawler, Steph, editor. *Mothering the Self: Mothers, Daughters, Subjects.* Psychology Press, 2000.
Love, Barbara, editor. *Feminists Who Changed America*, 1963-1975. University of Illinois Press, 2007.
Sheriff, Michelle, and Ann Weatherall. "A Feminist Discourse Analysis of Popular-Press Accounts of Postmaternity." *Feminism and Psychology*, vol. 19, no. 1, 2009, pp. 89-108.
Tuffery, Heather. "Are You Looking at Me? The Reciprocal Gaze and Art Psychotherapy." *Art Therapy OnLine*, vol. 1, no. 3, 2011.
Wade, Eti. "Refracting the Maternal Gaze: Mirroring and Mothering in Contemporary
Photographic Practices." *The International Journal of Social, Political and Community Agendas in the Arts*, vol. 7, no. 1, 2015, pp. 29-38.
Weinbaum, Batya. "Painting through Trauma." *Rain and Thunder: A Radical Feminist Journal of Discussion and Activism*, no. 61, 2015, pp. 29.
Weinbaum, Batya. "Feminist Spirituality and the Isla Mujeres." *Rain and Thunder: A Radical*
Feminist Journal of Discussion and Activism, no. 63, 2015, pp. 16.
Weinbaum, Batya. "Madhubani Art: What Do Women Experience Painting Durga and Kali?" *Femspec*, vol. 14, no. 1, 2014, pp. 14-73.
Weinbaum, Batya. "*Feminina Sube.*" *Triviavoices*, no. 16, 2014,
triviavoices.com/femenina-sube-my-aquarian-age.html#.WEHX-f4WcESU.Accessed 23 Oct. 2017.
Weinbaum, Batya. "On Tour with the Goddess." *Goddess Alive*, no. 24, 2013, goddessalive.co.uk/issue-24-home/on-tour-with-the-goddess/. Accessed 23 Oct. 2017.
Weinbaum, Batya. *Islands of Women and Amazons: Representations and Realities.* University of Texas Press, 1999.

8.
Sitting with My Mother's Bones

CHARLOTTE HENAY

> *Poetry is not only dream and vision; it is the skeleton architecture of our lives. It lays the foundations for a future of change, a bridge across our fears of what has never been before.*—Audre Lorde, *Poetry Is Not a Luxury*

Creek

Moments of note in coming to this work have me riddled with ambiguity in the telling.[1] Conceptualizing resurgence and social movement theory reaches through ancestry for me and begins, always, as do all my stories, with my mother. This piece is a collection of experiences, words, and remembrances that blurs disciplinary boundaries, and opens up differences inside theories of Indigenous resurgence and Black diasporic feminisms.

---

[1]This writing is an affirmation of the belief that our stories matter because we matter. Throughout this piece, I use the term womon/womyn/wimmin in the context of womanist, as referenced by Alice Walker in *In Search of Our Mothers' Gardens.* Womanist 1. From *womanish* (Opp. Of "girlish", i.e. frivolous, irresponsible, not serious.) A Black feminist or feminist of colour. From the Black folk expression of mothers to female children, "You acting womanish," i.e., like a woman. Usually referring to outrageous, audacious, courageous or *willful* behaviour. Wanting to know more and in greater depth than is considered "good" for one. Interested in grown-up doings. Acting grown up. Being grown up.

My mother said she hated secrets. Yet we lived a life replete with them, all different kinds belonging to all different people. In thinking through the secrets, in wondering about the stories that belong to the people the secrets were kept about and for, I find a history of myself. My family is people's stories upon story on top of stories. Sometimes, I am just tired. I wonder, how do I divest myself of my mother's compromises and still keep her jewelry?

Interchangeable with another Black folk expression: "You trying to be grown." Responsible. In charge. *Serious.* 2. *Also*: A woman who loves other women, sexually and/or nonsexually. Appreciates and prefers women's culture, women's emotional flexibility (values tears as natural counterbalance of laughter), and women's strength. Sometimes loves individual men, sexually and/or nonsexually. Committed to survival and wholeness of entire people, male *and* female. Not a separatist, except periodically, for health. Traditionally universalist, as in: "Mama, why are we brown, pink, and yellow and our cousins are white, beige, and black?" Ans.: "Well, you know the coloured race is just like a flower garden, with every colour flower represented." Traditionally capable, as in: "Mama, I'm walking to Canada and I'm taking you and a bunch of other slaves with me." Reply: "It wouldn't be the first time." 3. Loves music. Loves dance. Loves the moon. *Loves* the Spirit. Loves love and food and roundness. Loves struggle. *Loves* the Folk. Loves herself. *Regardless.* 4. Womanist is to feminist as purple is to lavender (xi-xii).

I qualify my use of the term womon as uncompromisingly queer beyond Alice Walker's cited gender binaries. In *The Resurgence of Indigenous Women's Knowledge and Resistance in Relation to Land and Territoriality*, Leanne Simpson states the following:

> Indigenous women and LGBQ2 people have been involved in resistance, dissent, mobilization and resurgence since the very beginnings of colonial occupation.... The logics of colonialism, however, have consistently denied and obfuscated these interventions, attacking the power of Indigenous women and LGBQ2 people by framing these issues outside of the political sphere and placing them firmly in the place of perpetual victimhood. Too often, the

In *Coyote Wisdom: The Power of Story in Healing*, Lewis Mehl-Madrona talks about telling our stories as "a creative act of community formation." He continues, "When we speak relationships form. Telling is an act of relating. Connections are created. Responses are expected. A community arises, made up of us and our audience. The audience is never passive" (131). Spirit is the common denominator in the processes I understand as Indigenous resurgence (Little Bear). These processes are replete with uncertainty, contested meanings of Indigeneity, and twisted recountings of land and labour at the root of settler colonialism. The work begins, then, as an affirmation of spirit in sharing and building community—a series of conversations with my mother after her death[2]—that frame resistance to oppression within a context of agency versus trauma (Tuck 409). I find solace in a method so

---

> 'activism' of Indigenous women has been reduced in the academic literature to issues regarding identity, violence, and discrimination—in a context that removes these issues from their colonial roots....This does a tremendous disservice to our collective work. (1-2)

How I read Blackness and Indigeneity is relevant to the contextualization of this scholarship. I am not interested in "racializing the identity of Blackness" (Dei, "African Scholar" 167) or Indigeneity (engaging in the "pursuit for an essential Black or Native subject," skin colour politics or intellectual essentializing). I want to complicate how Black and Indigenous praxis—intellectual and lived experience combined to form axes of intervention in our everyday lives—is informed by a shared history and the politics of the body (168). Our bodies matter, as do their presences and absences. This work reflects where I speak from, how I understand myself as an Indigenous womon, and situates that in a reclaiming of Indigeneity, as a political act of resistance. In writing for Afro-Indigenous futures, I aim to begin unwrapping the misperceptions, grounded in misinformation and erasure of Black and Native relations that route my Indigeneity, and that of many Black/African/Native folks in the geopolitical space known as the Caribbean and the Americas. There is, to quote Dei "a deeply complicated, complex and thoroughly organized socio-historical and political context of

chaotic it can find expression only in poetry, in a hermeneutics Chela Sandoval embraces as oppositional. I want to think, together, in the artificial sort of conversation that this is, my part being directional and yours, silent, about the peculiarities of voices heretofore extinguished, the collectivizing of the memories that are my mothers' secrets, and now mine, and the imaginaries they may offer for a different future. There is another essay offering a critique of heteropatriarchy in resurgence movements, (Simpson et al.) nationhood and sovereignty, expressing frustrations with Euro-dominant cultural abstraction, questioning methodologies of tribalism uninterrupted that decry "urban mixed-blood Indian and American writing" as self-indulgent (Cook-Lynn 338-39), excessively individualistic and irrelevant to sovereignty and Native intellectualism,[3] countering the fetishization of damage and celebrating our *survivance* as Indigenous wimmin and peoples, in the footnotes (Vizenor 93).

---

how Black people came to be" (*Reframing* 2) in the Americas, and how Native peoples came to be and continue to be dispossessed in their homelands. A thorough discussion of the history and specificities of colonial and Black/Native relations in the Americas is outside of the scope of this essay. It is essential to clarify, for my purposes of resurgence and remembrance here, that Indigeneity is an international category and a political site of intersectionality that Black/African and Native folks share. Neither of the latter identities should be collapsed into Indigeneity or erased by and/or within the other.

[2]It is significant that these conversations took place and take place, after my mother's passing. In inhabiting this space and time together there was no room for candid talks about being Indian (as my mother *whispered* the word) or Black. Ruled by heteronormativity/patriarchy and a commodification of the Black female body, sold and resold across generations of our family in multiple manifestations, ranging from chattel slavery to the expectation of exogamy and encouraged miscegenation underwriting contemporary Black-Native identities, the indoctrination of our exchanges revolved around status being conferred through filiation. My father was white, and so—according to my mother—that was

This is an invitation to resignification and a transgressive poetics. Some readers may find it easier to navigate than others, shifting between poetry and subtext easily. Yet others may find they have to negotiate a new way of reading that works for them. The subtext is not limited to the pages on which it appears. As footnote, the words are contingent at their beginning and unbound in their continuity as well as interpretation (Mol ix). It is not a luxury (Lorde 39); it is an alignment with Grace Hong's affirmation, in *The Future of Our Worlds*, that the work of culture, of imagining, is revolutionary (108).

This parallel conversation may serve to interrupt, deepen, question, or add a dimension to the thinking around anti-Blackness in Indigenous resurgence, the decentring of Black and Indigenous wimmin's stories, embodied experiences and practice of being and becoming. I insist on the stories of living in the in-between, in the hyphen, between people, between ideas, between one knowing and another (Harrison). Inhabiting the experience across space, place and time as a viscous sort of restoration, taking up space in the future with death as a catalyst for activism (Simpson, A.).

---

the identity I could, should, and *must* lay claim to. Anything less would be to refute the *agentive* exile and near madness she had condemned herself to, rejecting our matrilineal Creole Indigeneity (Jackson) in favour of the dominant ideology of paternal belonging and identification. At the time of this writing, the Bahamas is engaged in a process of constitutional reform. One of the issues on the table is gender parity. Children born outside of the Bahamas to Bahamian mothers, wed to non- Bahamian fathers, cannot claim Bahamian citizenship. My cousins and I living in Canada, children of Bahamian mothers and non-Bahamian fathers, born before 1973 are unbelonged.

[3]Resurgence mandates addressing state violence in developing strategies for resistance and movement building. Andrea Smith, in *Heteropatriarchy and the Three Pillars of White Supremacy*, affirms that white supremacy is organizing our continued oppression as Indigenous peoples and peoples of colour (POC), requiring a more thorough understanding of ways in which white supremacy works and is maintained. Smith's treatment of heteropatriarchy

Where Do I Begin?

miscegenated into dominance
creolized
touristified[4]
craving childhood reminiscence
glue repels
worn out
even my own veins are anathema they itch on the inside
i can see them stretched out over continents and honey-comb rock
beach ocean building
limestone stair
draped

---

and white supremacy recognizes that anti-Black racism can be reflected in racial organizing, and underlines the notion of value/labour in marking and commodifying the Black body. She suggests reenvisioning a politics of solidarity, in developing more complex strategies that have the potential to transform the political and economic status quo. Smith's work replies to Elizabeth Cook-Lynn in that she addresses the lack of a nuanced approach to the structure of white supremacy that "obscures the centrality of slave logic and reifies the Indigenous/Settler binary" (71). Smith denounces what she calls "secondary marginalization," prevalent in heteropatriarchally dominated praxes of Indigenous nationhood and settler colonial studies. Chela Sandoval's hermeneutics of love is necessary in negotiating Smith's pillars differentially, else they remain siloed, precluding a complex consideration of Red-Black relationships foundational to the Americas. See Sylvia Wynter's triadic model, a "dually antagonistic and interactional dynamic" of African-descended population, European whites and Indigenous folks in the Red/White/Black relationships reiterated by Eve Tuck and Wayne Yang as Settler/Native/Slave (9). Jack Forbes's *Africans and Native Americans: The Language of Race and the Evolution of Red- Black Peoples* and Jace Weaver's *The Red Atlantic* complicate the white supremacist and fundamentally divisive history of settler colonialism in the Americas. This analysis invites a con-

pulsing over canopy beds and louvred windows
in their imaginary absence i feel the ache
nostalgic of a lost limb
i want to toy with
the stump of my identity before i am snuffed out
whoooooooooshhhhhhh
into extinction
recognition and repair for stitched arteries leak into the
in between[5]

---

versation about resurgence in Black-Native identity and relations, false sovereignty, and the legitimation of nationhood. These are relationship-based terms I can work within, refuting the irreconcilable discourse of who has paid the greatest price for "being kept in this system of symbolic representations and its model of being and behaving" (Wynter 41), Black folks through slavery or Indigenous folks through genocide.

[4]In considering resurgence and a context of cultural reclamation, it occurs to me that some relatively stable frame of reference, in the face of assimilation and colonial legacies, is a precondition for asking ourselves how we can, as Brock Pitawanakwat phrases it, "live Indigenous lives in a colonized setting and remain faithful to our ancestral ways while rejecting the seduction of settler society" (Simpson 138). How do those residing in the in-between recognize ourselves and who we have become? This *whereiamnow* taking up of identity discourse is an integral part of re-culturation, faced with a "sense of colonial alienation as the root cause" of work that is about survival and writing ourselves out of shame as much as re-sistance and re-constitution of peoples (162).

[5]"A hybrid is a cross between two species, such as the mule and the hinny, which are female-male and male-female crosses between horse and ass ... both the mule and the hinny are infertile, which results in the species remaining distinct, held separate by an apparent natural check" (Young 15). The in-between is a hybrid space. *Mestiza*, womon, hybridity, ethical space (Ermine et al.), and differential consciousness (Sandoval) are terms and methods that trouble the notion of boundaries and of mixed-race identity. These terms and methods imply that there is a new imaginary to be

time space place[6] mothers' land-ed periwinkle ackee johnny
cake
flickering across world views
is a wake
for my grandmothers
they come
when I call
nighttime vigil for my child wrapped in bright made from
anguish
transmuted hatreds
bred into coffee cream
set aside the gin
in a heartbeat
burn for spirit
breathe for mothers
is there another story for me in there?
sick handed down
healing policing ourselves so industrious we are relieved

---

forged from relationality across boundaries. Young's definition of hybridity is sufficiently facetious as to defy its conceptualization as literal, opening the door to recognizing the possibility that hybridity reinforces liberal multicultural notions of universal POC identity, which negates the specificities of anti-Blackness and Indigeneity at the same time as it opens a space of fluidity by virtue of its mutative and flux nature.

[6]Little Bear and First Rider talk about how time, space, and place converge in Indigenous Knowledge traditions: "native philosophy consists of and includes ideas of constant motion/flux, all creation consisting of energy waves, everything being animate, all creation being interrelated, reality required renewal" (Little Bear). The common denominator is spirit. In comparing Western and Aboriginal thought, Little Bear says of space as a major referent in Aboriginal thought to time in Westerners' minds, "The constant flux notion results in a holistic and repetitive view. If everything is forever moving and changing, one has to look at the whole of being to discern developing patterns." He quotes Benjamin Whorf in stating that time is, "a realm of expectancy,

even of our own agency
tired
I ride bitch alongside my own freedom *wordsajumbleof-progress* in my
mouth teeth unbound i come to meltdown
silver shackles
molten anger and memory
I want
those trees and degrees very badly
discovered
bags of Bacardi caps and beetle runs no exception
to the craving that has powe-red
this reconstruction resurgence becoming
i don't need you
to tell me this is my
inheritance
i recognize it on the death certificate

floating
i have never lived
Arawak Pequot Taino Creek Seminole ways spinning
through blue holes *lickuhduhtarbrusssssssh*

---

of desire and purpose, of vitalizing life, of efficient causes ... one of the implications arising out of this notion of time is that the ancestors are only two days away. The stories, the songs, the ceremonies, the teachings are never more than two days old in the memory of the people" (Little Bear). Tiffany King names it a:

> simultaneous and syncretizing way of seeing and knowing ... an epistemic tradition of Black and women of colour cultural workers, spiritualists, and intellectuals ... a decolonial sense of time relies on the palimpsest and other non-chronological modes that can appear to congeal centuries and eras into a viewable frame ... temporality seeks to make eras and events that seem remote and unrelated into proximity ... the ways that they produce knowledge often work outside the epistemological frames of coloniality. (17)

waiting under water eyes open
sucker
fish hitches onto my hips i don't see
the barracuda
until
the only recourse is to
scamper leaping snagged propeller
bleeds diluted ancestry into salt
uncle not my uncle spear his only companion *down down down* no breath
dancing with our mother for dinner
trailing fingers in night sea skimmed by hungry mouths
yellowtail come up
half gone disappeared by the tickle beneath my fingers over gunwales
rocked by waves
headless
snatched back i cradle what's left
my cousin swims with sharks
guffaws at my foreign sensibilities
settles
almost went back but for intergenerational manferrence
hisfatherandmymother gave a whole new meaning to us *callineachudduhsistabruddah*
love affairs marred by cockroaches and vegas showgirls widely available
blackness
be-come home legacy insufficient to repatriate
me singlehandedly caught tossed fruit drove drunken revels home to gunpoint encounters
under lamplight and thought this was ancestral
practice well
by that time
that's what we had left
my mother capers beneath liquid
merciless thieves of our children's bones
you can drink these finite ripples in a land where i keep dogs' and white folks' secrets

swallow the lost
escapees diasporic neocolonial self-mutilating
nation states hand over heart we are all
punishing each other believe it
is a form of love
will my hands cramp with arthritis jagged with dysplasia
tongue twisted
with acculturation and appropriation
soaked in an inland sea of lies
genetically marked into authenticity on landscapes of souls
spill that milk don't touch each other love each other know
each other
sever *rightfromthegetgo*
filth
reprobates
ancestry to cut your teeth on
my
that looks lovely
better[7]
i watched that bird flip broken wing longer than i could bear
couldn't leave it
couldn't help it
called in a rescuer
provided a box
cold as shit why daydream about faraway folks who look

---

[7]Specific to southern Black and Native borderlands, in *Reconstructing the Native South: American Indian Literature and the Lost Cause* (2011), Melanie Benson Taylor engages in a reconstructive project. I find this quote useful in representing the confluence of Black and Native identities and projects in a postbellum south: "while the peculiar institutions of slavery and segregation did much to bring southerners together, it did nearly as much to drive them irrevocably apart ... until recently the border *between African and Native groups* had been policed studiously by ideological inertia, which James F. Brooks describes as 'the colonial incentive to keep the two peoples apart,' and hence protect the white power base from a colored coalitions" (77, my emphasis).

like me smell like me
come on
brown emergent from purulent chrysalis no iridescence here
it's a bat
looks like a moth
excruciating stretching wet
wings spitted roasting someone *lickitup*
there's a piece stuck
between
your teeth

eyes close
hold my belly
trees fall spirit walkers culled not indigenous
to
this
land
decisions made by creole bankers developers citizens
related to me by choices some others made now
i understand what she meant
said she came to realize she lives in a black country
home not her own since she don't belong
the way they say we ought to since she won't crawl
into the skin they've stretched out for us
a moulted remnant of my-the-ological proportions
can i get an amen

Black Seminole

i've been listening
i've been thinking
about this seemingly privileged chaos
under tone
ofsurvivalofabuseofaddictionoftoday
relatively comfortable compared to survival
uprootedness commodification *bodyfamilyidentity-sexyoualitygendher*
walking down the street to bring home him's car

paid for it
don't make it yours
in front of *anothermother's* house
grateful he hits the walls
until his knuckles bleed
better
than you *lookaway*
every cardinal rule of relatedness is violated
thisisyourmealticket
if you begin to pay
attention
what you have buried
is reborn
eight *chirren* dead
husband
burndownyourhouseinsurancemoney
marry off spring
trade them
for life
style
fifteenbeeninschoollongenough maybe it was
thirteen *childrennumbersruntogether*
owned renamed reclaimed
givenyouyourfreedom
last two babies left
is that profound thankfulness to have them
with you
as you *travel*?

grandmothers' stolen names

so you are adrift always
withouttribewithoutlandwithoutsongs
without gardens
bush medicine soursop breadfruit avocado
pear cherries bay lavender sapodilla mango sage sour
orange lime jujube guinep
sugar

apple ackee orchid hibiscus periwinkle
match-me-if-you-can
papaya sunflower,
scorpion tail.

Fertile ground for a hermeneutics of decolonial love (Sandoval 143), Indigenous Methodologies, (de)colonizing projects. In resurgence,[8] re-storying, re-searching our memories, individual and collective, what terms exist for our theoretical work? I am wondering what memory and presence look, feel, and sound like in being and becoming Indigenous, in visioning Afro-Indigenous futurities. To whom does this matter? And in what places? In engaging in a conversation about Indigenous resurgence, I'm locating the movement as multiple and manifold processes. How might transformative praxes that are counter-hegemonic and my grandmothers could get behind be envisioned?

---

[8]Resurgence is a collective and relational process. It may be experienced through individual practices while not being limited to or defined as such. Colonization and decolonization are likewise structures that require collective deconstruction. Patrick Wolfe in *Settler Colonialism and the Elimination of the Native* describes settler colonialism/invasion as the following:

> a structure, not an event ... elimination is an ongoing principal of settler-colonial society rather than a one-off (and superseded) occurrence. The (positive) outcomes of the logic of elimination can include officially encouraged miscegenation, the breaking down of native title into alienable individual freeholds, native citizenship, child abduction, religious conversion, resocialization in total institutions such as missions or boarding schools, and a whole range of cognate biocultural assimilation. (388)

This structure commodifies the relationship to land and conceptualizes it as contingent, in the present, upon possession, exploitation of its resources in a corporate fashion and continuous occupation. This obfuscates what Wolfe calls "glaring inconsistencies" such as the sedentary Indigenous communities

fight where you are you don't need to go looking
beyond your own doorstep
it's all in need of changing he said
grey ghosts hair powerful
re-membering
what of the language that is home
language that teases us and leaves us hungry
strips us of clarity and conviction
imprisons us in brightness that is a veneer
reduced by strategizing to gain minimal ingress
into a system we are not meant to walk in
throwing down words of possibility opening new windows
of hope
that don't feed my children yet bleed into my nightmares
waking hours to be borne in questing for alternate realities
indigenisms[9]
formica
underground gardens bloom with red flowers drip with rain
clandestine conversations with my mother in a parking lot
driving someone else's truck
i sure don't recognize it
botanical dreams
wailing aunties
mother holds court while i can barely muster a whisper
we were sure i would bellow
when the time came

---

across the Americas—the fact that settlers themselves came from somewhere else and that creating homesteaders out of Natives and Blacks hasn't conferred citizenship status or belonging upon either (396).

[9]Rinaldo Walcott, in the *York University Faculty of Social Work International Day for the Elimination of Racial Discrimination Annual Lecture 2014*, used the term "Indigenisms" as futurity, underlining the cooptation of equity and diversity theories and tactics into mainstream institutional cultures. He invoked a conversation about multiple Indigenous futures, speaking Indigeneity as a process and not an identity.

can't access anger
it's entombed along with her
carried me over oceans and universes driven by hybridity
sought safety in places where everyone else was righter
whiter
shackled in offspring
bones ache before they find cold earth
come out tree frogs
call your name
i need you to show me story
under my tongue sandpaper tickles hope
behind my eyes i see global dialogues opening[10]
in the cavity of aching bellies
vomiting boundaries never knew they were ceremonies
stand
beside me not behind me
you can't do that
i won't allow it
i am not a megaphone
to speak of return we just got here
too soon
sit with me this once
song for the morning
sugar without feathers adorning the rope
too much
buried in a daughter's flesh
some call it violation I prefer *habitcompanion*
found lurking in disenfranchisement should one have the
absolute misfortune to be called
Adelaide
spitting the seeds of together

---

[10]There are dangers in entangling less-than-specific terms for Black/Native folks and their interrelations, risking obfuscating specificities of anti-Blackness, replicating oversimplified Black-white and Native-settler binaries and ultimately reentrenching static extinction dialogues of savage Natives, imminently and always enslaveable Black folks.

learning to ride the turtle
turn inward
between layers of our own memories[11]
more and less than all these wimmin want
wrapped up in mite ridden cloth and other people's words
being and becoming a public act of continuity
show your work
algebraic functions of endless travel
offering yourself up for dissertation
this is my method
slow plodding inside a hermeneutics of shapeshifting
back and forth across *timeplacespace* multidimensional
transnational
all twisted up
backkneeme
from the outside in
an-other story
there is a spot at the back of my head
where it sometimes meets the pillow or a hand
where *thehairmyhair* is particularly nappy
springs un-rez-trained from the root defiant
CALLS OUT no pick no comb
tolerates an occasional caress
refutes advice *whatimaynotlikebutisbesttodo*
relax
get it to lay down
take it horizontal

---

[11]Considering the multiple complications of the imaginary and the recorded—mutually interchangeable given genocide and slavery as ideological frameworks—Daphne Taylor-Garcia's *Decolonial Historiography* speaks of "complex and nuanced dynamics" (18), obscured by an analysis that fails to recognize "shifting designations" (18) of cultures, instead representing non-Western peoples as homogenous. Taylor-Garcia calls for a "more complex telling of history that respects memory, imaginings and feeling" (5). We have to ask what documenting people means and how we write down identities.

along with the rest of my head
lends itself to shaping malleability
GET OUT i say to them
haven't got much left pushing up against a stone has pressed
the sour out of me
mostly pasty resignation occasional sadness
leave me to pick out the bush medicine *aks* for brown
nipples children returned standing up proud
sweet sop juice milk from home tickles my fingertips kisses
my palms
reliably returns to its ancestral form
come to my kink with the appropriate reverence
if you cannot find it in you
imagine

To Sit with My Mothers' Bones

renewal
women sand water blood
breathe in the *nevermind*
what will we eat
you can't drink memory
i prefer
crayfish
conch
lungs full of water I can wrap
my head around how to let go
of return to flotilla cities of salt
and burn
where do we rebuild
why are we talking inevitabilities
was their exile prescient
did they know we would drown how can I write without
breathing
nopausebetweenthoughts
it's out
theses don't come to me ceaselessly
moments convenient for someone

else neverending repairs cannot give back
mynamemygrandmothersmyequanimity
i must take it
coat myself in its stickiness
roll in shards of your failed occupation
regurgitate your indignation
strut crowing around
your arrogance
pluck you
sugar coated intestines deep fried in ancestral fat
you can't possibly repay your debt
gulps your indifference in a toothed maw rising
from betwixt islands
vortex you into a whirlpool of tactics
green your artful indigenizing of
spirit paths
you may go
leave your children and waistcoast behind
we will have need of clothing and labour
i want bromeliads in bathrooms
to watch for snakes in toilets
digested by mothers' fierce appetite for strangers
balance foam rollers as keeper
doan wan fight no more
wan laff mout open teet showin
memorystorywaterstone
go without me
i insist
too much to carry
detangle it from that grandmother's hair
washed in mangrove root
speckled green light at dawn
she dances there when she is alone
shiftstwistsshapes herself into
stump path box tendril
flowsliquidthroughdark spaces
something else
when you look again always herself

recognizable to those who have known
her bespeaks bush medicine and children
calls me gently while I gather my fear
cradles it in gnarled fingers enfolds it into
her centre
it beats there
junkanoo
dances with remembrance
across circles of time
she has waited while we quested
breathing connection
enough wondering
clothe yourself in your custom
strip the pieces grafted
toxic on top of flesh
gaping holes filled now see
thisshapenewshapetrueshape
until next shape
you can hide in dark holes
simpering it comes creeping nonetheless
in skin folds and potted plants
we all crawl into each other slightly acid
takeupallthatcomes
i just want to hold you in speckled green light
watch the play of your skin over stones
across genealogies and water
call you home when its time
witness
gnarled twisted theories envelop
you in slightly brackish backwater
interstellar without a manual or a prescription
she won't talk to me now
wanders alone amongst post it notes to her self
talking dirt to strangers
burned down the old house of bodies as currency
don't those Indians have any damned names
can't you trace your blood
quantum

in those stickies
take the memories with you when you leave to find your stories
don't forget me
how many cups of coffee until
revolution and imagination wake up together.[12, 13]

---

[12]Resurgence mandates that we "challenge ourselves and our political communities to be conscious of the ways in which (social movements) become institutionalized and inadvertently reproduce patterns of isolation, stifle radical possibility and growth, and lead to forms of commodification that often typify nonprofit and academic culture" (Bierria et al 9).

[13]Sections of this work have been previously published in Henay, Charlotte. "Becoming Indigenous: Hybridity and diasporic writing." *Feral Feminisms,* vol. 4, Summer 2015, pp. 69-73, http://feralfeminisms.com/hybridity-and-disaporic-writing/.

WORKS CITED

Benson Taylor, Melanie. *Reconstructing the Native South: American Indian Literature and the Lost Cause*. University of Georgia Press, 2011.

Bierria, Alisa, et al. "Community Accountability: Emerging Movements to Transform Violence." *Social Justice*, vol. 37, no.4, 2014, pp. 1-12.

Cook-Lynn, Elizabeth. "History, Myth, and Identity in the New Indian Story." *Handbook of Critical and Indigenous Methodologies*, edited by Norman K. Denzin, Yvonna S. Lincoln, and Linda Tuhiwai Smith, Sage, 2008, pp. 329-46.

Dei, George Sefa. "The African Scholar in the Western Academy." *Journal of Black Studies*, vol. 45, no. 3, 2014, pp. 167-79.

Dei, George Sefa. *Reframing Blackness and Black Solidarities through Anti-colonial and Decolonial Prisms*. Springer Nature, 2017.

Ermine, Willie, et al. *The Ethics of Research Involving Indigenous Peoples: Report of the Indigenous Peoples' Health Research*

Centre to the Interagency Advisory Panel on Research Ethics. Indigenous Peoples' Health Research Centre, 2004.

Forbes, Jack. *Africans and Native Americans: The Language of Race and the Evolution of Red-Black Peoples*. University of Illinois Press, 1993.

Harrison, Teva. "In-Between Days: First in a Series of Comics About Living with Metastatic Cancer." *The Walrus Comics*. The Walrus, 15 Mar 2015. thewalrus.ca/in-between-days/. Accessed 15 June 2015.

Henay, Charlotte. "Becoming Indigenous: Hybridity and Diasporic Writing." *Feral Feminisms*, vol. 4, Summer 2015, pp. 69-73, feralfeminisms.com/hybridity-and-disaporic-writing/. Accessed 23 Oct. 2017.

Hong, Grace K. "The Future of Our Worlds: Black Feminism and the Politics of Knowledge in the University Under Globalization." *Meridians: Feminism, Race, Transnationalism*, vol. 8, no. 2, 2008, pp. 95-115.

King, Tiffany, Jeannette. *In the Clearing: Black Female Bodies, Space and Settler Colonial Landscapes*. Dissertation, University of Maryland, 2013.

Little Bear, Leroy. "Traditional Knowledge and Humanities: A Perspective by a Blackfoot." *Contours Journal*, vol. 2, no. 3, 2012. Accessed 27 June 2016.

Lorde, Audre. *Sister Outsider: Essays and Speeches*. Crossing, 1984.

Mehl-Madrona, Lewis. *Coyote Wisdom: The Power of Story in Healing*. Bear, 2005.

Mol, Anne-Marie. *The Body Multiple: Ontology in Medical Practice*. Duke University Press, 2002.

Pitawanakwat, Brock. "Bimaadziwin Oodenaang: A Pathway to Urban Nishnaabe Resurgence." *Lighting the Eigth Fire*, edited by Leanne Simpson, Arbeiter Ring, 2008, pp. 161-75.

Sandoval, Chela. *Methodology of the Oppressed*. University of Minnesota Press, 2000.

Simpson, Audra. "Decolonizing Our Minds: Life is a Protest Event." University of Toronto, 28 Feb. 2015, Multi-Faith Centre, Toronto, ON. Keynote Address.

Simpson, Leanne. "Queering Resurgence: Taking on Heteropatriarchy in Indigenous Nation-Building." *Leanne Betasamosake*

Simpson, 1 June 2012. www.leannesimpson.ca/writings/queering-resurgence-taking-on-heteropatriarchy-in-indigenous-nation-building. Accessed 15 Feb. 2016.

Simpson, Leanne, et al. "The Resurgence of Indigenous Women's Knowledge and Resistance in Relation to Land and Territoriality: Transnational and Interdisciplinary Perspectives." *Intensions*, vol. 6, Fall/Winter 2012, pp. 1-7.

Smith, Andrea. "Heteropatriarchy and the Three Pillars of White Supremacy: Rethinking Women of Color Organizing." *Color of Violence: The INCITE! Anthology*, edited by Andrea Lee Smith et al., South End, 2006, pp. 66-73.

Taylor-Garcia, Daphne V. "Decolonial Historiography, Thinking About Land and Race in a Transcolonial Context." *Intensions*, vol. 6, Fall/Winter 2012, pp. 1-24.

Tuck, Eve, and Wayne K. Yang. "Decolonization Is Not a Metaphor." *Decolonization: Indigeneity, Education & Society*, vol. 1, no. 1, 2012, pp. 1-40.

Tuck, Eve. "Suspending Damage: A Letter to Communities." *Harvard Educational Review*, vol. 79, no. 3, 2009, pp. 409-27.

Vizenor, Gerald. *Fugitive Poses: Native American Indian Scenes of Absence and Presence*. University of Nebraska Press, 2000.

Walcott, Rinaldo. "In This Moment: Thoughts on Decoloniality, Social Justice and Radical Collectivities." York University. 25 Mar. 2014. School of Social Work, Toronto, ON. The International Day for the Elimination of Racial Discrimination Annual Lecture.

Walker, Alice. *In Search of Our Mothers' Gardens: Womanist Prose*. Harcourt, 1984.

Weaver, Jace. *Red Atlantic: American Indigenes and the Making of the Modern World 1000-1927*. University of North Carolina Press, 2014.

Wolfe, Patrick. "Settler Colonialism and the Elimination of the Native." *Journal of Genocide Research*, vol. 8, no. 4, 2006, pp. 387-409. Accessed 15 Feb. 2016.

Wynter, Sylvia. "1492: A New World View." *Race, Discourse, and the Origin of the Americas: A New World View*, edited by Vera Lawrence Hyatt and Rex Nettleford, Smithsonian Institute Press, 1995, pp. 5-57.

9. Daughters of the Dust

DORSÍA SMITH SILVA

As daughters of the dust,
we spring from the same womb,
aching under the newday field sun.
We seek the drum birthed by Queenie and Nanny,
hoping to emerge like true Ashanti, Yoruba, Guinea women
to chant up the spirits.

As daughters of the dust,
we wail for the spilled blood across oceans,
later poured out and measured in beads.
We mourn for those who ate dirt, swallowed their tongues,
had cane burned into skins.
How we try to cut the bitter taste from our mouths,
willing a change to free.

As daughters of the dust,
we gather to fly unharnessed by salt,
stretch to Africa and rewind,
reaping new rock-island formations.

As daughters of the dust,
we dance across the waters, scattering seeds,
bidding welcome like true Ashanti, Yoruba, Guinea women
to our ancestors called drum.

II.
MOTHERS AND DAUGHTERS IN OUR MEMORY

10. Across the Divide

Contemporary Anglo-American Feminist Theory on the Mother-Daughter Relationship

ANDREA O'REILLY

Sometimes it seemed as if we were engaged in an Olympic competition to decide whose mother was absolutely the worst. We ground them up in our long conversations and spit them out.
—Anne Rophie, *Fruitful: A Real Mother in the Modern World*

I cannot forget my mother. Though not as sturdy as others, she is my bridge. When I needed to get across, she steadied herself long enough for me to run across safely.
—Renita Weems, "Hush Mama's Gotta Go Bye-Bye"

"The cathexis between mother and daughter, essential, distorted, misused," wrote Adrienne Rich in 1986, "is the great unwritten story." I am a daughter and mother of two daughters, twenty-eight and thirty years old. My feminism as it is lived and as it is practised in my scholarship and teaching is decidedly mother centred; its aim is to recover, narrate, and theorize the unwritten stories of mothers and daughters. What I discovered close to thirty years ago, when I began my work on motherhood and the mother-daughter relationship, was that our stories as mothers and daughters had in fact *already* been written—narrated by the larger patriarchal culture that scripted the roles mothers and daughters were expected to play. The received view of mothers and daughters—or what author Toni Morrison calls in another context, " the master narrative"—is that this relationship, particularly in the daughter's adolescent years, is one of antagonism and animosity. The daughter must distance and differentiate herself from the mother if she is to assume an autonomous identity as an adult. The mother, in turn, is perceived and understood only in terms of her maternal role, viewed either as devouring shrew or devoted Madonna, bitch, or victim; her own subjectivity as woman is eclipsed by her maternal identity. The mother represents for the daughter, according to the received narrative, the epitome of patriarchal oppression that she seeks to transcend as she comes to womanhood, yet the daughter's failings, as interpreted by herself and the culture at large, are said to be the fault of the mother. This is the patriarchal narrative of the mother-daughter relationship.

The lives of mothers and daughters are shaped by these larger cultural narratives even as mothers and daughters live lives different from, and in resistance to, these assigned roles. The aim of my research and teaching is to deconstruct this patriarchal narrative by first exposing this narration as precisely that: a narrative, an ideology, which, by definition, is a construction not a reflection of the actual lived reality of mothers and daughters, hence neither natural nor inevitable. Second, my work is concerned with how daughters and mothers may unravel the patriarchal script to write their own stories of motherhood and daughterhood. As part of this larger project, I designed a first year course on mothers and daughters that I taught at York University for several years in the mid-1990s. The objective of this course, titled "Mothers and Daughters: From Estrangement to Empowerment," is to situate the mother-daughter relationship as a *cultural* construction. Students are taught to think critically and consciously about the cultural meanings assigned to the mother-daughter relationship; they are taught to explore how their own experiences of being mothered—and their perceptions of motherhood in general and of their own mothers in particular—are shaped by the larger patriarchal narrative of motherhood and daughterhood. The course aims to identify, challenge, and dismantle the patriarchal narrative of mother-daughter estrangement; in particular, it asks students to uncover the historical and psychological origins of this narrative. Students track the manifestations of the patriarchal narrative in various cultural practices as diverse as media, education, government policy, and psychological theory; analyze its workings in their own personal relationships; imagine ways it may be deconstructed; and finally construct an alternative mother-daughter narrative scripted for empowerment as opposed to estrangement.

An in-class writing assignment at the beginning of the course asks students to reflect upon their relationship with their mother. They are asked to describe this relationship at three points in their lives and are given a series of instructions and questions to help them do this: describe your mother both inside and outside her role as mother; what do you want or need from your mother?; what does she want or need from you?; are you like your mother?; do you want to be like your mother?; and describe how your mother has helped or hindered you in achieving your life goals. This assignment serves as the first entry in the students' course journals: a weekly written reflections on course readings, discussions, and so forth. One student, reflecting upon this assignment at the close of the course, commented:

> *When I look back to the beginning of the course only eight months ago I realize how different I was—how naive I was. To gain some perspective as to how my attitudes have changed concerning my own mother, I reread my first journal entry. I still agree with most of what I wrote, however after looking at the questions you asked us to answer, I realized that I had overlooked the most crucial of all the questions posed. I neglected the questions, "Do you know your mother as a person other than your mother? Who is your mother?" I think at the time I didn't really understand the significance of these questions nor could I have answered them for I didn't know my mother as a person. I didn't even know that I didn't know.*

This student's reflections, and in particular her comment "I didn't even know that I didn't know," serve as an appropriate epigraph for the positioning of daughters in the patriarchal narrative of mother-daughter estrangement. So thoroughly do daughters identify with this script that its cultural staging has been rendered invisible to them, and daughters see it as merely "the way things are"—hence natural and inevitable. African American essayist and poet Audre Lorde once said we must "name the nameless so that it can be thought" (37). The aim of this course, for daughters and mothers alike, is to render visible the "invisible hand of patriarchy" so as to see how thoroughly our lives are produced and shaped by patriarchal ideologies that are not of our own making.

MATROPHOBIA, MOTHER-BLAME, AND DAUGHTER-CENTRICITY

I begin the course with Nancy Chodorow's (1989) classic essay "Family Structure and Feminine Personality," and a lecture on her "reproduction of mothering" thesis as it is developed in her book of the same name (Chodorow 1978). Nancy Chodorow, as Penelope Dixon has noted in her feminist annotated bibliography on mothers and mothering, "was one of the first to write on the subject [of mothering] and subsequently has authored more books and articles on this subject than any other feminist writer" (4). Indeed, Chodorow's writings, particularly her now classic *The Reproduction of Mothering*, have influenced the way in which a whole generation of scholars has viewed motherhood. Less acknowledged, however, is how this influential writer, who is identified as a feminist, reinscribes the patriarchal narrative of mother-daughter estrangement even as she seeks to dismantle it. Chodorow contends that female mothering constructs gendered identities that are both differentiated and hierarchical. The pre-Oedipal mother-daughter attachment, she argues, is more prolonged and intense than the mother-son relationship. Because the daughter and the mother are the same gender, the mother perceives and treats her daughter as identical to and continuous with her self. The sameness and continuity of the pre-Oedipal mother-daughter symbiosis engenders a feminine psychic structure that is less individuated and differentiated. The daughter's sense of self is relational; she experiences herself as connected to others. The relational sense of self that women inherit from their mothers and bring to their own mothering, Chodorow goes on to argue, exacerbates female self-effacement and frustrates women's achievement of an authentic autonomous identity. Relationality, Chodorow concludes, is problematic for women because it hinders autonomy, psychological and otherwise, and since daughter-mother identification is the cause of this relationality in women, it is, in her words, "bad for mother and [daughter] alike" (*Reproduction* 217).

Chodorow's argument has been widely critiqued in the forty years since the publication of *The Reproduction of Mothering*. What concerns critics most is Chodorow's bracketing of the "real" world in her psychoanalytic abstractions of family patterns and gender formations. Critics have rightly pointed out that Chodorow's mother-involved, father-absent family is quite specifically a white, urban, middle-class family structure of the First World. The gendered personalities that this specific family structure might create should not be used, as Chodorow does, to account for universal male dominance and gender difference. Moreover, Chodorow's theory of mother-daughter mutual psychological over-identification, used to explain women's subordination, far too readily glosses over women's lived powerlessness in a patriarchal world. While I argue wholeheartedly with the above criticisms, I am nonetheless disturbed by the fact that among the hundreds of articles written about Chodorow's theory only a handful take as their focus of critique what I find to be the most troubling premise of Chodorow's reproduction thesis—namely, the pathologizing of mother-daughter identification and intimacy, particularly in positioning it as the cause of women's inadequacy, psychological and otherwise. One early critic of Chodorow, Marcia Westkott has faulted Chodorow for failing to understand that women's relationality and dependency result not from psychology but from culture: "The need of mothers to remain close to their daughters arises because mothers are given few other choices, not just because of an infantile personality structure" (17). Here, as with Chodorow, mother-daughter identification is construed as a liability.

In *Don't Blame Mother*, Paula Caplan writes, "women love connection. But in a society that is phobic about intimacy and extols the virtues of independence, we mistakenly regard connection and closeness as dependency, fusion, and merging" (113). The aim of the introductory section is to expose the pervasiveness of the pathology of mother-daughter intimacy and identification in contemporary culture. As one student commented, "It greatly disturbs me when women, such as Chodorow, write powerful stuff which influences a lot of people. I expect it from Freud but not from someone who calls herself a feminist." The sanction against mother-daughter intimacy observed in Chodorow is one of the many cultural practices that render mother-daughter estrangement natural and inevitable. It also originates from and reinscribes other central tenets of mother-daughter estrangement—mother-blame and the devaluation of motherhood.

In *Of Woman Born*, Adrienne Rich distinguishes between two meanings of motherhood: "the *potential relationship* of any woman to her powers of reproduction and to children; and the *institution*, which aims at ensuring that that potential—and all women—shall remain under male control" (13, emphasis in original). I use the term "motherhood" to refer to the institution of motherhood, which is male defined and male controlled, and mothering to refer to experiences of mothering, which are female defined and female centred. According to Rich, the reality of patriarchal motherhood contradicts the possibility of empowered mothering. Across cultures and throughout history most women mother in the institution of motherhood—that is, women's mothering is defined and controlled by the larger patriarchal society in which they live. Mothers do not make the rules, Rich emphasizes—they simply enforce them. Whether it is in the form of parenting books, a physician's advice, or the father's rules, a mother raises her children in accordance with the values and expectations of the dominant patriarchal culture. Mothers are policed by what theorist Sara Ruddick calls the "gaze of others." Under the gaze of others, mothers "relinquish authority to others, [and] lose confidence in their own values" (111). Ruddick calls this an abdication of maternal authority. "Fear of the gaze of others," she continues, "can be expressed intellectually as inauthenticity, a repudiation of one's own perceptions and values" (111). The institution of motherhood is predicated upon inauthentic mothering and the abdication of maternal authority.

A daughter, Rich emphasizes, perceives this inauthenticity and understands the powerlessness that underpins her mother's compliance and complicity. In *Of Woman Born*, Rich speaks of the rage and resentment daughters feel toward this powerlessness of their mothers. However, at the same time, the daughter feels rage toward her mother, she is expected to identify with her because the daughter is also a woman who, it is assumed, will someday become a mother and wife as her mother did. The daughter resists this identification because she does not want a life like her mother's, nor does she wish to be aligned with someone who is oppressed and whose work is so devalued. "Thousands of daughters," writes Rich, "see their mothers as having taught a compromise and self-hatred they are struggling to win free of, the one through whom the restrictions and degradations of a female existence were ... transmitted" (235). Rich calls this distancing between mothers and daughters "matrophobia": "the fear not of one's mother or of motherhood but of *becoming one's mother*" (emphasis in original, 236). "Matrophobia," she writes, "can be seen as a womanly splitting of the self in the desire to become purged once and for all of our mothers' bondage, to become individuated and free. The mother stands for the victim in ourselves, the unfree woman, the martyr. Our personalities seem dangerously to blur and overlap with our mothers, and in a desperate attempt to know where mother ends and daughter begins, we perform radical surgery" (236). When daughters perform this radical surgery, they sever the selves from their attachment with their mother.

The institution of motherhood and the cultural devaluation and subordination of mothers, and the practice of inauthentic mothering on which they are predicated, gives rise to mother-blame. Paula Caplan argues that mother-blame is rampant in contemporary culture, among both professionals and the population at large. "The biggest reason daughters are upset and angry with their mothers," writes Caplan, "is that they have been *taught* to do so" (empahsis in original, 20). Similar to the feeling of matrophopia identified by Rich, mother-blame distances daughters from mothers because mothers come to be seen not as sources of empowerment but as the cause of all and any problems that may ail the daughter. In *The Mother/Daughter Plot: Narrative, Psychoanalysis, Feminism*, Marianne Hirsch argues that the feminist theory written in the 1970s is characterized by a daughterly perspective or subjectivity that Brenda Daly and Maureen Reddy call "daughter-centricity"

(2). "It is the woman as daughter," Hirsch writes, "who occupies the center of the global reconstruction of subjectivity and subject-object relation. The woman as mother remains in the position of other, and the emergence of feminine daughterly subjectivity rests and depends on that continued and repeated process of othering the mother" (136). She goes on to say, "The adult woman who is mother continues to exist only in relation to her child, never as a subject in her own right. And in her maternal function, she remains an object, always distanced, always idealized or denigrated, always mystified, always represented through the small child's point of view" (167). Hirsch argues that such ambivalence expresses itself in the rhetoric and the politics of the 1970s movement:

> Throughout the 1970s, the metaphor of sisterhood, of friendship or of surrogate motherhood has been the dominant model for female and feminist relationships. To say that "sisterhood is powerful," however, is to isolate feminist discourse within one generation and to banish feminists who are mothers to the "mother-closet." In the 1970s, the prototypical feminist voice was, to a large degree, the voice of the daughter attempting to separate from an overly connected or rejecting mother, in order to bond with her sisters in a relationship of mutual nurturance and support among women. With its possibilities of mutuality and its desire to avoid power, the paradigm of sisterhood has the advantage of freeing women from the biological function of giving birth, even while offering a specifically feminine relational model. "Sisters" can be "maternal" to one another without allowing their bodies to be invaded by men and the physical acts of pregnancy, birth, and lactation. In this feminist family romance, sisters are better mothers, providing more nurturance and greater encouragement of autonomy. In functioning as mutual surrogate mothers, sisters can replace mothers. (164)

Thus, while mothering as nurturance was celebrated among 1970s feminists, real mothers and the biological processes of mothering were displaced and disparaged.

Hirsch identifies four reasons for the "avoidance and discomfort" with the maternal in the 1970s. First, for daughters, motherhood represented a compliance with patriarchy of which they wanted no part. Second, feminists feared the lack of control associated with motherhood. Third, feminists suffered from what critic Elizabeth Spelman has identified as "somatophophia"—fear and discomfort with the body (qtd. in Hirsch, 166). And nothing, as Hirsch has observed, "entangles women more firmly in their bodies than pregnancy, birth, lactation, miscarriage, or the inability to conceive" (166). Fourth, and characteristic of much feminist theorizing in the 1970s, was an ambivalence about power, authority, and anger—all of which are part of mothering and associated with the maternal. "Feminist theoretical writing in the U.S.," writes Hirsch, "is permeated with fears of maternal power and with anger at maternal powerlessness" (167). Caplan argues that men fear maternal power. It would seem that women, too, fear it. The sisterhood metaphor of the 1970s, thus, may be read as a gesture of displacement or containment. The maternal power that is feared is rendered safe by transforming it into mothering between sisters—no power imbalance—and by objectifying and "otherizing" the person who seems to wield this power, the mother.

To a young child, the powers of the mother appear limitless. Our own individual flesh-and-blood mother is also connected to the primordial Great Mother, who held very real life and death powers over mortal men. In our individual and collective unconscious, we remember that time when we lived under the mother's power in the pre-Oedipal and pre-patriarchal world. In *The Mermaid and the Minotaur*, Dorothy Dinnerstein argues that the fear of maternal power and the hatred of women generally originate from infant experiences, which, in turn, come to structure adult consciousness. The mother, Dinnerstein reasons, cannot satisfy all of the child's needs and desires. The inevitable dissatisfaction, discomfort, frustration, and anger felt by the child directs itself at the person whose responsibility it was to meet those needs. In contrast to Dinnerstein's view, I would suggest that the experiences of infancy, given that they include both pain and pleasure, engender not necessarily misogyny but a deep ambivalence that becomes organized around polarized constructions of the mother. The Good Mother and the Bad Mother become created; all that we find desirable about mothers is signified by the former, and all that we fear and hate is marked by the latter. This delineation is, I would suggest, mapped along an already established historical topography of separation and specialization. I refer here to what we speculate occurred at the dawn of patriarchy when the many diverse qualities of the original Great Goddess were separated and used to create several distinct goddesses. What mortal men feared in the original Goddess—particularly her powers over life and death—was displaced upon a terrible mother goddess, like the Hindu goddess Kali who represented death and destruction, whereas what was desired was retained and assigned to a beneficent power. In Catholicism, for example, Mary, the mother of Jesus, is such a woman. The polarization and specialization of the maternal self continue to structure our ambivalence.

The fear of maternal power is at the heart of such disparagement and idealization. However, as Ruddick reminds us: "All power lies at least partly in the eye of the beholder. To a child, a mother is huge—a judge, trainer, audience, and provider whose will must be placated.... A mother, in contrast to the perception her children have of her, will mostly experience herself as relatively powerless" (34). However, as we speak to and about the very real powerlessness of mothers, we must not forget the power a mother does possess. Ruddick writes:

> There are many external constraints on [a mother's] capacity to name, feel, and act. But in the daily conflict of wills, at least with her children, a mother has the upper hand. Even the most powerless woman knows that she is physically stronger than her young children. This along with undeniable psychological power gives her the resources to control her children's behaviour and influence their perceptions. If a mother didn't have this control, her life would be unbearable. (35)

Mothering is a profound experience of both powerlessness and power; it is this paradox of motherhood that helps explain women's ambivalence about motherhood. This ambivalence about maternal power—along with fear of the maternal, mother-blame, cultural devaluation of motherhood, and matrophopia—distance daughters from their mothers and scripts the relationship of mother and daughters as one of disconnection and estrangement.

MOTHER-DAUGHTER CONNECTION AND EMPOWERMENT: THEORIES AND NARRATIVE

Once students have identified these cultural practices that distance daughters from the mothers, they explore the ways these practices may be resisted. The sanction against mother-daughter identification, with which I began this chapter, is challenged by Elizabeth Debold, Marie Wilson, and Idelisse Malavé in their important work *Mother Daughter Revolution*. They argue that psychological theories of development are organized around the assumption that adolescence is a "time of separation when daughters are struggling to be independent, particularly from their mothers; and daughters in adolescence don't want to listen to their mothers or be like them in any way" (36). Separation from parents is mandated in developmental theory to enable the emerging adult to achieve an autonomous sense of self. *Mother Daughter Revolution* calls into question this "sacred cow" of developmental theory—the equivalency of separation and autonomy—and argues that it constitutes a betrayal of both mothers and daughters:

> Separation and autonomy are not equivalent: a person need not separate from mothers emotionally to be autonomous. Under the dominion of experts, mothers are urged to create a separation and disconnection from daughters that their daughters do not want. Early childhood and adolescence are the two stages of life where separation has been decreed as imperative to the independence and autonomy of children. To mother "right," women disconnect from their daughters and begin to see them as society will. Rather than strengthen girls this breach of trust leaves girls weakened and adrift. (22)

Mothers want to "do right" by their daughters so, as dictated by developmental theory, they distance themselves from their daughters when the daughters reach adolescence. At the same time, they propel the daughters out of the maternal space of childhood and into the heterosexual realm of adulthood. What is most disturbing about this pattern of separation and betrayal is its timing. "In childhood, girls have confidence in what they know, think, and feel" (Debold et al. 11). With the onset of adolescence, girls between the ages of nine and twelve come up against "the wall": "The wall is our patriarchal culture that values women less than men ... To get through the wall, girls have to give up parts of themselves to be safe and accepted within society" (Debold et al. 12). Before adolescence, girls are "fully themselves," but at the crossroads between childhood and adolescence, girls come to label their vitality, desires, and thoughts as "selfish," "bad," or "wrong." Debold et al. continue:

> They lose the ability to hold on to the truth of their experience.... They begin to see themselves as others see them, and they orient their thinking and themselves towards others.... [They] have to give up their relationship with the world of girls and women, the world that they have lived and loved in, and also give up the relationship with parts of themselves that are too dangerous to keep in the adult world of male desire. Girls give up these relationships for the sake of the relationships that have been prescribed for them in male-led societies. The wall of patriarchy expects girls to separate from what they know, from each other, and from the women who care for them. (15)

Central to *Mother Daughter Revolution* is the belief that mothers can help their daughters resist being influenced by the wall. With her mother beside her, the daughter is empowered and can learn to compromise less of herself. The key to the mother's ability to do this is the reclamation of her own girl self:

> If mothers decide to join with daughters who are coming of age as women, mothers must first reclaim what they

> themselves have lost. Reclaiming is the first step in women's joining girls' resistance to their own disintegration. Reclaiming is simply the process of discovering, describing, and reappropriating the memories and feelings of our preadolescent selves.... The goal is not to become a preadolescent girl. That wouldn't be desirable even if it were possible . . . But women can reclaim and, thus, reintegrate the vital parts of themselves that they discarded or drove underground. (Debold et al. 101)

This reclamation empowers the mother and enables her to help her daughter in her resistance. If mothers reclaim their driven underground prepatriarchal selves, their reclaimed selves can join their daughters, and empower them to withstand the loss or compromise of their own female selfhood. Mothers and daughters together "can claim the power of connection, community, and choice. And this power just might bring down the wall" (Debold et al. 38).

Another contemporary theorist read in my course who champions mother–daughter connectedness as a mode of resistance is Miriam Johnson, the author of *Strong Mothers, Weak Wives*. Johnson examines how daughters may connect with their mothers to withstand what may be called the heterosexualizing behaviour of the father. In Chodorow's psychoanalytical account, the differential treatment of sons and daughters by their mothers is said to be the cause of both gender difference and male dominance. Johnson challenges this argument. She writes: "It is the wife role and not the mother role that organizes women's secondary status" (6). Women's secondary status, she maintains, originates not from the maternal core of women's subjectivity (Chodorow's relational self) but from their heterosexual identity as wives of men. In contrast to Chodorow, Johnson maintains that male dominance originates not from the mother-child attachment but from the father-daughter relationship.

The relationship of father and daughter, Johnson asserts, "trains daughters to be wives who are expected to be secondary to their husbands" (8). She argues that fathers often romanticize the father-daughter relationship and interact with their daughters as a lover would. Fathers feminize their daughters: daddies teach their girls to be passive, pleasing, and pretty for men. In Johnson's words, the father-daughter relationship "reproduce[s] in daughters a disposition to please men in a relationship in which the male dominates." In other words, "daddy's girls are in training to be wives" (184). Because daddy's girls are trained and rewarded for pleasing and playing up to men, they grow up to be male-defined and male-orientated women. In most so-called normal (male-dominant) families what is experienced is psychological incest. "The incest ... is psychological, not overtly sexual. The father takes his daughter over. She looks up to him because he is her father. He is the king and she is the princess. It is all OK because the male is dominant in 'normal' adult heterosexual relations" (Johnson 173).

Johnson argues that these princesses are in need of rescue and that the rescuer is the mother: "If daddy's girls are to gain their independence they need to construct an identity as the daughters of strong mothers as well" (184). In *The Reproduction of Mothering*, Chodorow attributes women's lack of autonomy to the feminine-related sense of self which the mother-daughter relationship engendered. In contrast, Johnson argues that women's lack of autonomy originates from the daughter's psychological dependency on her father as a male-orientated daddy's girl. According to Johnson, a daughter's identification with her mother, far from prohibiting authentic female autonomy, produces and promotes that authenticity and autonomy. Chodorow suggested in her earlier sociological work that daughters are empowered by identification with their mothers in matrifocal cultures. Johnson believes that an empowering mother-daughter identification is also possible under patriarchy if the daughter relates to her mother as a mother and friend, not as the father's wife. Johnson contends that the mother-daughter relationship is the key to overcoming women's psychological inauthenticity as daddy's girl and, by implication, women's social oppression in patriarchy. Thus the daughter achieves authentic autonomy not through greater involvement with the father, but through a heightened identification with the mother.

For Johnson, the daughter must identify with the maternal part of her mother's identity rather than the heterosexual one. This identification empowers the daughter in two ways: first, it allows her to step outside her oppressive daddy's girl role; and second, it allows her to identify with an adult woman's strength rather than her weakness. In Johnson's view, women are strong as mothers but made weak as wives. In identifying with her mother as mother, the daughter may construct a strong female identity outside of the passive heterosexual one patterned for her by her father and by society at large. In *Mother Daughter Revolution*, the emphasis is on the mother joining the daughter, whereas the focus of *Strong Mother, Weak Wives* is the daughter connecting to the mother. Though different, both positions are mapped along what feminist writer Naomi Ruth Lowinsky calls "the motherline." In *Stories from the Motherline*, Naomi Ruth Lowinsky explores "a worldview that is as old as humankind, a wisdom we have forgotten that we know: the ancient lore of women—the Motherline" (1). She goes on to say:

> Whenever women gather in circles or in pairs, in olden times around the village well, or at the quilting bee, in modern times in support groups, over lunch, or at the children's party, they tell one another stories from the Motherline. These are stories of female experience: physical, psychological, and historical. They are stories about the dramatic changes of woman's body: developing breasts and pubic hair, bleeding, being sexual, giving birth, suckling, menopause, and of growing old. They are stories of the life cycles that link generations of women: Mothers who are also daughters, daughters who have become mothers, grandmothers who also remain granddaughters. (1-2)

Most women today, Lowinsky contends, are cut off from their motherline; they suffer from what she calls "the feminist ambivalence about the feminine" (30). "Women," she writes, "seemed to want to live their father's lives. Mother was rejected, looked down upon.... In the headlong race to liberate those aspects of ourselves that had been so long denied, we left behind all that women had been." "Many of us," she continues, "who joyfully accepted the challenge of new opportunities discovered in retrospect that we had cut ourselves off from much of what was meaningful to us as women: our mothers, our collective past, our passion for affiliation and for richness in our personal lives. We felt split between our past and our future" (29). Lowinsky asks that women integrate their feminine and feminist selves: women "must connect the historical self that was freed by feminism to live in the 'real' world, with the feminine self that binds us to our mothers and grandmothers" (32).

Daughters of the so-called baby boom are the first generation of women, at least among the middle classes, whose lives are radically different from those of their mothers. These daughters, Lowinsky argues, have "paid a terrible price for cutting [them]selves off from [their] feminine roots" (31). By disconnecting themselves from their motherline, these daughters have lost the authenticity and authority of their womanhood. Women may reclaim that authority and authenticity by reconnecting to the motherline:

> When a woman today comes to understand her life story as a story from the Motherline, she gains female authority in a number of ways. First, her Motherline grounds her in her feminine nature as she struggles with the many options now open to women. Second, she reclaims carnal knowledge of her own body, its blood mysteries and their power. Third, as she makes the journey back to her female roots, she will encounter ancestors who struggled with similar difficulties in different historical times. This provides her with a life-cycle perspective that softens her immediate situation ... Fourth, she uncovers her connection to the archetypal mother and to the wisdom of the ancient worldview, which holds that body and soul are open and all life is interconnected. And, finally, she reclaims her female perspective, from which to consider how men are similar and how they are different. (13)

Virginia Woolf writes in *A Room of One's Own*: "We think back through our mothers if we are women" (72). Writing about Lowinsky's motherline in her book *Motherless Daughters: The Legacy of Loss*, Hope Edelman emphasizes that "motherline stories ground a daughter in a gender, a family, and a feminine history. They transform the experience of her female ancestors into maps she can refer to for warning or encouragement" (201).

These stories are made available to daughters through the female oral tradition, or what we call gossip and old wives' tales. These feminine discourses, however, have been trivialized, marginalized, and discredited; they are, to borrow French theorist Michel Foucault's term, "subjugated knowledge[s]" that circulate outside the master narrative. Moreover, the language of the motherline is rendered in a specifically feminine discourse or dialect that has been discursively and culturally marginalized by patriarchal culture.

In *Motherless Daughters*, Edelman studies daughters who lost their mothers between infancy and their early thirties, and considers the impact this loss had on the daughters' lives. The daughters' narratives speak of feelings of incompleteness and fragmentation. "Our mothers," Edelman explains, "are our most direct connection to our history and our gender. Regardless of how well we think they did their job, the void their absence creates in our lives is never completely filled again" (61). When the mother dies, daughters lose their connection to the motherline. "Without a mother or mother-figure to guide her," writes Edelman, "a daughter has to piece together a female self-image on her own" (xxv). A girl who loses her mother has little evidence of the adult feminine to draw from. She has neither a direct guide for sex-typed behaviour nor an immediate connection to her own gender. Left to piece together her own feminine identity, she looks to other females for signs that she's developing along an appropriate gendered path (178).

Motherless daughters long to know and to be connected to, what Lowinsky calls, "the deep feminine," or in Edelman's words: "that subtle unconscious source of feminine authority and power we mistakenly believe is expressed in scarf knots and thank-you notes but instead originates from a more abstract gendered core" (179). "Without knowledge of her own experiences, and the relationship to her mother's," Edelman continues, "a daughter is snipped from the female cord that connects the generations of women in her family, the feminine line of descent ... the motherline" (200).

Adrienne Rich writes in *Of Woman Born*, "The loss of the daughter to the mother, the mother to the daughter, is the essential female tragedy" (237). In Edelman's work, this loss refers to the daughter losing her mother through death, abandonment, or neglect. In these instances, separation occurs as a result of the mother's leaving the daughter. More frequent, in patriarchal culture, is the loss of the daughter to the mother: daughters become disconnected from their motherline through specific cultural practices, notably the devaluation of motherhood and the reinforcement of maternal powerlessness, fear of the maternal, mother-blame, and matrophopia, discussed earlier.

Journalist Marni Jackson calls maternal space "the mother zone; [the] hole in culture where mothers [go]" (13). Motherhood, she writes, "is an unexplored frontier of thought and emotion that we've tried to tame with rules, myth, and knowledge. But the geography remains unmapped " (9). She emphasizes that "motherhood may have become an issue but it's not yet a narrative" (3). Maternal stories are forgotten and lost before they are spoken because "mothers in the thick of it have not the time or brain cells to write it down, to give it life. [When they] have the time, amnesia moves in ... all the raw extremes of emotion are smoothed over and left behind." "Culture," she continues, "encourages this amnesia, by excluding mothers from its most conspicuous rewards—money, power, social status" (4, 9). Because our mothers' stories remain unspoken, she argues, "the true drama of mother and child is replaced by the idealization of motherhood" (4, 9). Julia Kristeva identifies the maternal with the unspeakable. The maternal is found outside and beyond language, "spoken" only in the extralinguistic, nonverbal discourse of the semiotic. Perhaps, the maternal is, as Hirsch speculates in *The Mother/Daughter Plot*, "unnarratable" (179). Or, as Ruddick writes, "maternal voices have been drowned by professional theory, ideologies of motherhood, sexist arrogance, and childhood fantasy. Voices that have been distorted and censored can only be developing voices. Alternatively silenced and edging toward speech, mothers' voices are not voices of mothers as they are, but as they are becoming (40).

Much of current feminist writing and activism are concerned with the recovery of the maternal voice. While recognizing how difficult it is to speak that which has been silenced, disguised, and marginalized, writers today seek to make the maternal story narratable. In earlier times the ancient lore of the motherline was told around the village well or at the quilting bee; today, the oral tradition of old wives' tales is shared through written narratives. In *Writing a Woman's Life*, Carolyn Heilbrun observes, "Lives do not serve as models, only stories do that. And it is a hard thing to make up stories to live by. We can only retell and live by stories we have heard.... Stories have formed us all: they are what we must use to make new fictions and new narratives" (32).

Recent writings on the mother-daughter relationship call upon the mother to speak and the daughter to listen. Debold, Wilson, and Malavé argue in *Mother Daughter Revolution* that the compromise of the female self in adolescence may be resisted or, at the very least negotiated, when the mother connects with the daughter through stories. The mother, in recalling and sharing with her daughter her own narrative of adolescence, gives the daughter strategies of resistance and, hence, an alternative script for coming into womanhood. Caplan, in *Don't Blame Mother*, emphasizes that only by speaking and hearing the mother's story can women move beyond mother-blame. In turn, Lowinsky and Edelman argue that a daughter's very identity as a woman is acquired through connection to, and knowledge of, her mother and the motherline of which she is a part. Rich writes, "mothers and daughters have always exchanged with each other—beyond the verbally transmitted lore of female survival—a knowledge that is subliminal, subversive, pre-verbal: the knowledge flowing between two alike bodies, one of which has spent nine months inside the other" (220). The lore Rich refers to here is, of course, the lore of the motherline that constructs female experience outside the patriarchal narrative.

CONCLUSION

The theories and narratives read by the students in this course expose the cultural practices that underpin the patriarchal narrative of mother-daughter estrangement including sanction against mother-daughter intimacy, mother-blame, daughter-centricity, matrophopia, and fear of maternal power—and offer various strategies by which mothers and daughters may deconstruct the patriarchal narrative so as to write their own stories of motherhood and daughterhood, ones scripted from relations of empowerment as opposed to estrangement. As another student remarked in her journal at the conclusion of the course:

> *I want to tell you how much your course has meant to me and how much my life has changed because of it. I feel almost as if I am a different person now. You helped me break the cycle instilled in me by a patriarchal society that I was doomed to repeat. Most significantly, you provided me with the means to eliminate mother–blame from my life, and for that I am eternally grateful.*

Through this course, I hope to create a dialogue between mothers and daughters that in turn will help them build a bridge over which they can cross the patriarchal divide that separates them. By doing so, mothers and daughters can construct a truly lasting politics of empowerment.

WORKS CITED

Caplan, Paula. *Don't Blame Mother: Mending the Mother-Daughter Relationship*. Harper and Row, 1989.

Chodorow, Nancy. "Family Structures and Feminine Personality." *Women, Culture, and Society*, edited by Michelle Zimbalist Rosaldo and Louise Lamphere, Stanford University Press, 1974, pp. 43-65.

Chodorow, Nancy. *The Reproduction of Mothering*. University of California Press, 1999.

Daly, Brenda and, Maureen Reddy. *Narrating Mothers: Theorizing Maternal Subjectivities*. The University of Tennessee Press, 1991.

Debold, Elizabeth, et al. *The Mother Daughter Revolution*. Addison-Wesley, 1993.

Dinnerstein, Dorothy. *The Mermaid and the Minotaur: Sexual Arrangements and the Human Malaise*. Harper Collins, 1976.

Edelman, Hope. *Motherless Daughters: The Legacy of Love*. Delta Press, 1994.

Heilbrun, Carolyn. *Writing a Woman's Life*. Ballantine Books, 1988.

Hirsch, Marianne. *The Mother/Daughter Plot: Narrative, Psycho-*

analysis. Indiana University Press, 1989.

Jackson, Marni. *The Mother Zone: Love, Sex and Laundry in the Modern* Family. MacFarlane Walter and Ross, 1992.

Johnson, Miriam. *Strong Mothers, Weak Wives: The Search for Gender Equality*. University of California Press, 1988.

Kristeva, Julia. *Revolution in Poetic Language*. Translated by Margaret Walker, Columbia University Press, 1984.

Lowinsky, Naomi Ruth. *Stories from the Motherline: Reclaiming the Mother-Daughter Bond, Finding Our Feminine Souls*. Jeremy P. Tarcher, 1992.

Rich, Adrienne. *Of Woman Born: Motherhood as Experience and Institution*. W.W. Norton, 1986.

Rophie, Anne. *Fruitful: A Real Mother in the Modern World*. Houghton Mifflin, 1996.

Ruddick, Sara. *Maternal Thinking: Toward a Politics of Peace*. Beacon Press, 1989.

Weems, Renita, "Hush Mama's Gotta Go Bye-Bye." *SAGE: A Scholarly Journal on Black Women*, vol. 1, no. 2, 1984, pp. 25-28.

Weskott, Marcia. "Mothers and Daughters in the World of the Father." *Frontiers*, vol. 3, no. 2, 1978, pp. 16-21.

Woolf, Virginia. *A Room of One's Own*. Granada Press, 1977.

11.
Glow

DORSÍA SMITH SILVA

On the night when you were born,
you came falling out around me
like graceful water.
You became my yellow twilight,
when the pale earth gently stirs
and streams of splendored light
smear across the sky.
I heard your voice—
the sunup of morning,
new blades of grass
mixed with dew.
How you glistened in shark-white linens
looking like you had been touched
by the lips of the moon,
drawn into the flowering of the world,
washed down with soft gold.
For me, the green centre of dreams.

12.
Isthmus

DONNA SHARKEY

> *Isthmus*: a narrow passage or strip of land connecting two larger areas of land, of great significance in the world as they offer important connecting paths. The bodies of water on each side of the path present a threat of tides rending apart the two land masses.

It started this way. As it turned out, both of us were thinking a lot about it.

Nobody here has a mother, except two sisters who go out with their mother one Sunday afternoon a month. Each time they say they won't come back, but they do. One thing I know is that we all had mothers—of course. I have a best friend, Tania, and she's really nice.

Three weeks before my mother's terminal illness diagnosis and half a year before she dies, I start the process of adopting a child. I never share my plan with her. It seems too cruel to discuss my future life without the prospect of her being a part of it. Just before she dies, my mother tells me how hard it had been to birth me, to move me through her birth canal into the world.

Some of the bigger girls are mean and bossy. They can hit you and punch you if they want. I hate all the rules. Everyone here is strict, even Sister Maria Teresa, but she's smart. She speaks English.

When the representative from the adoption agency phoned to tell me about an eight-year-old girl, I sat back in my chair. Eight? I was interested in adopting a toddler and had not considered adopting a child older than that. I hesitated. Then suddenly I thought, yes, that's my daughter. That's her. What's her name? I asked. Tell me about her.

Sister Maria Teresa calls me into her office. No one ever goes there unless they're in big, big trouble. I walk in, scared, but I'm not shaking. Sister Maria Teresa smiles. She asks me, "Do you want to have a mother?" I'm confused. She knows that all the kids want to have a mother. "Do you want to go live in Canada?" I can barely look at her. "Yes," I say. "I do." I don't ask her, what's Canada?

I forward an album of pictures of myself, my home, my dog, and my neighbourhood to the orphanage. An eight by ten picture of the girl arrives in the mail shortly after. The girl looks forlorn, her curly hair close to shaved, her legs long and thin. But her eyes look directly forward. I like that. I place the photo on the mantle to greet whenever I enter my living room. Hello, Alessandra.

Sister Maria Teresa shows me the album. She says she will keep it safe in her office, and I can come after school on Thursdays and look at the pictures. I like the pictures of my mother and the house. I don't like the dog, even though it's not very big. I don't tell my friends I'm afraid of dogs, but I am.

I think about her a lot. Is she thinking about me? The next month goes by slowly until I hear from the representative: "Everything is set for you to fetch your daughter and bring her home." Sunnily, I go off to Brazil to bring Alessandra home.

Sister Maria Teresa tells me my new mother is coming soon. I run to tell my best friend, Tania. She says, "What if she's not nice?"

I have never been inside an orphanage. I remember the enormous stone orphanage in the city I grew up in. When I was small, we drove past it from time to time, my parents in the front seat of our family Vauxhall, my sister and I tucked into the back. Each time as we approached it, my sister and I got ready to stare. Riveted, we took in as much as possible. The sight of the building, larger than a castle, kept us in its spell. The what-if we lived there, the what-if our parents died, the thrall of how different the lives of the children living there must be from ours. In the backseat we mused about what they wore and ate, whether they were poor, and how many slept in one room. Back in our bedroom, we used the orphanage's captivation to taunt each other: "they're going to send you to the orphanage!"

I keep thinking about what it will be like to leave here. I might be really lonely, but I'm not afraid. One of the bigger girls said it's too cold in Canada. "You'll die," she told me. "No," I told her back. "I'll never die."

Though exhausted from my flight and the heat, I'm filled with nervous energy in the small yellow taxi from São Paulo to the town where the orphanage is located. Drive on faster, I say in my mind at the driver. When we finally arrive, I see from the taxi the oversized wooden doors of the huge building. I pause. How similar they are to the doors of the orphanage my sister and I long ago drove by with our parents. Then walking up the lane toward these doors, I notice my stride slowing. Sueli, my interpreter, keeps pace with me. Tears lay waiting near the front of my eyes. I think, in a few steps I'll be inside. Whatever you do, I tell myself, don't cry inside the orphanage.

Kids aren't allowed to open the doors, but today I'm allowed. I wait a long time looking through the small side window for her to come. What if she's changed her mind? What if she doesn't come? All the kids will laugh at me if she doesn't come, and then I'll have to stay here. A taxi stops, and two women get out. I know which one is her. I know from the picture. I open the doors before she knocks, but I keep my head down. I'm too nervous to look.

A young girl solemnly opens the door before I have a chance to knock. She's looking at the floor as though she had just lost something. Is this her? Is this how I'm to first see my daughter? Sister Maria Teresa, the orphanage's director, quickly comes to greet Sueli and me. I glance around the expansive entrance area hoping to get another glimpse of the girl, but she has already gone.

I run to find Tania. My new mother's here! She came! Tania looks at me. "So what?" she says.

After a tour of the orphanage, I sign documents in the director's cramped office. Alessandra is then brought in. She looks fearful. The director tells her to count to ten in English. Determinedly, she does this. We are then awkwardly introduced. I smile. I say my practised Portuguese greeting phrases, and in a serious tone, she mutters a reply.

It was so hard to wait while they go into all the rooms, and then they stayed in Sister Maria Teresa's office forever. I keep counting to ten in English to not forget the numbers. Finally, I go into the office. I'm so scared. My mother looks nice, but the way she speaks Portuguese isn't very good.

The scar above her left eye looks cruel, and I notice there are several on her legs. The director assures me they were all as a result of play. It is then that I realize that I hadn't seen a playground on my tour of the orphanage.

I can tell they are talking about my scars. I wish she hadn't noticed. Maybe she won't like me.

We're brought into the assembly room. Alessandra pulls a girl called Tania over to me. "My best friend," she tells me. The girls of the orphanage are waiting to sing a farewell song to my new daughter. Plaintive cadence of a song of loss, dancing slowly in a circle around us, some holding hands, others not. I wonder how these children understand forever. Goodbye forever. Gone with her new mother. Never returning. I find myself fighting back tears, and I pick up my camera, hiding behind it as I take pictures. After the song, children surround me, ever so delicately touching my arms and hands—take me with you, take me with you. And shyly, will you be my mother too?

All the other kids are waiting for us in the assembly room. They all look at me and my mother. I hold Tania's hand to bring her close to my mother. While everyone sings the farewell song, I don't let myself cry. But I like that they're dancing; it makes me feel special. My mother takes pictures. When the song is over, all the girls crush around her. What if she takes one of them instead? What would I do?

We leave the orphanage. Alessandra has on red plastic flip flops, a t-shirt, and shorts. She carries a small paper bag containing a piece of embroidery and a sample bottle of hand lotion as a gift for me. I hold her passport tightly, her picture inside it seared with sadness. The director walks with us as far as the waiting taxi. Like a lightning bolt, Alessandra jumps in, her eyes straight ahead. As we drive away, she never turns to look back.

I had to make sure nothing would happen so that I wouldn't be allowed to go. I want the taxi to go fast, and it does when we get to the highway. I want to touch my mother's hand like the other girls did. When I look across the seat at her, she has tiny tears on her face. She smiles anyway and reaches out her hand. Soft, her hand is soft.

Alessandra and I are out of the orphanage, speeding along the highway. Going into the world together, I stretch my hand to hers. Isthmus.

And it went along this way.

We arrive in Ottawa in a snowstorm. Alessandra learns English quickly. She makes friends at school, and in a short time, she becomes great pals with our dog. A year and a half later, her sister Renata, five years younger, joins us. Our family is now complete. Hallelujah.

We especially love to all dance together, and we often do—in the kitchen after dinner, in the living room on Saturday afternoons, up and down the upstairs hallway. A marker of joy in our family, a language to share. Sometimes our dog joins in. Alessandra sings "That'll Be The Day." We dance to "Billie Jean," bop to the Minipops, and rock and roll with Little Richard, with Chuck Berry.

Then,

Two years later the unexpected emerges. Mental illness begins to mark the terrain of my daughter Alessandra's life, the landscape of my mind and heart, her sister's too, and the profile and contour of our small family. She is ten years old. My relationship with Alessandra more and more situates itself around the fulcrum of psychosis.

Her initial diagnosis of attention deficit hyperactivity disorder is followed by a finding of learning disabilities. At twelve, she experiences her first psychotic break, prompting her stay of six months—including her thirteenth birthday—in a psychiatric ward of a children's hospital. Her sixteenth birthday also comes and goes during a hospital admission, her third. Diagnoses are presented, retracted, changed, but none are definitive. Amid the churn of psychotic episodes, Alessandra's adolescence is marked by self-harming incidents, hospitalizations, and three periods spent in comas from suicide attempts. She experiences a narrowing of friendships and social possibilities and restricted agency to make life choices. Her containment seeps its way into my life as I ride with the roil of her situation and emotional location.

Our home is governed by chaos, and I live in constant vigilance, perpetual high alert. But there are also glorious periods of respite when Alessandra's health sparkles, and during these, my hopes soar with my desire that each of these remarkable periods will become the norm. I hold on to this desire each time in spite of the past having illustrated something different: that her illness is in fact cyclical.

Nevertheless, Alessandra and I keep dancing. It holds us together, keeps us in rhythm with each other, makes us laugh. It's play. It's in the moment. Rockabilly, doo wop; Bill Haley and the Comets, Buddy Holly, and Elvis; "Always on My Mind"; our at-home sock hops. The wild music from the wild guys to us. We sing the words. We change the words to fit us. We make up words. I love you, ya ya, ya ya, yaaaa.

Once, on my birthday, Alessandra and I eat in a restaurant with juke boxes at the banquettes. We are the last people there that evening, playing music and chatting with the waitress. At closing time, the waitress locks the doors, turns down the lights slightly, puts the CLOSED sign outside. We jive with the waitress and the cook around the restaurant, up and down the aisles. "Twist And Shout," "Ring Of Fire."

But my daughter's mental illness becomes more and more a source of containment for her: long wait lists for appropriate and safe housing; more hospitalizations; medications, often changed and at times exhausting her spirit and her body. My energy, too, is draining from me. Diagnoses continue to shift by circumstance and psychiatrist. No diagnostic determination lasts.

Several years later, during her twenties,

Alessandra is living in a high rise apartment with her boyfriend. One Sunday afternoon in January, suicidal, she goes on her own to a hospital emergency room but is sent home. Later that day, she attempts suicide, jumping from her apartment balcony.

In a wheelchair with paraplegia and in constant physical pain, Alessandra's options narrow even further. Her needs for support amplify. Finding housing for her becomes more challenging with few possibilities available and wait lists spanning years. Making her way around the city in winter is often impossible. Accessing restaurants, shops, people's homes and buildings for appointments—all prove formidable. Nevertheless our bond, significantly centrepieced by mental and now physical illness, continues to strengthen. So, too, do my efforts to manage the interplay between grieving the persisting toll of her increasingly complex situation while, despite that, attempting to maintain a positive approach and to mine hope.

Throughout shattering experiences, Alessandra's joy of engagement with the world, her love for her family, her laughter, her delight in spending time with animals, and her resolute gusto—all these are never crushed. Throughout various diagnoses and an uncovering of early childhood trauma, her goals, her potential, and her life possibilities taper. But her personality—determined, persistent, never giving up on what she sets her mind to, and always brave—remains.

Alessandra and I learn a new dance style, our own wheelchair style. "Thriller," "That'll Be The Day," "Are You Lonesome Tonight?" Alessandra joins Propeller Dance, an integrated dance group, dancing every week and performing to sold-out audiences each June. After her first performance to an audience of six hundred people, she claims nervousness. The third year, she wheels to the centre of the stage, and with her dance group in a semi-circle behind her, she sings a cappella "What a Wonderful World." I sit in the audience crying, hugging a bouquet of flowers for her.

We talk a lot about our beginnings, our first days together.

Yet,

Alessandra died during a November night, alone in her room in a hospital psychiatric ward. Much later, the autopsy report would indicate no obvious cause of death. But just an hour after her death, I open the door of her room. She lies in her bed, intubation tube still in her mouth, emergency equipment left beside her. EKG grid paper strewn across the floor showing the long flat lines of her heart. Stilled. Leaning over the bed, I hold her hands tightly. Isthmus.

13.
Grandma's Husband

Parenting with My Mother

CHERYL CHAFFIN

One day my son, then four years old, said, "You're grandma's husband." I was taken aback. How to explain to your child that you are not married to your mother! "We're not married," I said. "She is my mom. She helps to take care of you, and we share a house with her." His little "Oh" gave me time to reflect on my choices that had brought us to this place—the possibility of marriage to my own mother, and all that implied (beyond my son's immediate knowledge of parenting). Had he somehow absorbed the idea that those who work in tandem to raise a child are always in some way male/female, husband/wife in their roles? Perhaps he had seen or heard these conceptualizations at school, and was trying to fit around our nontraditional relationship a normative view of parenting as he observed and felt it in the larger environment. Certainly, I had not taught him traditional conceptions of parental and martial relations, and in our liberal California community, there were many kinds of parental dyads. In a strange way, he was right however: my relationship with my mother has constituted a companionship of two women maturing (through joy and struggle), two women who had discovered feminist ideals only after leaving conservative Christian backgrounds, and who, within the frameworks of all we have learned, have tried to create together a space for a child to grow and thrive.

MY MOTHER'S TEACHINGS

My son's idea that we were husband and wife in our childrearing duties drove me to think further of the situation during my own childhood. My father had worked, travelled, and introduced me to the outside world and its rules. He had taught me how to make a way for myself in society. My mother had married at twenty-one and had me, her first child, by the age of twenty-three. She would advise me through my early adulthood to "see the world, meet men, and get educated. Don't do what I did," which was to get married early, forego a university degree, and spend the next years of her life raising her two children and tending to the domestic environment. My father was a politically conservative, "self-made" man who believed that if his wife worked, she'd raise his tax bracket. I wanted to see the world, meet many kinds of people, and have lots of experiences. I did not want anyone to tell me what to do. My mother fuelled my determination. I resolved that a husband and children were not in my immediate future. They would only hold me back.

My mother's voice resounding within me, I became a burgeoning feminist in college in the 1980s—a young woman who envisioned one day having a child on her own, a single mother travelling through Europe with a baby on her back. It was a romantic ideal that combined the robust masculinity of the nineteenth and early twentieth centuries with the bra-burning feminist revolution of the mid-twentieth century. Somewhere within that mix of robust masculinity and feminist revolt, my mother's teachings resonated. My ideal was a feminism that fought for not just equality with men but the right—and the psychic and physical space—for females to move in the world without fear and shame and with courage and independence.

At that time as I conjured my version of intellectual life combined with motherhood, I had not considered that I could contain both father and mother—and that others would help me to raise a child. Yet the will and one's imagination have less influence on reality than the material manifestations of experience, as life beholden to circumstance mostly takes a course of its own making. That my mother has been a lifelong friend as well as a parent and that she has helped me from the outset to raise my child is no small matter. The joint project of raising a child with my mother has altered and reconfigured our relationship. To find some rationale to better understand the change in our mother-daughter relationship, and to my son's idea of my mother and me as a husband and wife team, I turn to Jacques Lacan's idea of the necessity of the father in that he is a figure that represents what Lacan terms "the Law." How, I have wondered, does the psychoanalyst's theory apply when two women raise a child together?

BENDING AND BREAKING THE LAW

In considering Freud's analysis of sexuality as shaped by family and society, French psychiatrist and psychoanalytic theorist Jacques Lacan wrote in the mid-twentieth century of the necessity of the father. The father breaks "the asocial dyadic unit of mother and child.... [the] relation of mother and child cannot be viewed outside the structure established by the position of the father" (23). Since Lacan's writing on sexuality in the 1950s and 1960s, feminist theorists such as Simone de Beauvoir, Julia Kristeva, Hélène Cixous, Jacqueline Rose, and Toril Moi have shown the diversity of women's experience as they reconfigure notions of Freud's ever-elusive female subjectivity. Contemporary readers of Freudian psychology know that there are many ways to view and to experience the relationship between mother and child. Numerous factors constituted in the social and political ramifications of race, culture, economics, sexuality, and ideology (to name a few) influence a child's development.

For Lacan, The Law (with a capital "L" for its authority) represents a permanent impossibility or prohibition. The Law finds its expression in social norms and taboos (embodied in those close to us), as well as in the signifiers that shape our reality as translated into language. Lacan writes that the role of the father is a representation of The Law. This law not only is the voice of authority for the child but provides structure, guidance, and purpose to life's activities. Traditionally, in Western cultures, the father has symbolized a kind of intelligence transferred to the child. That intelligence ideally consists of knowledge of how to be in the world, how to function, how to make money and survive, how to socially relate with others, journey outward, and learn new things.

I learned how to be in the world through both my father and my mother, of course, but from my father I learned the world of work, the possibility of career, how to think about finances, and, when young, the rules by which I was to live. I learned these rules also in the patriarchal church and through the notion of a benevolent and judgmental Father God. The role of the father was everywhere around me, and I imbibed it without much thought but with a feeling of need and duty. I was born in 1963 and came into adulthood experiencing the hard-won benefits of American feminism. My parents divorced (my mother's choice), and my family left the evangelical church, a church into which I'd been born and raised. My whole life had changed radically by the time I'd completed college. I was no longer a practising Christian. I had travelled, had begun what was to be a succession of romantic affairs. Influenced by secular ideas, I no longer felt a need for religious doctrine. I had left behind the notion of redemption through salvation.

The discoveries of the past twelve years since the inception of my child have led me to the realization that because the father role is metaphoric and symbolic—in Lacan extended to language, to speech, to social roles and taboos—I no longer conceptualize and read "the father" as an energy housed exclusively in a male body and delivered within the parameters of a traditionally patriarchal (authoritative and imposing) style. The awakenings I have experienced through conception, pregnancy, birth, my child's infancy, toddler, elementary, and now middle-school years have revealed to me a distinct sense of feminism and what it means to parent as a "feminist." Feminism means to create (with full knowledge of the masculine history of The Law) a way of life that insists not on the gendered, binary nature of The Law, but one that exists in conscious relationship to the daily tasks and demands of the world, both familial and social, without the rigidity of parental roles assumed along gender lines. In this way, I consider my teaching role in relationship with and to my son. I model behaviour and, in part, provide options of how to be in the world, ways to think about situations and problems, and ways to interact successfully with others. Early on, I defined my place as parent in relationship to my son. My work was to provide him an environment to develop his knowledge—academic, spiritual, and practical—so that he could function well and with satisfaction in the world. I wanted him to have the skills to navigate his way through difficulty, struggle, confusion, and suffering—the inevitable experiential elements of human embodiment.

I took Lacan's idea of The Law and remade it for my own situation. For example, The Law for me regarding my own mother was to protect my young son's development so that he did not receive information that he could not cognitively understand and so not critically process before his appropriate developmental age. The determination and practice of these parameters have taken on a degree of sensitivity and intuition, subtle qualities and discrepancies intrinsic to attuned parenting and to the idiosyncrasies of my particular child. I did not want my mother to detail extreme social and political violence in front of my son. She (voracious reader of news headlines that seem to thrive on sensational details) responded to my objections with, "You don't need to protect your son! This is the reality of the world." Yes, but her timing was off, so that one night my nine year old went to bed with images of a beheading. What does a child, sleepy and turning to bed, make of such narrative? What repetitious images persist through his sleep? "It took me awhile to sleep," he told me the next morning. "I kept thinking of the man without his head and how afraid he must have been."

At the same time, I'm a realist. I want to parent cognizant of the world's realities, not to push them into a silent corner where a monster of ignorance may develop. I want my son to grow into an intelligent citizen, an informed and contemplative person. I, his parent, should reflect a tender pragmatism to/for him, one that says: this is the world in which you live, child. My questions arise as follows: who will guide you through the rigours and violence of this world that we have unwittingly inherited? The father? The mother? Any trusted, caring, wise being? For there are laws in the world that are not of an individual's making. Too often someone else dictates The Law. It imposes itself on us as something other than personal choice, something undesired and constricting. Growing up is a coming to terms with the limits the material world imposes on one's interior world, the things one wants for oneself but, because of others and the way circumstances unfold, is sometimes unable to attain. Someone is always imposing to the best of his ability his Law on another's freedom(s).

Someone or something is always trying to disturb our human tendency to what Lacan calls "asociality," the dyad of the two. Specifically, he references the symbiosis of mother and child, which psychologically over one's lifespan represents the longing for home, its comforts, familiarity, and safety. The symbiosis of mother and child signifies a longing to return to gestation, the warmth and insularity of the womb. It is to this breaking that the child is abruptly and gradually awakened, and to this breaking that he is put to bed. This breaking constitutes the formative years of his undoing, his unraveling into the world, as gradually, step by imperceptible step, the world intervenes and distances him from his initial need of home, his familiars, from his parent(s) and from all those who love him. It is not such a sad thing, this necessary and inevitable separation from the first symbiosis with the mother. Rather it happens by nature of human embodiment and growing into that body, carried away with the body as it grows. Yet the sense of this first inextricable connection lingers within us, something familiar yet remote and barely remembered.

In my parenting, I try to revise and merge the role of father and mother, not as a commanding God or an eternally nourishing source, but as a narrative of a father-mother that encompasses no particular gender but assumes the full responsibilities of parenting—responsibilities always shared with others across genders and generations. These responsibilities include sustained teachings in relation with my child of how to be in the world with others and how to develop a fruitful and rewarding relationship with oneself. The parent helps to teach the child how to enjoy the pleasures of solitude, to find solace in his own company, and to discover and manifest through life what he most loves.

VULNERABILITY AND REIMAGINING SELF

How is it that my mother and I came to trust one another so deeply? On whom else could I rely when the desire for a child arose and two months later (terrified, subconscious of my desire for a child) found myself pregnant? There are things that I remember now, like our twined vulnerabilities and how throughout the years we've come to one another's aid. That July when I was five months pregnant we stayed for a few days at Tassajara Zen Center in the Santa Lucia Mountains in a box canyon behind Big Sur. My mother fell in the creek. It was to be a hike across the creek and to a swim hole. Not to swim, just to make the hike and to look at the swimmers and the place, which was supposed to be beautiful. She was sixty-four and had had an onset of rheumatoid arthritis a year earlier while travelling in Myanmar by herself. Now her knees gave out over slick creek stones in steadily moving water. Suzuki Roshi who founded Tassajara in 1966 had also fallen in the river (at the swimming hole) and nearly drowned. Several students had rescued him. He was calm, unshaken. I erased the few feet between us. Her wrists buried in the creek, the water rushed around her shoulders. She seemed unafraid but she had surprised herself, and me.

My mother recovered, her knees scraped, her wrists tender. My son came at the end of November. She stayed with me throughout induced labour and steadily over five days in the hospital after Caesarean section. The baby's father came and went: home fifty miles to check voicemail messages, to eat lunch, to rest. My son was lifted from my body just before two on Tuesday afternoon. His father stayed in the OR during Caesarean for the arrival of the baby. That night he slept in the hospital room on a foldout bed. The baby slept next to me. I woke at four in the morning, milk rushing in and filled with longing to connect with another human being. "Would you marry me?" I said, thinking it was possible, that we could make it work (part of a long history of people who, in particularly poignant and charged moments, have felt the same). I spoke toward the dark corner where I knew he lay awake. "It will be okay," he replied. It was good he comforted me but did not take my question seriously. We both knew we would not stay together. We would learn to parent cooperatively, but we did not have an intimate future.

My son's coming into the world, the new moments of vulnerability and fear in the face of the unknown, had created for me a forceful passion to bond. But no such merging would come. It was to be that I would raise a child on my own. That was what I had wanted; yet, for the first year or two of my son's life I wanted to be with a man who would love me with my child. Slowly the desire for a man dissipated. One day on a neighbourhood walk, I passed a house I had long admired. A young couple and their toddler lived there. I imagined they shared a partnership in raising their child that I did not have. They had sex and intimacy, they were making a life together and that connection likely deepened as they watched their child grow. That sort of situation felt incredibly rich and engaged to me. How did people attain it? I wanted what I did not have. I called it envy and wrote a poem about the terrible state such envy induces. It took nearly two years until I did not long for what they had. It was a day of passing the house and not feeling desire but a state of acceptance and calm. I was not alone. I was raising my child with my mother and in tandem with other parents and people I knew and loved. I was doing just fine.

When I had discovered my pregnancy, my mother said, "You can live with me. I'll help you raise the baby." She was ecstatic. She was going to be a grandmother for the first (and only) time. I liked my mother—her independence, her determination. She had been married to my father for a quarter of a century and had had total clarity that for the next half of her life she would remain single. I trusted her. We had been roommates off and on throughout the years. I had supported her emotionally through her divorce, and we had travelled for weeks at a time in Europe and the Western United States. My best conversations happened with her. She was a friend, a confidant. I pushed her to return to school. She went reluctantly, with trepidation but anticipation. She attended community college and the university. I helped her with papers. We simultaneously attended graduate school. She studied for a master's degree in East/West psychology while I worked towards an MFA in creative writing.

My mother had been trapped, stifled like so many housewives of the mid and late twentieth centuries. Many women had preceded her. She contained multitudes. But she did not know of those other women because they had been silent, their voices lost to history. Those women had written books my mother was only just discovering. Attending community college thirty years after my birth she would discover literature and writers that spoke to her and made her realize that she had experiences worth writing. Conservative Christian culture and the time of her childhood and adult maturation—the forties, fifties, and sixties—had stunted her development, made her afraid, insecure, aggressive, impulsive, and sometimes angrily outspoken. I would do well to describe myself emerging from the church with some of those same traits. My mother was proud when she inquired of our pastor why women served punch and cookies at church socials while men served as deacons on the church governing board. The pastor replied, "Give us time," and she, in her rhetorical manner, answered, "How's two thousand years?"

I wanted an intellectual mother, one interested in studying, reading, improving her mind. Not in the sense that men had wanted women for centuries to be educated enough so that they were decent conversationalists, but a smart mother, a mother who cared about thinking and reading. "I was hungry to become a good critical thinker," she tells me as I write this essay. I, her daughter, had grown up in a house where intelligent, thoughtful conversation was not a staple, where politics and literature did not matter. I wanted those things to matter, and I wanted my mother to share—in her own style—that journey with me.

Our stories are linked in vulnerability: Mom in the creek, me in the hospital room; Mom with rheumatoid, me birthing a child. There has been support, even rescue—Mom in the creek, me erasing the distance; me, in the hospital after birth, Mom encouraging me through pregnancy, into birth, and supporting me through the demanding first years of my son's life. The ambience and energy surrounding his birth brought a sense of great change: turmoil and angst with his father, creating the baby's new room with my mother, everything centred on the coming child, uncertainty about my swelling body and raising a child. Not that I was incapable. But fear came in a looming sense of vulnerability—as a pregnant woman, a mother. Fear, too, that I had sacrificed, and hence lost, the freedom for which I had labored. Yet in those first years of the child's life, I wrote a whole collection of poems, which I aptly titled *Heat: Poems from Early Motherhood*. When he was four I went on to get my PhD. "Apply for the doctoral program," my mother had said, "You've wanted this advanced degree. I will help you." The program entailed six years of in-depth study, and simultaneously I worked. I have over the years felt my mother's selflessness, her knowledge of my need to accomplish certain things in life, and, ultimately, her support. Just as I have wanted certain things of and for her, she has wanted things of and for me. Our lives have been entwined, even enmeshed, in finding fulfillment in the endeavours and successes of the other.

FATHERING/MOTHERING WITH MY MOTHER

The baby came in November 2003. Now a new and foreign life arose: the daily labour of raising an infant, quickly becoming a toddler, who was dependent upon me. I was a mother, the figure of nurture and care emblazoned on my child's psyche, reflected in his social and emotional development for the remainder of his life. My mother and I became parents, co-parents together, even while his father visited on weekends and spent time with his son. The child became the centre of our daughter-mother and mother-son-grandmother relationship. The daily friendship I had had with my mother was put aside for parenting and awareness of a child. If my mother and I were speaking (usually in the car) and he was not immediately included, he interrupted. He asserted himself into our awareness, usually speaking directly to me, competing with his grandmother for his mother's attention. My mother responded with frustration. "He's a child," I would say. "My attention goes to him first." The daughter-mother relationship of close and ongoing communication fell away. My mother rebelled against this loss. For years, I tried to hear two voices at once and to participate in more than one conversation. This work tired me; its effects linger. It is the reason I am on silent retreat just now.

Many people commented that my son would mature into a feminist man. The assumption was that having been raised by two women, he would understand women. I agreed. It was my hope. But I also felt compelled to counter hope. Outwardly, I laughed and joked with others: "Either an enlightened feminist man or an impossibly spoiled and difficult to please adult male!" No guarantee that in understanding women he would like them, or they him! In the new millennium, cultural journalism has focused on women's independence and has examined the implications (for children, for the economy, for the legal system) of the growing number of single mothers. A recent issue of *The Economist* describes children of single mothers as coming from "broken homes" (in an ironic twist on Lacan's theory of the Father as the one who breaks the union of child and mother), and reports that children of single mothers do poorly in comparison to children from intact families. The intact family is described as the dual parent and usually dual gender household. Neither of these descriptions—broken, intact—fit my own immediate family situation, at least in the conceptualizations of mothers and their parenting situations put forward by *The Economist*. I'm by definition a single mother—never married, not living with his father. Mine is not a traditional (two parent, two gender) nuclear family, but I live in a thriving family household. We are not *broken*. Are we *unbroken*? Does aloneness and/or a terminated relationship imply brokenness or indicate malfunction? I insist it does not. Where does *my* family fit then? How to discourse my parenting situation as it affects my son's life if not by these popular definitions and their implied assumptions? That is in part what I'm figuring out here in exploring the reality of once having been "Grandma's husband." Of course, it is high time that cultural commentators rethink their conceptualizations of family. Women increasingly choose to raise children without men's help, especially if men are unreliable or abusive, but, too, when men are undesirable, in that they are not emotionally or physically available in the fulltime process of raising a child.

The newer idea touted in the media is that women prefer to be alone, given the dire choices of available men; such is the argument in Hanna Rosin's "The End of Men," published in *The Atlantic* in 2010. Women, now the majority of college and graduate students in the United States, often have a stable income and satisfying professional work. Rosin writes, "for the first time in American history, the balance of the workforce tipped toward women, who now hold a majority of the nation's jobs. The working class, which has long defined our notions of masculinity, is slowly turning into a matriarchy, with men increasingly absent from the home and women making all the decisions" (*Atlantic*). As a result of this developing socioeconomic situation, concerns of parenting may not centre so much on the child's need of a father, but that the child is cared for by responsible, thoughtful, and loving adults.

When my son was very young, many well-intentioned people remarked, "He will need males around [in that my mother and I were raising him full time]. It's good he has your brother [his uncle]." I mentioned a male friend. I assured people that he saw his father every couple weeks and that his grandfather (my father) lived just forty miles away. Why did I make these assurances? Did I, too, believe that a male child needed men in his life? I felt that in my mother and me he had steady, daily presences in his life. But the social wisdom and pressure revolved around the importance of male presence for male children. Yet I realized that families in which a father and mother lived together were no guarantee against dysfunctional, disturbing, and unsupportive environments. According to Rosin, there's more: women have acquired power in the form of educational and professional opportunities. Educated women are intelligent, skilled, and, frequently, financially independent of men. Media reports bemoan the trend of missing and disengaged fathers. "Children need fathers," journalists claim, as do my students in their papers on women's growing social and economic power. Yes, children need diversity in all forms, including mentor males (whether teachers, uncles, grandfathers, friends, coaches). Finally, in Western countries, we are increasingly defining family as a community of supportive adults—regardless of gender—who participate with time and resources in the enormous task of raising a child. That community should and need not be exclusively women, but many times it is women who assume the majority of the momentous efforts needed to raise children. Many men want to be a part of that community. In dialogue with men, women need to find beneficial ways to include men desirous of caring for children and participating in their lives. It's important for children to know who loves them and a man's dedicated parenting should never be curtailed or truncated when it helps a young human being thrive.

In particular, my mother's help has nourished my son's growth and has permitted me to develop a successful teaching career and to earn my doctorate. The house she bought twenty years ago is also my home and the house my son has known from birth. I have discovered how I embody both father and mother. I work and come home to cook dinner. In parenting, at home, and in the world, I enjoy practising kindness, love, sensitivity to self and others, and practice attunement to the mystery and beauty of the unspoken. I have learned to read others with care and with consideration. My readings allow me to navigate situations, and as a parent, these readings help me forge the way with my son, to make decisions for him, but always in dialogue with him, and often with my mother and his father. I have worked diligently to develop professional success in my ability to make my own money and to support my child, as well as in continually cultivating my intellectual abilities (both as pleasure and professional endeavour). I have devoted sustained attention to cultivating my emotional equanimity, part of which includes setting boundaries with others and clarity in decision making. There is no father or grandfather that lives with us on a daily basis. There is a grandmother and mother who fulfill parental roles and provide a home foundation, a centre of love and knowing for a child who is (all too soon) growing into a man.

ANGER TO LOVE

For my mother and me, the long road to recognizing our full abilities has given rise to anger—shared, fueled, fanned, and cooled over the years of our late-growing feminism, our travels, our graduate degrees, our sharing of Buddhist practice, and our increasing independence in thought, body, and mind. It has been no small undertaking that together we've raised my son in a shared house at the edge of the Pacific Ocean and that it was given to us to nurture a boy into the world. This undertaking has helped my child to grow into an intelligent, thoughtful, compassionate, and energetic male. It is my hope that his early experiences with his mother and grandmother will serve him well as he continues through life to his old age. Likewise, the young male in our presence has taught us much about the delightful and active energy of a growing boy's curiosity and his connection with others as he discovers the world. It is because of my child that I have come to appreciate men's presence with renewed vision, a sense of possibility and an awareness of men's beauty in the world.

It does not take a father to separate the supposedly asocial unit of mother and child. The world intervenes, the dynamic, ever impermanent, transmogrifying world into which my son is growing. Who is this child? That is the mystery. When I imagine the life he has ahead of him, I envision my son running knee-high in wild grass, coastal oaks dotting the hills on which he runs. We are always running toward a view to things and, so, I have him reach a boundary, a rim, a border where he might see ahead and where his hungry heart asks, "What's next?" in the anticipation and thrill of youth as it charges into the wild and painful and lovely swirl that is life.

WORKS CITED

Lacan, Jacques. *Feminine Sexuality: Jacques Lacan and the Ecole Freudienne*. Edited by Juliet Mitchell and Jacqueline Rose. Translated by Jacqueline Rose. Norton, 1982.

Rosin, Hanna. "The End of Men." *The Atlantic*, Jul/Aug. 2010, www.theatlantic.com/magazine/archive/2010/07/the-end-of-men/308135/. Accessed 11 Oct. 2015.

"The Weaker Sex: Blue-Collar Men in Rich Countries Are In Trouble. They Must Learn to Adapt." *The Economist*, 30 May 2015.

14.
For the Child

DORSÍA SMITH SILVA

To some people love is given,
to others only Heaven.
—Langston Hughes, "Luck"

Honeybee buzzed over to my African violet

entered the uterus root

a discharge

androecium to the gynoecium

seed planted—

molecule in my womb

maybe i should have waited for another honeybee
or hornet

or wasp

maybe i should have told that honeybee to go inside of a daisy

maybe i should have ignored my ovary's blue-red burning

honeybee flew off

with a swarm

of other lovers

Tiny seed

from between my stem legs

your fetus buds

were handed over—

put into a jar

germination

stopped

i sent you back to the spirit field

wanted you to be more than a bastard bloom

to be reborn

15.
The Worst is Not the Worst

Memories of Motherhood and Multiple Miscarriages

ALMA SIMOUNET-BEY

And worse I may be yet: the worst is not
So long as we can say "This is the worst."
—Shakespeare, *King Lear*

Sailing ahead into the waters of narrative discourse was not an easy prospect after many decades of producing strictly academic writings. I discovered that this exercise of bringing forth memories that have not been exposed for some time to the reality of my existence, remembrances of the four pregnancies that never came to fruition, became a crucible harder to surmount than the losses themselves.

I do not wish to wake up dormant dreams of the lost children that I yearned to guide through life. I know that I have purposefully rejected any attempt at resuscitating my memory so as to drown the pain of loss. But that pain is so deeply ingrained in the empty pages of those fertility years that any hint of the recovery of memory is bound to be the waking call for uncontrolled rivers of sorrowful remembrances. Still, I need to revisit those moments. I must heal the pain, for I am now approaching the winter of my life. My time is running out, and my spirit seeks reconciliation, so as to end this existence in the peace that acceptance gives.

As I put my head down, I force myself to think back, to move in time and space toward those years of soul searching, wondering once more about the what and the why of my lost babies. My own self tries to engage in an Armageddon-like fight to create a disconnection with those years of what seemed to me as a continuous flow of unending pregnancies and unending losses. Not to mention the sense of guilt that my Puerto Rican culture planted early in life. I know that through the course of this writing, the dreams will come back, and I will wake up trying to ascertain if I have just lived through a true episode of my life or if what I saw in the hallways of my mind was reawakened thoughts of wishes gone bad.

Still, I must share these failed attempts at motherhood after my first child was born and the lessons they entailed. They constitute my legacy to all mothers and mothers-to-be. Truly, if my life had been different, I may have raised a daughter to receive this legacy as a possible future mother in her own right. Instead, I hope my story will ensure that other daughters-becoming- mothers may cherish this precious gift of bringing forth life.

My first baby was the result of a flawless pregnancy and delivery. He came into our lives in San Juan, Puerto Rico, on 16 January 1974. The family rejoiced. And at that time, the family was constituted by anyone who came for lunch to Mami Carmen's house on Sundays. Eugenio was "*el principito*" to everyone, and he behaved accordingly. Four months had barely gone by of so much to be thankful for when the first loss occurred. I was just three months into my second pregnancy when a short trip to the bathroom ended in the fear that comes when one is not in control of the kind of knowledge that puts into the right perspective what is truly happening.

Why would such light bleeding be of great consequence? I arrived at the doctor's office somewhat worried, but not seriously, as a result of my own ignorance. My obstetrician was off-island, so another physician received me in his office. He immediately hospitalized me. I could not understand the reason for the hospitalization until the next day arrived, for the pain that I felt as I lay in bed was almost impossible to bear. My entrails were engaged in a battle in which I could literally feel rugged hands inside of me, violently pulling my organs and ripping them apart for hours, and there was not a single drop of the heavenly pain-killing potion that would stop it. Hours went by in the midst of this horrendous manipulation of tissue and blood vessels until all of it came to a sudden stop like the blissful ending of a nightmare. The happiness that was brought about by the termination of this inextricable physical pain became in itself the death knell for my baby. By giving up the last breath of life, he or she had infused joy and comfort to my fatigued body.

No one, not even my own doctor could explain scientifically the reason for the spontaneous abortion. "It's one of those things that happen in pregnancy." I can still hear the comment and see the lips moving as they were uttered in an authoritative voice. No one could give me a convincing explanation as to what had gone wrong, and all this time I still believed in science and in the wonderful discoveries about reproduction.

I came back home empty handed, devastated, juggling feelings of loss and joy at the sight of my boy. He was a four-month-old child who looked at me with the expressions of happiness that only a baby can express, a headful of blonde hair and penetrating dark eyes awaiting me at home, too young to know if he really missed me or who apparently felt good about seeing the familiar face of the person that fed him and gave him physical and spiritual warmth. And I was glad. Besides, I was still young, healthy; more children would come. I would not waste time thinking about impossibilities. The memories of the two days at the hospital and the accompanying, insurmountable pain would soon vanish from my mind.

That Thanksgiving, my husband decided to take me on vacation to Haiti so we would have some time to ourselves. The flight over was quite short. The hotel van picked us up at the airport and drove us up the mountain where the villas were located. Driving through the city of Port-au-Prince was one of the most depressing rides I have ever had; there was so much poverty. I saw mothers washing their babies in the filthy water of the gutters; I could not utter a word. We arrived at the hotel, built on Marie Antoinette's former estate, in a very remote area of the mountain. The seclusion, exclusiveness, and ostentation of this hostelry in the midst of unimaginable poverty turned into such an unbearable weight inside me that when we arrived at our assigned villa, I pulled myself into the shower to cry with contempt and sorrow for this world of inequities, suffering, and injustice. I thought of the baby I had lost and cried. The stay was short but laden with the emotional weight of memories. I spoke to my husband, and though saddened that he had tried to make me happy but instead produced the opposite result, he understood how I felt. At least the trip was a short one.

Eugenio was about a year and a half old; I felt fortunate because my teaching career provided me the time that I needed to be with my son and my husband. Life was good to me: I was pregnant again. The first loss had already passed to the dimension of long-term memory, so there was nothing I should be worried about.

The initial three months, crucial to any pregnancy, moved along free from any outstanding event. We travelled in the summer; a stop in Ann Arbor revived many experiences of college life, but the environs was not the same. College life seemed to be different; the students, now attending summer school, looked different and acted differently. It seemed as if the university itself had entered a different zone. As postuniversity adults, we think that we are the only ones that experience and witness the passing of time; the world we left behind must stay the same, vegetating in a complacency of its own. We do not expect anything to change, and when we become aware of our error, we want to modify our interpretation of life so the newfound experience fits a particular truth. Yes, Ann Arbor looked different, so I left with the feeling that my time there was the best. This in no way affected me. My pregnancy was going along smoothly. Everything in my body said, Go ahead. We're doing fine.

After the summer, I sat down at my computer to resume my academic work, reflecting upon my recent experiences, writing them, and looking at the words on the screen as if I were scraping my life out of an iceberg. Reminiscing at that part I wish to let go, the remembrances of that pregnancy continued to haunt me.

Classes began early in August. We did not have to worry about snow days, but we did have to plan ahead for the real possibility of a hurricane, for this was the Atlantic hurricane season and the months of August, September and October marked that time of the year for the birth, and sometimes death, of these atmospheric phenomena. I met the students in my assigned sections, young *prepas* or freshmen, eager to begin a new stage in their lives at the main campus of the University of Puerto Rico. I said to myself, it's going to be a good semester.

Unfortunately, these thoughts did not last very long. I began to develop symptoms similar to those of my second pregnancy. Again, there were stains of blood, but this time they were larger, denser in texture, and of a stronger red hue. I was actually bleeding, not spotting; this time, I was concerned, very concerned.

For one month, I was bedridden, continuously bleeding heavily, in my sixth month of gestation. Classes, teaching, interacting with new students. Playing with Eugenio on the patio and looking closely at the beauty of the petals in the hibiscus, the oleanders, and the bougainvillea flowers, exhilarating experiences shared with a young child as he tried to make sense of what he saw and what I said. Going to the supermarket to buy strawberries. Teaching Eugenio that we could buy an inexpensive toy this week but not the next. Going to the beach and playing in the sand, feeling the coolness of the waves as they hit us smoothly. All of this went into oblivion. My mom and my sister Nancy looked after Eugenio and me during the day. My husband felt helpless. I could feel my baby moving inside of me, letting me know that he was still alive and that, like me, he was going to fight so that he could come into this world.

Weeks into this stage, I began to feel strong contractions. A dangerous sign. Back then, in the 1970s, it was believed that the only way to stop premature contractions was to begin a steady intake of alcoholic beverages—rum, gin, or vodka, mixed with soda or juice until the uterus relaxed and did not initiate a new set of contractions. Sometimes the intake had to be so strong that for the first time in my life, I knew what it was like to be drunk, but that did not matter because the contractions would stop and my baby was still alive, kicking and fluttering inside. How ironic that alcohol, which affected my body negatively health wise, would become the saving grace for my child. The family grew concerned that I would become an alcoholic in no time.

Cultural teachings in Puerto Rico, closely attached to Catholic Church dogma, have created for generations a distorted picture of the reason behind serious illness, death, sorrow, all natural outcomes of being alive and human. Anything that smells of great medical proportions, of suffering or tragedy, is immediately judged as the heavenly scourge for sinful behavior. Thus the same institution that teaches love and mercy and presents itself as the fountain of compassion and spiritual shelter becomes the source of condemnation, for it has traditionally viewed any kind of sorrow as the redeeming channel through which we provide a kind of payment for the commission of grave or mortal sin. How can the generative force of love place the pain and sorrow of seeing the life of a child slipping away as the offering of a human being to achieve redemption? It is a paradoxical teaching of redeeming punishment. (I am aware that this Church now sees life through different eyes. Are they the eyes of a more humane leader?)

On many occasions, we become so immersed in our own despair that we lose sight of the advent of more aggravating circumstances still. Shakespeare's Lear voiced this awareness in the midst of his suffering as a father. The worst is not the worst. In the afternoon hours of 15 September 1975, the impending approach of Hurricane Eloise to the island frightened everyone. I was not well; my young stepson had been sent over the weekend before, but he seemed to have arrived with a bad stomach virus. So that day, when I awoke in the morning, I knew the virus had been passed on to me, too. I suffered the uncomfortable effects of this nasty virus, burned in high fever, bled profusely as a result of frequent bowel movements in the form of diarrhea; yet receiving the loving care of Eugenio's godfather, Andrés, a dedicated neurologist and psychiatrist, and his wife, I settled down, feeling better and thinking that I had defeated another hurdle in this difficult and uncompromising road to childbirth. I had no contractions, and I was surrounded by my husband, Eugenio, my sister, my mother, and Andrés and his wife. I had nothing to fear.

Because I had not been able to ingest any kind of food, it was not until midnight that my body let me know that it needed a little nourishment, perhaps a sandwich. And that was what my sister brought me. Not an hour went by when I felt my water had broken. Hurricane Eloise was raging outside, and I could feel the blood slowly trickling between my thighs. It wasn't long before I realized that Eloise was a typical meteorological phenomenon of the season, but my internal storm was brewing into a larger, darker happening.

My husband decided to call for an ambulance because he was afraid that walking under these circumstances could cause a haemorrhage. The paramedics arrived, carefully moved me onto the stretcher, placed me in the ambulance under a heavy downpour, and rushed me to the hospital. I remember lying on the stretcher, afraid to move, facing backward, looking at large raindrops sliding down the glass of the ambulance doors and seeing how the traffic light at the intersection of Fernández Juncos and Todd Avenues moved abruptly back and forth, straining the wires that tried to hold it in place, fighting the strong winds and heavy rain. This sight slowly disappeared in the distance as the ambulance rushed unimpeded down the empty, wet road, but the memory of the red traffic light is ingrained in my mind. I don't know why erasure does not take care of obliterating these trifles. I guess the associations with what was going on were too strong to face.

We finally made it to the hospital. There was no electricity, but the lights were on. So the generator was working, one positive sign. I do not remember when the uterine contractions began—there was so much turmoil around me. The staff at the hospital had not been able to reach my physician because her phone had somehow gotten hooked up with that of the weather bureau at the airport. I knew she lived close to that area. Inside the hospital, the hours went by, but there was no sign of her. I prayed that my baby would make it, even if I did not.

She finally arrived in the early hours of the morning and immediately checked me. The bleeding was too heavy to induce a regular delivery, so there was no option but to perform a Caesarean surgical procedure. The nurse took me into the operating room. With the help of another nurse, he carefully pulled on the sheets under me to position my body on the table. I was asked to turn on my side and given spinal anesthesia.

Sometime later, the operation began. I cannot erase from my mind the words of my physician as she was about to initiate this final episode: "*En el nombre de Dios.*" That is when I realized the seriousness of my condition. "*Doctora,*" I said. "I can feel the scalpel. It feels like a razor cutting through my skin." The little food that I had had made it impossible for her to give me anesthesia any higher in my spinal column, she explained. The burning became so unbearable that I kept moving and churning. She decided to give me Demerol intravenously. It worked fast. Soon I must have fallen asleep because I suddenly woke up to her screams, asking the assistants in the operating room to summon a doctor to come and help. As if almost all the stars were against me, the uterine muscle, one of the strongest in the body, had contracted so intensely that her hand was caught with the baby's leg inside. I was so confused at the moment that to this day, I cannot remember the event clearly, and all that I am able to put together is that the muscle finally let go of her hand and of the baby's leg. She was now able to pull him out. When the baby was placed on the crib close to me, I was able to catch a glimpse of his face. He looked just like Eugenio, those big dark eyes, staring, just staring. ¡*Dios mío, gracias*! I had had my son against all odds.

When I woke up in my hospital room, it was dark. The curtains were drawn; the lights were out, and there was silence. A grave silence. I couldn't understand what was going on; I just thought of the baby. We had both made it. I murmured something; my husband heard me and came rushing to my side. I asked him to pull open the curtains, open the windows and turn on the light. Why was everything so grey? "How is the baby?" I asked. "He's okay. He's at *Centro Medico*, at a place for premature babies." Oh, yes, I remembered; I was barely seven months pregnant when he was born. I was too tired to continue talking, so I fell asleep again. The crucible was not over yet.

My husband visited the baby every day and reported back to me. He was doing fine. My stay at the hospital was longer than usual because of the many complications I had undergone. First of all, the diagnosis was total placenta previa—a dangerous condition in which the child's placenta adheres itself to the cervical canal through which it will eventually be delivered. I had the accompanying symptoms of strong contractions and heavy bleeding, but the day when my water broke, I developed a high fever and stomach problems associated with the virus I had caught. In addition, the situation with the hurricane warnings had aggravated an already ugly picture. To make matters worse, during the operation, I also had a haemorrhage, which forced my husband to rush to the blood bank with my sister in the middle of the hurricane. My life had been hanging from a thread while I slept, totally unaware of the life-threatening situation I was in. I send my blessings to the person who donated the blood that saved my life.

Halfway through my hospital stay, my doctor came to see me at a time when she did not normally do her rounds. I was wearing a red robe that my mother-in-law had sewn for my hospital stay and which I still have and wear after forty years. I treasure it because it stands for the love of my family and especially the love of my son. I asked her the reason for her visit. She did not hesitate one moment, her words coming out of her mouth like an unstoppable train: the baby had passed away. Had he survived, it would have been in a vegetative state. Now I had an angel who would be looking after me forever. She had come because my husband had asked her to do so. He simply could not tell me.

My crying over the loss of this baby has never stopped, not even now. The milk that was supposedly dried out in my breasts with an injection continued to flow out, for no one, for a void in life. I was still in the hospital when my son was buried next to one of his grandfathers.

So I went home and Eugenio, now seventeen months old, was once more waiting for me.

One would think that given this experience that took me to the brink of death. I would have given up on having more children. The year after, I was pregnant once more. I pretended to not be worried; however, insignificant things like the sight of a dirty napkin with ketchup in the waste basket made me shudder. I knew I was in trouble, but inside my mind, my own self kept telling me, You can. You paid your dues. So the scientific part of me rationalized that I was healthy and could do it. But my cultural and religious upbringing tempted me into thinking that I still had to pay back for something, but what?

This pregnancy continued for five uneventful months. Then, on a Saturday afternoon, after walking all day with the family in the historic district of the city, we returned home. I felt fine. There was no pain. I rushed out of the bathroom and called out to my husband. I was bleeding again.

After passing a day in bed, my doctor's associate saw me on Monday. She explained that given my history, she would have to hospitalize me immediately. What she did not tell me at the time was that my baby was already dead inside of me. Next day, in the operating room, I learned that the fetus could not be pulled out. Instead, I would need a Caesarean procedure. I asked the doctor to please check my organs visually. Did everything look "normal"? I don't remember if I was given medication to sleep or if I was half awake. All I remember is the doctor coming to my side and telling me that it was a girl, ¡*una niña*! I would have to stay in intensive care for a longer period of time because of the threat of a haemorrhage. My organs looked fine, to my joy and grief; my problem seemed to be functional. Functional! That things go wrong! What kind of scientific explanation is this?

So I went back home again, empty handed. But Eugenio was there, waiting for me, and he was now over two years old. I saw him and cried.

My last pregnancy did not last long. I believe I was just entering my fourth month when I started to bleed again—same shock, same fear. My spirit was low; I did not have the energy to fight. The doctor saw me, prescribed some injections to avoid a miscarriage, and ordered a sonogram.

The results showed the end had already arrived. The little sac that holds the baby was still in place, but the baby was gone; the bundle of flesh and blood had left my body in the bleeding. There was only one procedure left to end this medical condition, and it would have to wait until I began to bleed heavily again, a sign that the sac was ready to be discharged from my body. However, I could not bear going home to wait for blood to start flowing out. This was like going through double suffering, psychologically speaking. So I collected my papers and went to the bathroom before I left the doctor's office. Lo and behold I had already begun the bleeding. I asked the secretary to let me see the doctor again before I left her office, so I went in and told her she could now order my hospitalization process. She could not believe how fast my brain had commanded that the physiological process begin and said something to the effect that if I had just used that brain power to hold on to my babies, my whole picture would have been different. Had I not?

The trip to the hospital was my final one in this episodic tragedy.

It was a short stay that was marred only by the strange coincidence that I had to share my room—there were no other rooms available—with another woman with a similar last name to mine except for the letter "u" that was missing in hers. I would have to make sure I was given the right medication. The curettage was successful. Why was the fetus discharged from the embryonic sac? No explanation.

And, once more, I went home with empty hands. But Eugenio was there. He was now three and asked me: "*¿No tienes que volver al hospital?*" (You don't have to go back to the hospital?). No, I responded.

Forty-one years later, looking back at all of these decisions and their consequences, I ask myself whether my obstinacy with having more than one child was foolish and absurd, given my medical history. Every occasion of miscarriage could have driven me to death and thus to the failure of enjoying the love of my husband, my son, and my grandchildren, Andrés and Ryan, throughout this longer life with which I have been blessed. I don't believe in the "eye for an eye, tooth for a tooth" teaching of my culture. However, I do believe that our tragic flaws—Othello's jealousy or Hamlet's indecision, my own stubbornness—drive us to obstinate, unyielding decisions that, unless curtailed, could drive us to our own psychological and physical undoing. This I have learned, not only as a result of my losses but also as the sensible consequence of remembering, grieving, and reconciling myself with life's predicaments. Writing this narrative has been part of the process.

The everyday dreams about my lost children have subsided. These thoughts now come less frequently, and when they do, they are images of playful instances, not of sadness. The pain and sorrow have not disappeared. Why should they? They are part of what I am today. At the same time, they have been placed in the right perspective so that they may be seen as experiences that have helped me heal and see myself and others as individuals with the capacity to surmount our flaws and develop into more mature, balanced human beings, not only emotionally but also spiritually.

The river of my life continues to flow steadily, aware of external forces that may rule the roughness or tranquility of its waters. I am ready to face these circumstances. There will be torrential rains, droughts, the unpredictability of storms that may surprisingly come my way, but I am now a seventy-five-year-old river whose new spiritual and cultural knowledge has overcome old teachings, immersed in the fluidity of memories, still forging ahead and blessed in the warmth of tropical sunshine, providing sustenance to the shores upon which I end. My waters now touch others with kindness and understanding, I hope, and the memories of my life whisper to me that I will endure in the vast ocean of life.

16. The Facsimile of Existence

Mothers and Daughters in Perpetual Reproduction of Identity and Image

MARY BRONSTEIN

During the sea blizzards
she had her own
portrait painted.
A cave of a mirror
placed on the south wall;
matching smile, matching contour.
And you resembled me; unacquainted
with my face, you wore it. But you were mine
after all. (Sexton, "The Double Image" 38)

INTRODUCTION

In the poem "The Double Image," Anne Sexton describes the enthrallment, mystery, confusion, and horror of what it is like to be stuck in the middle of a mother-daughter identity continuum. Trying to decipher where one ends and one's mother begins is a theme that exists in the work of many female poets, but perhaps most exquisitely realized by Sexton, Marge Piercy, and Susan Griffin. It is notable that men, especially male psychoanalysts, have also long been interested in this specific, isolative, and shape-shifting relationship. This is a relationship in which men have no role. They must watch and analyze from the outside as their wives, partners and daughters engage in an involuntarily intense and confusing dynamic. Psychoanalyst C.G. Jung claims, "Every mother contains her daughter in herself and every daughter her mother, and that every woman extends backwards into her mother and forwards into her daughter" (149). Although Jung is touching upon some truth in the way he discusses mothers and daughters as existing on a continuum of individualization and identity, he is, of course, on the outside looking in. This can only be seen as an act of speaking for women, instead of as or to them. Because of this, the process of feminist inquiry requires suspicion of this statement as a male speech act. Is there an implication that no woman ever possesses a true Self and is simply a transient being defined by relationships? In the context of Jung's body of work, this may be true. Of course, in reality, women are true and complete human beings with all the complications of identity that this entails. In this chapter, I place myself, female poets, feminist theorists, and male psychoanalysts in dialogue with each other while I argue that when a woman becomes a mother to a daughter, the *part* of her that is a mother and the *part* of her that is a daughter are ignited in a struggle with time, place, identity, and Self against her actual mother and daughter. The mother of a daughter is many selves at once: The Daughter, The Mother and Her Own Mother. Yet she is one individual woman. She does not forgo her personhood for this struggle; however, this struggle becomes part of it in an in-extractable way. The mother of a daughter exists in a constantly shifting triune state. In a three-dimensional universe, the mother of a daughter transcends the dimensions of reality and time simply by being.

Before proceeding in this examination, I must acknowledge that women become mothers in many different ways, such as adoption, fostering, surrogate, and egg donations. I also acknowledge that women exist as daughters in various ways as the result of adoption, absentee mother, deceased mother, stepmother, same-sex parents, familial guardianship, or various other familial arrangements. All of these types of daughterhood are valid and are personal realities for many women. As such they deserve careful theoretical studies in regard to the daughter's experience in her own mothering of a daughter, but I will not be speaking about them. In this chapter, I am primarily concerned with women who were raised by the woman who gave birth to them because of the extremely complicated and unique phenomenology produced by this type of dyad. It is only in this specific type of relationship that the holy trinity of identity confusion and reproduction, as I speak to it, exists.

THE QUESTION OF IDENTITY AND FORMS

According to Plato's theory of forms, that chair in your living room is not a real chair at all. It is an inferior copy of The Chair—the intangible, perfect, original, *true* chair that exists beyond this dimension and which all other chairs are merely imitative descendants of (253-55).[1] In a study of forms as Plato defines it, mothers and daughters are not actually mothers and daughters at all. They possess motherness and daughterness but can never be considered absolute definitions of these terms. Just like in the positioning of a trifold mirror, a woman with a daughter can look backward into infinity and observe that she is merely a copy of a copy of a copy of The Mother. She can also look forward to her daughter and see herself. Accordingly, it is impossible to know where the original Self lies for women who give birth to female children. As Jung asks, "Whose children are we?" (121).

In Sexton's poem, her mother's face becomes a cavity in which Sexton should be able to find herself, but it is too vast, too cavernous to ever see a clear reflection. Who is the woman at the end of the cave? She also describes her daughter as wearing her face, which positions the whole dynamic as one similar to entering a hall of mirrors. As such, mothers have laid claim to their children, projecting onto them their own selves and shadows of the mothering they themselves received. But they project while wearing a reflective apron so that the woman is caught in a constant psychic ponglike pattern of identity and image with her mother. When this woman gives birth to her own female child, she repeats the pattern, trying to find herself in her daughter while mothering, as both her mother's daughter and an individual. Sexton writes, "I made you to find me" (42). If a woman is a daughter and a mother to a daughter at the same time, where exactly does the "me" she is trying to find lie?

REFLECTIONS

Five years ago, I lay on an operating table with my abdomen severed and my uterus being stitched up on a table next to me. I asked my husband to go behind the curtain to look at our daughter. "Tell me what she looks like," I called as he left my side. I realize now that I was actually asking, "Tell me who she is." Who just emerged from my body? He took a video of the baby and ran back to show it to me. When I looked at the image of the wiggling, slimy, crying baby my first thought was, "Yes, that's her." I *recognized* her. This baby was no stranger; she was not a new sight. I had seen her before and knew this baby. The feeling was akin to looking in a mirror or sorts. Yes, that is she. Yes, that is *me*. But how could this feeling happen if in reality this baby was as much of a stranger to me as any other baby born that day? When my late grandfather-in-law met my daughter for the first time he said to me, "You have been reflected." It was true. Birthing my daughter felt like standing in front of a prism and a mirror at once. When I looked at her, my self bounced off of the prism and beamed a tiny version into the mirror to look back at me. In this I knew her. When my mother held the baby for the first time she laughed and said, "I feel like I am holding you, it is so strange." I wondered then, what did it mean to feel like she was holding me? When I was born did my mother feel the same sense of metaphysical familiarity? If my mother experienced me as her reflection and I experienced my daughter as mine, when my mother held my daughter did my mother see herself? Did that also mean that my daughter was not a reflection of me, but in fact a reflection of my mother? Whose daughter was she really?

> My mother is my mirror and I am hers.
> What do we see? Our face grown young again,
> our breasts grown firm, legs lean and elegant.
>
> Our arms quivering with fat, eyes
> set in the bark of wrinkles, hands puffy,
> our belly seamed with childbearing.
>
> Give me your dress so I can try it on.
> Oh it will not fit you, Mother, you are too fat.
> I will not fit you, Mother. (Piercy 29)

Being reflected by a daughter means more than a daughter physically resembling her mother. In fact, I doubt it is even necessary and one must not take Sexton's face-stealing daughter as literal. Rather, it is a product of both the unique physical and metaphysical positions a mother to a birthed female child experiences. When a female fetus develops inside a woman that woman is not only carrying her own ovaries, uterus and fallopian tubes; she is also carrying a second fully developed reproduction system belonging to her unborn daughter. The woman now is walking around with all the eggs she will ever have inside of her ovaries, representing potential children, in addition to all the eggs her daughter will ever have, representing her own potential grandchildren. Imagine then that this woman also developed inside her own mother's uterus. And that mother developed inside her mother's. What we have is a set of nesting dolls that illustrate an essential issue for women of daughters: who is the biggest doll and who is the smallest? Who is The Mother? As in Sexton's portraits, there is a difference in view and perspective based on which place in the nest we are occupying. A daughter looks backward to the mother to learn who and what she is, should be and could be. A mother looks forward to the daughter, trying to find the same answers in the newest addition to the maternal nest. If a woman exists as both a mother and a daughter, she is constantly pivoting, backward and forward, projecting and reflecting both actively and passively over and over again. Psychoanalytic theorist Carl Jung applies some meaning to this idea by expounding on the existential tie between mother and daughter: "The conscious experience of these ties produces the feeling that her life is spread out over generations, the first step toward the immediate experience and conviction of being outside time, which brings with it a feeling of immortality" (149). If mother and daughter are spread psychically over time and space, the idea of bodily reality and possession becomes problematic. To whom do these two bodies belong to at any given time? Are both bodies communal by nature of the relationship or can they be individually possessed and boundaried? Poet Susan Griffin speaks to the primal struggle women have with their mothers over both their status as a copy of a copy of a copy and the dual essential truth that one's mother once was one with her daughter physically, but remains one with her psychically:

Mother
I write home
I am alone and
give me my body back. (Griffin, "Mother and Child" 99)

DOUBLING THE SELF IN BODY AND MIND

It is a taboo in American culture to openly announce one's gender preference while pregnant: "To the mother it is not supposed to matter if her child has a penis or a vagina. And yet the truth is that when one woman gives birth to another, to someone who is like her, they are linked together for life in a very special way" (Friday 20). But what is this special way? Before I was even pregnant, I pictured myself with a little girl. I pictured myself playing all the same games with her that I had played as a child. I pictured her studying ballet as I had. I pictured watching her sit in a corner drawing or weaving on a child's loom. What I really was imagining, of course, was giving birth to myself. How wonderful it would be to birth yourself, to get an opportunity to raise yourself so that one can be present with an adult's mind in the same space with one's own childhood self. Wishing for a daughter may be the manifestation of a narcissistic fantasy to know oneself from the ground up and perhaps experience being mothered once again by dividing the self into the triad of existence. Adrienne Rich warns that, "The self of the mother threatens to intrude upon that of the daughter" (62). In her poem, Sexton seems to lament her reasons for "making" her daughter Joyce with the purpose of finding herself, for committing an intrusion on Joyce's self. She sees her quest for self-discovery through motherhood as an incredible burden on a child who cannot possibly have the answers. As Nancy Friday explains, "If the reason for having a child is to give yourself an identity, the daughter cannot be let go because she is doing something for you" (401).

Friday also writes, "The first thing it can be said a mother honestly feels in relation to her child is a kind of self-love. The child is essentially a narcissistic extension of herself" (19). This can be true for children of both genders of course, but the idea of child-love as disguised self-love is complicated when the child is female.

Rich expounds, "Mothers and daughters have always exchanged with each other (beyond the verbally transmitted lore of female survival) a knowledge that is subliminal, subversive, preverbal: the knowledge flowing between two alike bodies, one of which has spent nine months inside the other" (220). The energy that Rich calls knowledge flows both ways, backward and forward through time, as in Sexton's portraits. The energy flow is inherently narcissistic because of the reproduction of both body and self that the daughter represents. When a woman looks at her daughter, there are a number of complicated processes happening. First, the woman sees the daughter as the happening that has turned her into a mother. But she does not simply turn into *a* mother. The woman has taken the space of *her own mother* in the metaphoric matrilineal nesting dolls. From this position, the woman can mother her daughter while going back in time as she feels what it was like for her mother to mother her. Second, the woman sees herself in the daughter. The daughter is her but also an other. She takes care of herself by mothering her daughter. She looks to the daughter for clues about her own identity, her own truth, because now she is privy to her very start of the development of herself. Third, the woman buries her own identity as a daughter deep within herself so that when her own daughter looks to her she does not see herself (a fellow daughter), she sees Mother.

> And this was the cave of the mirror,
> that double woman who stares
> at herself, as if she were petrified
> in time-two ladies sitting in umber chairs.
> You kissed your grandmother
> and she cried. (Sexton, "The Double Image" 41)

Sexton diminishes the singular identities of herself and her mother when she describes them as a singular double woman. We might imagine conjoined twins or perhaps a woman with one body and two heads. As Marianne Hirsch asks, what if every mother and daughter actually shared the same body, what if they are the same person, speaking with two voices? (Lawler 3). This double woman stares *at herself* in perpetuity because her divided self is locked in position, facing off for eternity. By having this image serve as a definition for the cave mirror she previously mentions, Sexton positions the double woman as living out some sort of hell or punishment, as from a Greek myth. Her use of the word petrified here cannot be ignored: the mother and daughter are at once both meanings of the word. They are mummified in place through the existence of the other and experience a state of terror when caught in a reflective loop.

The Matrophobic Imperative

You scrape your knee. You learn my name,
wobbling up the sidewalk, calling and crying.
You call me *mother* and I remember my mother again,
somewhere in greater Boston, dying.
(Sexton, "The Double Image" 41)

In American popular culture women receive messages that turning into one's mother is an undesirable and even horrifying thing. Rich identifies a phenomenon called matrophobia (235) where the prospect of turning into one's mother fills a daughter with intense dread and anxiety, which is different from the more prevailing understanding of the term as a fear of the overpowering mother. The fear of turning into one's own mother is a direct product of the patriarchy and simply serves to warn women not to get old, to stay a sexualized being and not to turn into the *father's* mother, lest he ceases to be attracted to the mother of his own children. Women are encouraged to become mothers, but are taught to fear turning into Mother. This fear is also fueled by a fear of one's mother in the abstract. As Nancy K. Miller explains, many women don't fear turning into their own actual mother but rather a composite mother: "The mother we think didn't love us, the mother we don't think we loved" (Miller 71). In reality, for better or worse, every mother *is already* her own mother by virtue of being her daughter and reproducing. She becomes the embodiment of everything the term Mother means to her, positive and negative. It is disturbing to imagine a woman's identity being ripped from her simply because a baby has passed through her womb. On the contrary, when a woman becomes the mother to a daughter she does not cease being "herself;" she adds a layer of identity to her Self. As Kim Chernin notes, "I feel there are two of me—I, myself, and close beside me, wearing the same skin, there is my daughter's mother" (3). But there is another version of the self that coexists: her mother's daughter. By becoming a mother, the woman has simultaneously given birth to herself in the form of the baby and the mother of her childhood in the form of herself. Instead of fearing her own mother, women need to understand that by the time they give birth it has already happened.

In Oscar Wilde's *The Importance of Being Ernest,* the character Algernon expresses, "All women become like their mothers. This is their tragedy. No man does, and that is his" (Wilde 15). In so much as that the word "tragedy" means an event that causes great suffering, I do not agree with this sentiment. Women can certainly have negative feelings about reproducing mothers in themselves, depending on the quality of the mothering they received in childhood, but it is an inevitability rather than a tragedy. Wilde exposes in this line a paradox in which it pains men to realize they will never truly be one with their mother, whereas women feel the oppression of its utter inevitability. Wondering how a male child fits into the mother-daughter cycle is beyond the scope of my work, but perhaps the difference between becoming *like* somebody and becoming *the spiritual embodiment* of somebody is paramount here. Both men and women can be like their mothers, but only a woman can actually become her mother through birthing a child herself.

Having become her own mother, the mother of a daughter resurrects the mother of her childhood. The individual mother in the present reality is inconsequential, as is whether she is alive or dead. Friday asserts, "In the unconscious where the first connection was forged, the mother of our infancy never dies" (407). This is one way to interpret Jung's aforementioned comments about motherhood being a way to exist outside of time in immortality: becoming the mother of a daughter is a process of constant resurrections of past realities and roles. Writer Kim Chernin sees it as a recreation rather than a resurrection: "She recreates her real mother or she recreates a symbolic mother to hold and foster her psychological and emotional development" (xiii). Through this resurrection or recreation, the mother simultaneously becomes the mother to a new daughter and the mother to herself, as the baby now replaces her role as The Daughter in her relationship with her own mother. When the baby cries, the mother experiences it at a certain level as the new daughter "screaming at her mother for love" (Friday 397). This is the opportunity for the mother to care for herself, to relive the experience of being mothered at the same time as it serves to keep the mother of her childhood alive. Through the act of mothering a daughter, Lawler describes these processes of existence as "a rupture in women's selfhood, a breach of the autonomy which is held to be constitutive" (157). I clearly remember a moment after my daughter was born when I was walking through my city, pushing a stroller with nowhere to go. As in child psychoanalytical theorist D.W. Winnicott's famous assertion that there is no such thing as an infant, it occurred to me in this moment that there is no such thing as a mother. In this moment, I could not find my Self in space, I was my daughter's mother, I was my mother, my daughter was a stranger, my daughter was me. I did not exist. My mother called and asked about the baby: what was she doing? What was she wearing? How was she eating? She was mothering her through me from a distance. I exclaimed, "What about me? Why aren't you asking how *I* am?" She replied, "By asking about her I *am* asking about you." In this moment the change in my status as an existing entity became solidified. To my mother, and perhaps to the world, I was a vessel, a conduit, a pathway, connecting my daughter to everything and everyone.

> You came like an awkward guest
> that first time, all wrapped and moist
> and strange at my heavy breast.
> I needed you. I didn't want a boy,
> only a girl, already loved, already loud in the house
> of herself. We named you Joy.
> (Sexton, "The Double Image" 41)

Sexton describes here the intense hope and promise that only a daughter can bring to a mother. She literally names her daughter as *her* happiness. Her daughter is her joy at the same time that she is Joy, the individual human being. For Sexton, Joy is a chance to know a better version of herself while injecting her with love and purpose, so that she might get these things back in return. Albeit complicated, it is not insidious or inherently cruel, but is often misinterpreted as such. Jung feels that the tragedy of the daughter is always that "the mother lives out for her beforehand all that the girl might have lived for herself. The daughter leads a shadow-like existence, often visibly sucked dry by her mother, and she prolongs her mother's life by a sort of continuous blood transfusion" (117). An image of a vampire and a helpless shadow-baby engaged in an eternal relationship of cyclical dialysis comes to mind. Mothers feeding on their daughter's youth or seeing the daughter's life as a way to perfect her own are stereotypes of mothering that are alive and well in American culture. But what if it was accepted that on an abstract level the daughter *must* first exist as a mother's shadow because she is in fact her own mother, merely mimeographed and printed in three dimensions? I do not believe that the daughter is sucked dry. Instead, the daughter and mother become entwined in a dynamic in which the survival of each is dependent on the survival of both. As in my answer to Winnicott's nonexistent infant, there is no mother without a baby and there is no baby without a mother. Both must look to the other in order to see themselves. The daughter sees both her future and past when looking at the mother, but the mother sees the same thing when looking at the daughter. A new daughter does not just keep the mother alive; it keeps the entire set of matrilineal nesting dolls breathing.

My daughter likes to play a game in which she pretends to emerge from my womb as mysterious baby-guests. These babies can talk from birth and say to me, "I came from inside of you, you are my mommy!" as my daughter directs me to be confused and sad that this new baby might not be mine, but ecstatic when it actually is. These babies represent all of her imaginings of how she was seen by me as a helpless infant: some are sweet, others are annoying, some are clingy and overly involved in my body, and still others are abusive. I asked my daughter after playing one of these games where all these babies are coming from, how can I take care of all of these babies? She answered, "I am the mother of all these babies, but you are the mother of me, and so they come from your stomach. But they want you to be their mom." In this game, my daughter is enacting in somewhat literal terms the metaphysical blurring of maternal lines, bodies and identities that I speak of. These imaginary babies belong to both of us, but are of my body. They also claim me as their mother as if I have no idea who they belong to, even though they have passed through my body. Just as I recognized my daughter as a familiar being upon birthing her, my daughter expressed her otherworldly knowledge of me. In this game, she quite literally enacts giving me the identity of mother and seems to be making the statement, "I knew you before you knew me."

> My twin, my sister, my lost love,
> I carry you in me like an embryo
> as once you carried me.
> (Piercy, "My Mother's Body" 30)

THE DAUGHTER-RIGHT

Radical feminist writer Mary Daly talks about a "daughter-right" that all women must claim and assert in order to become one with their mothers, daughters, and other women in general. Claiming one's daughter-rite is dependent on accepting and valuing the truth that women's true bond is not that they are all female, but that they are all daughters. Recognizing that the maternal ancestral line is more important than the patriarchal line for understanding where the Self lies is also required. Daly explains, "when we reach the daughter within the mother we can bond with ourselves... when a woman comes to recognize the Daughter in her self, in her mother, she comes into touch with her own tradition ... sharing this recognition, mothers and daughters become sisters in struggle" (347). Reconciling the part of herself that remains a daughter and exposing that part of the multifaceted Self to her daughter and her mother while effectively maintaining the role of Mother is an extremely complicated task for a woman. Being a daughter denotes smallness, weakness, vulnerability, and dependency. Mother denotes caretaker, omnipresent protection, unconditional love, and knowledge. Once a woman becomes the mother to a daughter, her place in the maternal line is moved up by one and everyone in that line is renamed according to their relationship with this new female infant. Her mother is now the grandmother to her daughter, and she takes the space of Mother. With all attention focused downward toward the new daughter, the former daughter (the new mother) loses the point of matrilineal focus and secures a spot as someone the daughter can look backward to in time. The new mother hides away her daughterness so that she may become The Mother to her new daughter. Jung posits, "A woman lives earlier as a mother, later as a daughter" (149). Exposing daughterness as a mother takes time during the relationship with a daughter.

Early psychoanalytical and developmental theories focus on the importance of a daughter switching her primary bond from her mother to her father. In Erik Erickson's stages of development, the focus is on moving away from both parents in favour of independence and agency. Much feminist work has been devoted to deconstructing these theories and recognizing that it is through the relationship with her mother that a daughter comes to understand herself and the world. Feminist psychologist Carol Gilligan writes, "Girls experience themselves as like their mothers, thus fusing the experience of attachment with the process of identity formation" (8). She argues that girls do not develop through separation and individualization; they develop and understand themselves through relationships. I add that deep engagement with a mother is essential for a daughter's identity formation simply because the mother is the daughter with no beginning and no end, like clockwork gears in which two distinct pieces do not exist alone so much as they exist by feeding into one another. The mother and daughter are one unit of body, mind, and essence.

As a daughter reaches adolescence and young adulthood, it is difficult for both women to contend with inevitable physical separation. Rich describes this as "radical surgery" (236), which is most commonly performed by the daughter in reaction to a growing confusion regarding "where mother ends and daughter begins" (236). This radical surgery, as Rich describes it, comes from the patriarchal and essentially Western doctrine that mothers are our caretakers, not our very blood, brain, and soul. Indeed, the facsimile of existence that uniquely marks the mother and daughter bond can also become too intense for the mother, who struggles to have a Self in the midst of embodying so many other existences and ascriptions. Aurelia Plath, mother of poet Sylvia Plath, gives words to this rarely mentioned feeling: "Between Sylvia and me existed—as between my own mother and me—a sort of psychic osmosis which, at times, was very wonderful and comforting; at other times an unwelcome invasion of privacy" (Plath 32).

> In south light, her smile is held in place,
> her cheeks wilting like a dry
> orchid; my mocking mirror, my overthrown
> love, my first image. She eyes me from that face,
> that stony head of death
> I had outgrown.
> (Sexton, "The Double Image" 40)

In 1931, Sigmund Freud asked, "What does the little girl require of her mother?" (235). Freud never attempts a meaningful, non-sexualized answer to this question during his life. He also neglects to realize that in the dyad of mother and daughter the daughter is not a Little Girl any more than the mother in this relationship is a Woman. They must remain named in relationship for the question not to be inherently false. Regardless, four decades later psychoanalyst Jacques Lacan responds to Freud by positing that what a daughter requires from her mother is "an impossible plentitude ... a demand which expresses an unfulfillable desire" (qtd. in Lawler 32). Both the question and the answer are wrong. A better question is, what do daughters and mothers require from *each other*? Although Freud may have a mother and daughter as a pair of concentric circles, daughter and mother are more like parts of a closed spiral of infinity, inclusive of all the mothers and daughters who came before them. In this spiral, knowledge and existence flow backward and forward. What is required by and of both mother and daughter is simply not to break this spiral—to be present in it and recognize all the meaning and purpose in each fluid state of identity. When he speaks of daughters as a glass that can never be filled, Lacan presumes that mother and daughter are objects of innate frustration for each other. In his imagining, the daughter as a syphon is not a participant in an interchange of epistemological questioning, answering, and acting. How do these men explain what the daughter does for the mother? And what the mother continues to do for her own mother? And what her mother continues to do for herself? Not recognizing the relationship of mother and daughter as one of infinite expansion is to deny that daughters are born from their mother's bodies and very selves.

CONCLUSION

Women are not taught to recognize or give heed to the otherworldly and intangible symbiosis that link mothers and daughters for eternity, so that women may function appropriately in a male-centric world. To concede to the Western master narrative of necessary psychic separation from the mother-daughter dyad is to deny the metaphysical state that exists between the two individuals. This does not mean that women need to live with their mothers for their whole life. In fact, to continue growing the spiral or enlarging the set of nesting dolls women need to reproduce themselves apart from the mother. Physical separation does not abet or lead to an automatic psychic separation; that is impossible based on the nature and meaning of this relationship.

My daughter recently asked me if we could be buried in the same tomb when we die. In her fantasy of the future she will marry me, have many babies that I will care for, and grow old with me until we die at the same time. I presently allow her this fantasy, as it is her way of expressing the desire for a continuation of the blurred existence I have described, which is most evident in early childhood. Through marriage, childrearing, and death she tries to name tangible bonds that represent the feeling of being the same person with me in existence and out interchanging roles. Nevertheless, I explain to her that we probably would not die at the same time because I am older than her, and older people generally die first. She responds, "You'll be my ghost and then when I die we can be ghosts together for the babies." And this is what mothers and daughter are: linked spirits embodied with meaning who have the ability to reproduce themselves throughout eternity, exist as each other without the rules time and space, and become invisible realities that shape more mothers and more daughters forevermore.

> When I grew well enough to tolerate
> myself, I lived with my mother. Too late,
> too late, to live with your mother, the witches said.
> But I didn't leave. (Sexton, "The Double Image" 36-37)

ENDNOTE

[1]Plato's theory of forms says that human beings hold images of the idea or essence of any given object. Any object or meaning ascribed from the image of the ideal form cannot be considered real. The only real thing has already existed and will never be seen again. Plato speaks of each object in the world as having three states: one existing in nature (the Real object), one made in imitation, and one represented in art. In relation to mothers and daughters, the mother holds the position of one made in imitation and the daughter is one step down in station as merely an imitation of an imitation. All of our ideas about Mother are passed from generation to generation, distorted and distilled. We cannot ever know what a real Mother is, according to Plato's theory.

WORKS CITED

Chernin, Kim. *The Woman Who Gave Birth to Herself*. Penguin, 1998.

Chesler, Phyllis. *Woman's Inhumanity to Woman*. Penguin, 2001.

Daly, Mary. *Gyn/Ecology*. Beacon, 1978.

Freud, Sigmund. "Female Sexuality." *The Complete Psychological Works of Sigmund Freud, Volume XXI: 1927-1931*. Translated by James Strachey, Hogarth, 1961.

Friday, Nancy. *My Mother My Self*. Delta, 1977.

Gilligan, Carol. *In a Different Voice*. Harvard University Press, 1982.

Griffin, Susan. "Mother and Child." *Like the Iris of an Eye*. Harper, 1976.

Jung, C.G. *Aspects of the Feminine*. Princeton University Press, 1982.

Lawler, Steph. *Mothering the Self: Mothers, Daughter, Subjects*. Routledge, 2000.

Miller, Nancy K. *Bequest and Betrayal: Memoirs of a Parent's Death*. Indiana University Press, 1996.

Plato. *The Republic*. 1894. Translated by Benjamin Jowett. Dover, 2000.

Piercy, Marge. "My Mother's Body." *My Mother's Body*. Knopf, 1985.

Plath, Sylvia. *Letters Home: Correspondence 1950-1963*. 1975. Edited by Aurelia Schober Plath, Harper, 1992.

Rich, Adrienne. *Of Woman Born: Motherhood as Experience and Institution*. Norton, 1976.

Sexton, Anne. "The Double Image." *The Complete Poems of Anne Sexton*. Mariner, 1999.

Wilde, Oscar. *The Importance of Being Ernest*. Edited by Stanley Applebaum, Dover, 1990.

17. Researching Death

RENEE NORMAN

I am researching
how to transport dead bodies
specifically my mother's
who's not actually dead yet
someone will think
I'm planning murder

I am researching
whether air carriers
transport dead bodies
from one city to another
specifically my mother's
from a Vancouver old age home
to a Calgary cemetery
beside my father
who is actually dead
I long to put a stone
on his grave

my sister conveys
my mother's wishes
at our holiday dinner
among friends and a turkey
who is also dead

we grieve our mother's
accelerating descent into dementia
masked by comic macabre

my sister wants
to be prepared
our mother is eighty-nine
there's not going to be
any miracles here
no oil burning
for eighty-nine days or nights
no Maccabees to fight
the battle of Alzheimer's

when I hear
the estimated cost
I say I'll drive her
one last trip to Calgary
like the grandpa
in Little Miss Sunshine
our lawyer relatives
remind us of legalities
dark humour aside

my sister
serious for a moment
looks me in the eye
will I come with her
to Calgary
bury our mother
beside our father
throw a handful of dirt on the grave

I agree
we have already been mourning
a mind lost
language gone,
the body last to go

our daughters murmur
they will come too
this and my sister's eyes
travel straight to my depths
no monetary cost
but oh,
so much currency spent

I am researching
how to transport
a dead body
write down quotes
remember the Talmudic words
in the hall
when I visit my mother:
"Do not cast me off in old age..."

a stone for the graves

18.
Exploring Pantsuit Nation

A Message for Our Daughters

DORSÍA SMITH SILVA

On the evening of November 8, 2016, I waited with eager breath to hear the news that the United States had elected its first female president. To my dismay, the election took a highly unexpected turn and the victory of hailing a woman into the highest office of power did not happen. My disappointment of women not finally breaking this elusive glass ceiling made me ponder several matters. I asked myself, "When would the United States join the ranks of other countries and have female leaders? When would history rewrite the script and say Mrs. President? If not in 2016, then when? And what do we tell our daughters?"

This last question gave me pause, especially when I envisioned the image of the numerous mothers who had told their daughters that women could do and be anything—including be the ruler and the commander-in-chief of the United States. In searching for ways to reconcile the aftermath of this presidential election and still empower our daughters, I thought of how we must reiterate the significant historical contributions of women to our daughters. In this context, I would tell our daughters that we come from a long trajectory of resilient women that have fought for equality; confronted and challenged gender, social, political, economic, and racial barriers (among many other forms of discrimination); and amplified several generations to build the groundwork and change the landscape for women.

Abolitionist and former slave Sojourner Truth, for instance, in her speech delivered at the Women's Convention in Akron, Ohio in 1851 called "Ain't I a Woman" noted the strength of women and how we should be treated equally to men:

> Look at me! Look at my arm! I have ploughed, and planted, and gathered into barns, and no man could head me! And ain't I woman? I could work as much and eat as much as a man—when I could get it—and bear the lash as well! And ain't I a woman? I have borne thirteen children, and seen them most all sold off to slavery, and when I cried out with my mother's grief, none but Jesus heard me! And ain't I a woman? (31)

Truth also highlighted the endurance and fortitude of women when she stated, "If the first woman God ever made was strong enough to turn the world upside down all alone, these women together ought to be able to turn it back, and get it right side up again! And now they is asking to do it, the men better let them" (31). I would tell our daughters that long before women received the right to vote in the United States and before the first woman was elected to U.S. Congress, Victoria Claflin Woodhull challenged the gender barriers by running for president of the United States in 1872, one-hundred and forty-three years before Clinton's nomination. Exhorting for the right of women to vote, have control of their bodies, and receive an education, Woodhull decided to run for president with the backing of the Equal Rights Party and intention to be an advocate for women:

> I therefore claim the right to speak for the enfranchised women of the country, and believing as I do that the prejudices which still exist in the popular mind against women in public life will soon disappear, I now announce myself as candidate for the Presidency. I anticipate criticism; but however unfavorable I trust that my sincerity will not be called into question. (qtd. in Gabriel 55)

She also remained undeterred by public ridicule during her campaign and stated, "I shall not change my course because those who assume to be better than I desire it" (qtd. in Gabriel 91). Since the nineteenth amendment, which gave women the right to vote, did not become law until 1920, Woodhull was not permitted to be cast on the ballet in the presidential election. After losing the 1872 election, she informed a reporter that she was "too many years ahead of this age and the exalted views and objects of humanitarianism can scarcely be grasped as yet by the unenlightened mind of the average man" (qtd. in Braxton 97).

I would tell our daughters that we must pay attention to the women that tenaciously defied gender, social, political, economic, and racial limitations, and became agents of conscious change by reframing numerous yardsticks. Activist Ida B. Wells-Barnett, in particular, is an example of a woman who reshaped several barriers. When she felt unwelcomed in other suffrage groups consisting of white women, Wells-Barnett co-founded the Alpha Suffrage Club, an organization for African American women in Illinois in 1913. In that same year, she and other members of the Alpha Suffrage Club attended the National American Woman Suffrage Association's parade in Washington D.C. After being asked to walk behind the march's white organizers, Wells-Barnett objected and publicly derided the racism in the suffrage movement. Her comments initiated many suffragettes and suffragists to become conscious of the racism among the bridges of women—an issue that enriches our understanding of today's intersectionality. Women have multiple forms of identity and in our sisterhood we must acknowledge and respect these identities and critique any sites of discrimination.

I would tell our daughters to understand the necessary steps that Jeannette Rankins took when she became the first woman elected to Congress. In 1916, Rankins ran as a progressive for one of the two seats in Congress from Montana as a Republican. While promising to work for the women suffrage movement and improve social welfare, she became the first woman elected to the U.S. Congress and national legislature in any Western democratic state. She worked for several political reforms on behalf of women, including civil liberties, suffrage, birth control, equal pay, and child welfare. In addition to these notable accomplishments, Rankins also garnered esteemed recognition when she sponsored the Susan B. Anthony Amendment. After passing the House in 1917 and the Senate in 1918, it eventually became the nineteenth amendment, which gave all American women the right to vote.

I would tell our daughters to envision the dismantling of prescribed models of women, such as when Sandra Day O'Connor garnered the position as the first woman on the U.S. Supreme Court in 1981. While serving from 1981 to 2006, she ruled on several landmark cases, including *Planned Parenthood v. Casey* in 1992, which upheld *Roe v. Wade* in 1992, and *Bush v. Gore*, which resolved the disputed Presidential election in 2000. Her position began the transformative action for three women to become judges on the U.S. Supreme Court: Ruth Bader Ginsberg, Elena Kagan, and Sandra Sotomayor.

I would tell our daughters that our history is rich with women who have reshaped and redefined the roles of women: 1) Edith Wharton is the first woman to win a Pulitzer Prize in 1921; 2) Activist Alice Paul proposes the Equal Rights Amendment for the first time in 1923; 3) Gertrude Ederle becomes the first woman to swim across the English Channel in 1926; 4) Amelia Earhart is the first woman to cross the Atlantic in an airplane in 1928; 5) the All-American Girls Professional Baseball League becomes the first professional baseball league for female players in 1943; 6) Dr. Sally K. Ride becomes the first American woman to be sent into space in 1983; 7) Joan Benoit wins the first women's Olympic Marathon in 1984; 8) Madeleine Albright becomes the first female Secretary of State in 1997; 9) Kathryn Bigelow becomes the first woman to win an Oscar for best director in 2010; and 10) Sarah Thomas becomes the first female full-time official in the NFL in April 2015. In addition to the women mentioned in this essay, there are countless models of women positively reconfiguring the power of women and striving to instill how women are integral to society—these are the messages to our daughters. In this regard, we can think of our own mothers, sisters, aunts, cousins, grandmothers, neighbours, and teachers that break free from the rules of patriarchy and practice conscious empowerment. As mothers, we must lead the charge.

WORKS CITED

Braxton, Bernard. *Women, Sex, and Race: A Realistic View of Sexism and Racism*. Verta, 1973.

Gabriel, Mary. *Notorious Victoria: The Uncensored Life of Victoria Woodhull Visionary*. Algonquin, 1998.
Truth, Sojourner. "Ain't I a Woman?" Women's Convention, 1851, Akron, Ohio. *Crisis,* vol. 106, no. 1, 1999, pp. 31.

III.
MOTHERS AND DAUGHTERS IN LITERATURE

19. Daughter of the Disappeared or *Hija de la República*

Maternal Imagery, Daughterly Identity and Argentina's "Dirty War" in Carolina de Robertis's *Perla*

CRISTINA HERRERA

> Because there were no fetal remains found in Julia's grave, the forensic anthropologists assured Catalina that Julia's child was born. Whether it was aborted naturally, or, due to the conditions of the prison cells in which she was held, whether it was born dead or killed afterwards, or whether it was removed and placed in the home of a military family as many other children of the disappeared had been, is impossible to know. In the crowds of Buenos Aires, on the street, in the lines forming at bus stops, Catalina cannot be sure whether that seventeen-year-old girl she sees, smiling as she remembers her young daughter smiling, is or is not her grandchild. As she scans the crowd, she cannot know if she should be looking for a girl or for a boy, and among so many faces she does not know where to begin. (Eric Stener Carlson, *I Remember Julia* 25)

INTRODUCTION

The epigraph above describes a woman named Catalina, whose daughter Julia was one of the estimated thirty thousand disappeared victims of the Argentinean "Dirty War" that spanned the years from 1976 to 1983. Perhaps the most chilling element of Catalina's grief over her disappeared daughter is the uncertainty surrounding her grandchild's life, if indeed the child was born at all. This passage is found in Eric Stener Carlson's book *I Remember Julia* (1996), a text that is comprised largely of interviews the author conducted with people who knew this woman, referred to only as Julia. This important work asks complicated questions: what does it mean to "disappear"?; can the disappeared return, and if so, in what form?; Or perhaps, through memory, can the disappeared person return, a reappearance of sorts? These questions, and variations of them, centre the analysis of the 2012 novel by Carolina De Robertis *Perla*, a haunting and lyrical text that gradually unfolds the truth of the protagonist Perla Correa's true origins—stolen daughter of a disappeared couple who was adopted and raised by a Navy officer and his wife.

Perla is set in the decades after Argentina's infamous Dirty War—considered by some scholars to be the most brutal Latin American military dictatorship because of the disappearances of thousands of people and torture tactics that included stealing children born to imprisoned women, many of whom were later raised by military families. The novel's time frame alternates between the years 2001, when the bulk of the plot occurs, and in the present, as the protagonist and narrator reflects on that year, which would alter her life in a way she had never imagined. *Perla* is narrated by the protagonist of the title, Perla Correa, whose voice is at times supplanted by the voice of an unnamed "visitor," as she calls the man who appears soaking wet in her living room on 2 March 2001. This visitor's arrival forces Perla to at last confront what she has suppressed her entire life: she is not the daughter of a stiff naval officer and an emotionally distant mother, but in fact, the biological daughter of a married couple who were "disappeared" during the Dirty War. Although Perla recalls brief moments in her childhood that hinted at the truth of her lineage, her upbringing in a household that supported the military dictatorship helped to keep this fact of her birth buried and undisclosed.[1]

In this chapter, I examine the rather tense and emotionally distant relationship between Perla and her mother, Luisa Correa, a relationship marked by silences and resentment that hint at secrets surrounding Perla's birth. Through a close reading of this troubled relationship, I argue that Perla's discovery of her biological parents and the truth of her adoptive parents' theft forces her to choose and negotiate the daughterly identity she will claim for herself. I will also draw from research that has documented the two conflicting, warring images of motherhood and maternity that surfaced during this unstable period of military rule in Argentina to situate the complexity of Perla's buried identity and her search for her real origins. On the one hand were Las Madres de La Plaza de Mayo/The Mothers of the Plaza de Mayo, maternal activists who have protested the disappearances of their children; on the other hand were women like Perla's adoptive mother, Luisa Correa, "Mothers of the Republic," who were tasked with raising upright, non-"subversive" citizens who respected the military's authority. Perla's discovery of her birth parents and the trauma that accompanies this knowledge, I argue, places her within a conflicted space of daughterly identity that forces her to negotiate what kind of daughter she will be, with all the psychological and political consequences these identities entail: activist daughter of a disappeared woman or complicit daughter of the Republic who ignores the atrocities her country has committed in the guise of order and progress. Furthermore, as I show, choosing one daughterly identity over another encompasses not only mourning her biological parents but a symbolic mourning of an identity as daughter she had been expected to uphold as complicit bystander in a country that has killed and tortured its own citizens. In a sense, then, as I alluded to in the opening paragraph of the chapter, the novel suggests that, like her biological parents, Perla's birth identity has been disappeared as well; learning the truth of her origins is also a search for her own disappeared self.

"CRAZY WOMEN" AND "PROPER MOTHERS": MATERNAL IMAGERY DURING ARGENTINA'S DIRTY WAR

Military regimes have frequently occupied Latin America, and Argentina is certainly no exception. Although some scholars consider Argentina's most recent military dictatorship, which spanned from 1976 to 1983, to be one of the most brutal in the region, these tumultuous years had long been building. Prior to the military coup that occurred on 24 March 1976 (Arditti 7), "the country was governed by de facto military governments" (Sutton 22), making it primed for this takeover. As Rita Arditti comments, "This was not just one more coup; the bloodiest and most shameful period in Argentine history was about to begin during which Argentina became infamous for the atrocities of its government and its striking similarities with the Nazi regime" (7). Known as *El Proceso* ("The Process"), the major branches of the military—navy, army, and air force—declared themselves the country's rulers, immediately deeming anyone who challenged the military's rule as "subversives" and justifiable targets of kidnapping and disappearance (Arditti 8). In the years to come, the Argentine government would systematically torture, kidnap, and hold thousands of Argentine citizens in hidden prisons; these victims would later be known as *los desaparecidos*, the "disappeared" (Feitlowitz ix).

Following the coup that toppled Isabel Perón's presidency, the military quickly stated its role not only as leader of the country but as the "preserver of 'the moral and spiritual values of Western and Christian civilization'" (Graziano 19). Perhaps, what is most striking about the junta's declaration of itself as a model of civilization is how this rhetoric targeted women, specifically mothers, as responsible for raising proper citizens. In fact, motherhood and "proper" maternity were frequently mentioned in speeches given by military leaders throughout the regime's rule: "From its opening address, the junta made explicit that the maternal image of the Patria or Motherland justified the civil violence. The military claimed it had to save her, for she was being "raped, penetrated, and infiltrated'" (Taylor, "Making" 184). By describing La Patria as a raped, violated woman, the military's role as ardent protector must be secured. In addition to equating Argentina with a woman's body being brutalized by unruly subversives, the regime made clear that only certain types of maternity were allowed, such as those that unquestioningly upheld military rule. For example, in one speech given by Admiral Emilio Massera, considered to be one of the junta's masterminds, he urged Argentine mothers "to be mothers of the Republic; to teach it to walk, to teach [it] to think, to teach it to smile. Never as in these moments has Argentina so needed its women, because never as in these moments has Argentina so needed to be on the side of life" (qtd. in Feitlowitz 38).[2] Appealing to women's maternal responsibilities, television and radio advertisements asked questions, such as, "How have you raised your children? Do you know what your children are doing, *right now*?" (Feitlowitz 37, emphasis in original). By mandating that mothers were solely responsible for their children's behaviour, the new government essentially cast blame on them for failing as mothers in raising subversive children; the responsibility of raising upright model citizens were firmly placed on women's shoulders.

In using motherhood as a discourse to uphold La República, the years of the Dirty War thus resulted in warring images of maternity (Taylor 192). By defining good mothers as those who supported the military government, women who actively defied this authoritarian control were condemned as bad, crazy, and out of control (Taylor, *Disappearing* 78). These bad women were Las Madres de la Plaza de Mayo, mothers of disappeared children who protested the government's violence and terrorism. For not only was their morality questioned by the junta, but their very act of publicly protesting in Buenos Aires's main square in the centre of the city directly challenged the gendered maternal role of the private sphere (Bejarano 408). As Diane Taylor explains, "The very notion of the feminine was split in two—into the 'good' woman and the 'bad' woman. On the one hand, the junta honored the symbolic image of pure motherhood associated with the Patria, the 'good' woman.... On the other hand, active women were 'bad' women, associated with deviance and subversion" ("Making" 184). Furthermore, Las Madres were considered as "nonmothers" because they ostensibly had "renounced their right to motherhood by being bad mothers, mothers of subversives" (Taylor, *Disappearing* 83). Good mothers did not decry the military government; rather, they taught their children to respect, honour, and unquestioningly obey what their leaders did as moral and right. Within this framework, the military was seen as an appropriate leader because of its model of discipline. In their refusal to be silenced and carry forth the myth of El Proceso as necessary for the nation's salvation, Las Madres vocally condemned the government's abuses, and made their grief a public demonstration of mourning, loss, and maternal pain. They continue to protest and demand that their children be remembered. In their refusal to remain silent or simply go away, Las Madres serve as visible reminders of their country's darkest days.

"MY MOTHER, THE MASKED WOMAN": MATERNAL AND DAUGHTERLY IDENTITY IN *PERLA*

> As I walked up the noisy boulevard toward the university I thought of all the years that I had dutifully walked through the world with careful sanity, as though all were well, as though my family were well, as though nothing rotted beneath the surface (De Robertis 12).

Perla begins with a seemingly impossible scenario: a twenty-two-year-old woman named Perla Correa is home alone on the night of March 2, 2001, and discovers a naked and soaking wet man in her living room who arrives from apparently out of nowhere. He has "returned" from the ocean, where he, along with other Argentine victims, was thrown to his death from a helicopter during the first years of the Dirty War. His arrival not only raises questions about his identity, which is revealed near the end of the novel, but also questions regarding Perla's mental state. It becomes clear that this man is a ghost or possibly a figment of her imagination—a being only she can see, someone with whom she must reckon. If ghosts "represent the dreaded past and provoke anguished memory," according to Laurie Vickroy (170), then what does this strange visitor represent for Perla? This apparent supernatural appearance, in particular the random way in which he arrives in her home, suggests the impossibility of leaving a traumatized past in the past, until the traumatized person confronts what she has kept at bay (Herrera 62-3). In Perla's own doubts of her mental stability, as cited in the epigraph to this section, she points to one of the central issues in the text: the novel does not suggest that Perla's interaction with this ghostly presence is evidence of her descent into madness. Instead, Perla's forced containment of memories, clues, and trauma that lurk beneath her family's façade— the truth of her lineage that her adoptive parents have kept from her—is the real madness expected of her as daughter of citizens who openly supported the country's dictatorship yet denied the atrocities committed. The text's narrative style includes Perla's first-person voice as a twenty-two-year-old university student in 2001, as well as Perla's own monologue to her unborn daughter six years after the appearance of the wet man she discovers to be her biological father. In addition, the reader is given the man's own narrative voice told in flashback that includes harrowing details of his and his pregnant wife's kidnapping, torture, and death in the early years of the Dirty War. With these narrative techniques, the novel delves into the country's history of trauma, silence, and denial that function as a microcosm within her upbringing by the Correa couple.

Perla recalls that her life has been defined by rigid rules that demand silence and unyielding obedience to her parents' authority and rule, which she comes to see as factors that lead only to potential madness and desperation. In one memory Perla describes, Luisa Correa, in fact, points to the protesting Madres as examples of "craziness," warning her daughter against empathizing with these "hysterical" women: "Perla, Perlita, my mother said, don't believe the lies about the disappeared. You're going to hear things in school and I'll tell you now that they're not true, Perlita, these people are hysterical, they don't understand a lot of things. Don't say anything to them about it. Just stay quiet and remember they're confused" (20). While Luisa suggests that those who protest the government's torture of its citizens are "hysterical," Perla soon learns that these constant accusations of "crazy" protestors serve to mask, hide, and cover up the horrors committed during the Dirty War. Indeed, if these protestors are "crazy," as Luisa claims, why does she feel the need to draw attention to them? Ironically, Luisa's condemnation of the protestors as "hysterical" and "confused" hints at the possibility of unsavoury truths that she and her husband try desperately to keep Perla from discovering. Her repetition of Perla's name also suggests a tone of desperation, as if she is pleading with her daughter to not believe the supposed lies she'll be told in school. Moreover, in her caution that Perla not believe the "lies" and that she "stay quiet," Luisa attempts to mold her daughter into an unquestioning, yielding daughter of the Republic.

Yet Luisa herself wears a symbolic mask, and this hidden self she withholds from her daughter forms the crux of their emotionally distant, tense relationship. In contrast to her rather affectionate relationship with her father, Perla's relationship with Luisa is marked by secrecy and rigidity. Describing Luisa's appearance as a form of "armor" (97), Perla alludes to her mother's own suppressed secrets and desires that serve as a barrier to intimacy; in short, Luisa is a stranger to Perla. If masks are worn to protect and shield, much like armour, the obvious question arises: what is Luisa hiding? This is a question Perla ponders throughout her childhood and young adulthood. Her increased curiosity over her mother's past, the time before the mask, occurs when she begins to question the silences and denials surrounding Argentina's troubled past. Aligning a search for her mother's past self with this discovery of Argentina's hidden ills, Perla longs for an authenticity and truth to topple the façade created by her parents:

> Luisa grew up as a good girl, obediently Catholic, obediently quiet, with all her ruffles and smiles in place, though no one knew what churned and curdled under the surface. Then, when she was seventeen, she spent the summer with an uncle in Madrid, and in that summer, the summer of 1969, she found the nub of rebellion within her and made it unfurl. This was the period that fascinated and bewildered me, the brief version of my mother I could not comprehend, and longed to see. She confessed all of this to me right before I graduated from high school, the only night she ever told the story, the two of us alone on my bed.... On that night, I felt delicious hope that we'd stay like this now, mother and daughter, woman-friends, sharing secrets and delights. It seemed attainable. It was probably the wine. (131-32)

Describing this rare occasion of intimacy as a state of intoxication, Perla holds only fragments of her mother's past, revealed to her in a fleeting moment induced by alcohol. Perla's "delicious hope" for a maternal relationship that never comes to fruition demonstrates one of the major sources of struggle faced by the character. This memory is recalled with both longing and regret; it is revisited not only for what it contains, Luisa's confession of her rebellious adolescence, but also for the physical and emotional intimacy that makes such a confession possible. Clearly, then, Perla struggles with making sense of these memories that reveal her desire for maternal bonding—feelings she is uncomfortable admitting to herself, particularly after she condemns her parents' involvement and complicity with state-sponsored disappearances. As Adrienne Rich has famously stated in her foundational work, *Of Woman Born* (1976), the maternal relationship is often marked by ambivalence—the simultaneous attraction to and dread or fear of the mother—and in the case of Perla and Luisa, Perla's desire to learn more about her mother's past stems in part from her fear of Luisa's cold exterior she has cultivated through a shedding of her former adolescent self (235). Luisa's outer façade is meticulous, as Perla explains: "No one, on meeting my mother, Luisa, would imagine she had once been that earnest and ardent young woman, bent on becoming a painter, prowling the museums of Madrid. Even I, growing up in her presence, could not have imagined it. My mother the mystery, my mother the masked woman" (135). The irony surrounding Luisa's former self, of course, is that this rebellious nature—symbolized by the parted hair, marijuana, and aspirations of being an artist (131)—would have made her a target of the junta had she not adopted the identity of mother of the Republic via her marriage to Héctor Correa. An added source of irony is both women's possessions of two selves, one presented outwardly and the other hidden behind a mask, which serve as a major source of conflict and estrangement rather than connection. Because the women keep these hidden selves under guard, seldom uncovered except in spontaneous, drunken moments, any possibility of maternal bonding remains elusive. Even more significant is that it is only Luisa who divulges these secrets, however fleeting the moments may be, whereas Perla intuitively knows to keep her hidden self secret because it will reveal the long-held questions she has had of her parents' involvement in the dictatorship.

The recollection of this memory of maternal intimacy, however, is quickly replaced only a few pages later, as Perla recounts a time when, as a young girl, she spied her mother's bare face free of makeup, a rare occurrence that foregrounds the depths Luisa goes to quite literally mask herself. Significantly, both memories are recalled only after the man's ghostly arrival; his presence leads to the gradual unfolding of suppressed memories that long hinted at the possibility of Perla's connection to the disappeared.

While Perla reminisces the fleeting moment of mother-daughter connection and affection, her narration of this rare sight of her unmasked mother instead serves as a reminder of maternal cruelty and disillusionment:

> Mamá was half-finished: one of her eyes wore a perfect mask of black lines and blue shadow, while the other was naked and sunken, bereft of paint, staring wearily at its own reflection.
>
> "Mamá," I said.
>
> "What do you want from me?"
>
> She said this in a voice I had never heard before, the voice someone might use toward a stranger who is not to be trusted. The mirror reflected a single naked eye, cold, aggrieved, and utterly foreign…
>
> "You know what?"
>
> "What?" I said.
>
> "I wasn't made to be a mother…"
>
> "I often think you shouldn't have come." (136-7)

For Perla, this memory is striking not only because of her mother's icy demeanour, but because she crossed a taboo boundary by witnessing Luisa's unpainted face. As scholar Laura Gutiérrez Spencer argues, "Cosmetic masks serve as a barrier to a true representation of a woman's inner self" (77), which undoubtedly applies to Luisa's careful daily application of makeup. By walking in on her mother, Perla glimpses what is off-limits: Luisa's hidden self rather than the meticulous one painted to face the world as an upright citizen and wife of a naval officer. Although Perla is initially intrigued by this sight of her mother's uninhibited, unprotected face, her reaction later turns to fear at what she sees. Ironically, it is Luisa's bare face that is strange and "foreign," and it even suggests an element of horror and the uncanny. Perhaps the most pointed detail of Luisa's harsh words is what she is doing when the words are uttered: she is not looking directly at Perla but rather, staring at her through the mirror, avoiding direct eye contact. Although scholar Susan Elizabeth Sweeney suggests that the mirror "signif[ies] moments of self-recognition or self-discovery" for the woman gazing into it

(56), it is Perla who sees beyond the mirror's reflection, and later recalls the memory that reveals Luisa's own ambivalence toward motherhood. The rather vague nature of the words Luisa uses to describe Perla's presence in the family as a sudden arrival, rather than as a product of a typical gestation period, confirms to adult Perla that the circumstances surrounding her birth are questionable, suspicious, and secretive.

Perla's quest for answers, to make sense of "so many words, so many versions, always pushing back and forth" (22), begins in her childhood, shortly after the country's transition into a democratic government, and continues into her adulthood. Perla's doubt intensifies with the ghost's arrival, and his account of his and his wife's experiences as detained prisoners and disappeared victims shatters Perla's futile attempts to uphold her parents' truth. This search for truth, however, demands that she question her mother's narrative: "Mamá, after all, insisted that the accusations about *desaparecidos* were untrue" (37). Luisa's adamant denial of the disappearances falls within the deposed junta's ideologies of maternity, given that there were many mothers who not only supported the military rule but who also helped to propagate the denial of the military's abuses. As a mother of the Republic, Luisa denounces the weekly protests held by Las Madres, dismissing them as "*old bags* ... [with] *nothing better to do than try to destroy other people's families*" (177, emphasis in original). In fact, in several passages throughout the novel, Luisa's contempt at Las Madres is unleashed; as a mother of the Republic, Las Madres' public mourning and maternal activism are viewed with suspicion, even disgust. By reducing Las Madres to a group of insignificant "old bags," Luisa attempts to maintain the shaky binary of good-bad mother, teaching her daughter that ideal Argentine mothering does not question the government's actions. Luisa's accusation of Las Madres as merely existing to "destroy" families is ironic, but it nevertheless points to the shaky nature of the façade she and her husband have created to present themselves as Perla's biological parents. And, of course, if the Madres are the antithesis to family, then Luisa and Héctor are models of upright parenting.

Essentially, Perla is taught not only to deny but to forget the past completely. If remembering trauma is to relive it and to recall what struggles to remain contained (Portela 161), then Perla's constant battle with her mother's version of events results in their prolonged estrangement and conflict. Furthermore, the ghost's continued presence and their shared revelation that he is her biological father, forces Perla to at last confront that her upbringing, though marked by her adoptive father's affection, has been based entirely on denial, hidden truths, and buried secrets. However, this knowledge is unsettling and raises a number of questions that the text insists must be asked. What is she to do with these facts? Should she confront her parents and discard the only life and parents she has ever known? Or should she deny her biological parents' traumatic history, which by extension belongs to her as well? As if her identity is in limbo, Perla struggles to act on these troubling questions, particularly when she visits Las Madres during one of their weekly protests. Admitting that she wants "to be recognized," the sight of the Madres nevertheless incites fear; to admit that she is a stolen daughter, a product of a disappeared couple, is to create a new self she is not sure she is prepared to claim (159). Perla is reluctant to discard her identity as daughter of Luisa and Héctor; in short, she does not want this part of her life to disappear. When, with the encouragement of her boyfriend, she visits the office of Las Madres to seek out DNA testing to verify her origins, she is initially overwhelmed with the images of disappeared victims and the notion that her identity can be "restored": "*Restored*, the book said; as if the identity I had before birth were simply waiting for me, a folded piece of clothing, ready to slip back into, a perfect fit. As though I could simply become the woman who would have blossomed with her true parents if the nation had not fallen prey to the Process ... I recoiled from the notion" (201, emphasis in original). Adding that "however false my identity might be, it was the only one I had" (201), Perla complicates the many layers of her country's troubled reckoning with disappearance. On the one hand, citizens such as her parents deny the past atrocities committed, erasing the fact of the disappearances. On the other hand, activist groups like Las Madres also engage with their own type of erasure, warranted though it may be, as Perla suggests. Although the novel does not in any way compare these two modes of erasure, the text does, however, unveil the many complexities of what it means to disappear and reappear. Perla's discovery of her origins and her subsequent escape from the Correa home is itself a source of trauma, even if she does, at last, learn the truth of her origins.

As the novel suggests, discovering the truth behind her birth is only the first step in claiming a new identity. Admitting that she "tried not to think about" Héctor and Luisa only to "fail" at these attempts to forget them (226), Perla struggles with what to do with this former self. In many ways, the novel draws similarities between Argentina's systemic denial of past crimes and Perla's own difficulties in making sense of her former identity. Perla questions whether she should deny what she had once been prior to the discovery of her true lineage. In questioning whether these two selves can co-exist—Perla Correa, daughter of Luisa and Héctor Correa and Perla, daughter of the disappeared couple, Gloria Rossella Ramos and Adelmo Rossella—she imagines the possibility that through her own daughter's impending birth, she can create a version of herself that carries forth the past even as it is unburdened by it. As the newly discovered daughter of a disappeared woman and now a mother-to-be, Perla instills her baby daughter, Gloria, not only with her deceased mother's name but with the means to connect past trauma with a hopeful, though painful, future:

> Soon after I became pregnant, I learned that baby girls have all their eggs already formed in miniature while they are in the womb. So that the egg of you was in me before I was born. So that when I was in my mother, whose face I never saw, a fleck of you was there, a fleck inside a girl inside a woman. Which means that when she disappeared we both disappeared with her, and every reappearance—yours, mine, into the future—belongs to all of us as well. That is why I've spent the night here at this window, telling you this story, preparing you for the world or perhaps preparing the world for you. It is your story as much as it is anyone's. (232-33)

In giving birth, Perla finds a way—through the body, through memory, and through story—to connect with her mother and daughter, forging past, present, and future. By claiming her birth origins, Perla also passes on this "story" to her daughter as granddaughter of the disappeared. Not so surprisingly, then, it is through disappearance, her mother's and hers, that a new self, Gloria's, can reappear. Finally, Gloria's birth on 2 March, six years after the appearance of the ghost, is a symbolic merging of disappearance with appearance, past with future, trauma with new possibility. Perhaps most poignant in Perla's declaration of this story belonging to her baby daughter as well is the act of passing on the responsibility of truth and history to future generations. Although Perla grew up ignorant of her country's history and her adoptive parents' complicity with these atrocities, passing on this story to Gloria prevents such denials from ever taking place again and reclaims her birth parents' story as an official historical narrative. Transmitting this story is a deeply touching and emotional moment of maternal bonding that insists on remembering, speaking, and sharing to undo silences that initially robbed Perla of the truth of her parents' murders at the hands of a corrupt government.

CONCLUDING REMARKS

In the decades since Argentina's Dirty War, news stories have captured the reunions between children of disappeared victims with living family members, not unlike the end of *Perla*, which describes the heartfelt meeting between Perla and her biological grandparents. Although the novel in no way suggests that this meeting seals Perla's identity shut, this beautiful though painful exchange hints at the possibility of a new life filled with honesty, truth, and shared pain that may be lessened through the bonds of love. In closing the novel with Perla's loving and emotional letter to her baby daughter and her earlier meeting with her biological family members, Carolina De Robertis points to the necessity of shaping an identity that merges disappearance with rebirth. The past cannot be contained or forgotten, nor should it; and Perla's former identity serves as a reminder of the tragedies wrought by systemic denial of trauma. As a daughter of the disappeared, Perla adopts this identity to contest her country's ills even as she gives birth to a new generation that will continue to make sense of these past atrocities. Passing on her mother's name to her daughter is a symbolic though powerful mode of claiming her mother's life and disappearance, giving voice to this generation of victims. No longer *una hija de La República,* Perla proclaims herself daughter of the disappeared.

ENDNOTES

[1]*Perla* is not the only text by a writer of Latin American origins that has explored the traumatic and psychological consequences when a daughter discovers her father's role in a military dictatorship. See Haitian-American writer Edwidge Danticat's well-known novel, *The Dew Breaker* (2004), for example.

[2]As Francine Masiello notes in her study *Between Civilization and Barbarism: Women, Nation, and Literary Culture in Modern Argentina*, this idealized image of the mother of the republic owes its origins to nineteenth-century gender ideologies that deemed women's domesticity and maternal roles as "patriotic" duties (19). These ideologies were later encouraged by the junta to bring order" and "progress" to the troubled Argentine nation. See also Amy Kaminsky's article, "The Real Circle of Iron: Mothers and Children, Children and Mothers in Four Argentine Novels," for further discussion of maternal imagery in Argentinean history and literature.

WORKS CITED

Arditti, Rita. *Searching for Life: The Grandmothers of the Plaza de Mayo and the Disappeared Children of Argentina.* University of California Press, 1999.

Bejarano, Cynthia L. "Las Super Madres de Latino America: Transforming Motherhood and Houseskirts by Challenging Violence in Júarez, Mexico, Argentina, and El Salvador." *Violence and the Body: Race, Gender, and the State*, edited by Arturo J. Aldama, Indiana University Press, 2003, pp. 404-28.

Carlson, Eric Stener. *I Remember Julia: Voices of the Disappeared.* Temple University Press, 1996.

Danticat, Edwidge. *The Dew Breaker.* Knopf, 2004.

De Robertis, Carolina. *Perla.* Knopf, 2012.

Feitlowitz, Marguerite. *A Lexicon of Terror: Argentina and the Legacies of Torture*. Oxford University Press, 1998.

Graziano, Frank. *Divine Violence: Spectacle, Psychosexuality, and Radical Christianity in the Argentine "Dirty War."* Westview, 1992.

Herrera, Cristina. "The Madwoman Speaks: Madness and Motherhood in Angie Cruz's *Soledad*." *Journal of Caribbean Literatures*, vol. 7, no.1, 2011, pp. 51-67.

Kaminsky, Amy. "The Real Circle of Iron: Mothers and Children, Children and Mothers in Four Argentine Novels." *Letras Femeninas*, vol. 32, no.1, 2006, pp. 21-32. *JSTOR*. Accessed 20 Mar. 2015.

Masiello, Francine. *Between Civilization and Barbarism: Women, Nation, and Literary Culture in Modern Argentina*. University of Nebraska Press, 1992.

Portela, M. Edurne. *Displaced Memories: The Poetics of Trauma in Argentine Women's Writing*. Bucknell University Press, 2009.

Rich, Adrienne. *Of Woman Born*. Norton, 1976.

Spencer, Laura Gutiérrez. "Mirrors and Masks: Female Subjectivity in Chicana Poetry." *Frontiers: A Journal of Women Studies*, vol. 15, no. 2, 1994, pp. 69-86.

Sutton, Barbara. *Bodies in Crisis: Culture, Violence, and Women's Resistance in Neoliberal Argentina*. Rutgers University Press, 2010.

Sweeney, Susan Elizabeth. "Mirror, Mirror, on the Wall: Gazing in Edith Wharton's 'Looking Glass.'" *Speaking the Other Self: American Women Writers*, edited by Jeanne Campbell Reesman. University of Georgia Press, 1997, pp. 54-75.

Taylor, Diana. *Disappearing Acts: Spectacles of Gender and Nationalism in Argentina's "Dirty War."* Duke University Press, 1997.

Taylor, Diana. "Making a Spectacle: The Mothers of the Plaza de Mayo." *The Politics of Motherhood: Activist Voices from Left to Right*, edited by Alexis Jetter et al., University Press of New England, 1997, pp. 182-96.

Vickroy, Laurie. *Trauma and Survival in Contemporary Fiction*. University of Virginia Press, 2002.

20.
Her Mother's Ashes

South Asian Daughters Reimagining the Mother to Reimagine the Self in Diasporic Locations

DANNABANG KUWABONG

> My mother left me three legacies worth talking about. A black shawl she had been embroidering for me as a PhD graduation present. A long hair, blonde wig she bought herself when the wretched chemicals that were to cure her killed her hair. And she left me her friendship with Ushabehen. (Roshni Rustomji, "Porous Borders" 59)

The multifarious narrative reimaginings of diaspora South Asian mother-daughter relationships in North America—edited by Nurjehan Aziz, and published as *Her Mother's Ashes*, in three volumes 1994, 1998, and 2009—axiomatically demand multifaceted theatres of reading that transcend, unify, and consolidate their multiple geophysical, religious, and cultural boundaries. The voices in *Her Mother's Ashes* though transnational in their reach—covering Canada, the United States of America, East and South Africa, and South Asia—are not randomized in their narrative focalizations. These narratives display epigrammatic mother-daughter relationships among diaspora South Asian women's communities.

Fundamentally, I presuppose certain intertwining nuances of cultural, geopolitical, social, gender and transnational contiguities and cohesions while simultaneously recognizing the presence of certain centrifugal cultural forces that expose differences. In the "Introduction" to the inaugural volume, Arun Prahba Mukherjee states categorically that the volumes of *Her Mothers Ashes* do not posit a "South Asian essence" (x). Corollary, she stresses that "These stories by South Asian women, reporting on different geographic, cultural and historical aspects of the South Asian experience, make the diversity of South Asian communities quite apparent" (x). She examines certain signifiers of differentiation among South Asians women that must inform any reading of these daughter-mother narratives (x). Concomitantly, Murkherjee cautions against the pitfalls in academic circles to homogenize "the third world woman," or "the South Asian woman" into quantifiable and/or differentiable entities (x). Mukherjee's ratiocination provides the trajectory for my engagement of how comparative theories of gender, diaspora, transitional/ transnational relations, and generational conjunctions and disjunction encourage an understanding of the shifting cultural cartographies in South Asian mother-daughter affiliations. I posit that through these narratives, South Asian daughters reimagine their matrilineage inheritances through which they project aspects of their own self-images. I assert that the stories in *Her Mother's Ashes* are unfinished testimonials and reflexive examinations of personal and group meanings among diaspora South Asian daughters, and are structured on their relationships with their mothers: biological, cultural, historical, spiritual, psycho-emotional, and national.

Significantly, Glen Deer's lamentation that "Asian North America in Transit," particularly Canada, are continuously "interpellated as stereotypical and simplified *others* by an historical narrative that includes acts of exclusion, internment, disenfranchisement, and discriminatory taxation" is relevant to my thesis (5). Deer recapitulates the cultural and literary politics of underrepresentation(s) or total exclusion of invisibly visible "minority" North American literatures within the larger North American academic arena, except within eroticized and erratic liminal spaces into which they are squeezed and labeled as minority literatures of Canada or America, ditto: non-European Canadian/American literatures. I do not intend to regurgitate the perennial arguments in this debate. Rather, I explore what Eleanor Ty claims as the shift in narrative perspectives and themes among Asian Canadian authors at the end of the twentieth century and the early decade of the twenty-first century. Ty sees a shift among diaspora Asian writers from the "mainly auto-ethnographic . . . explanatory narratives often tied to ethnic and national identities" (xiii) of countries of origin, to more "experimental engagement with narrative forms, structures, and contexts ... with less identifiably Asian [character] whose plots, are not necessarily concerned with the struggle between the traditions of Old and New worlds" (xiii). Predictably, I endorse Pilar Cuder-Dominguez et al.'s advocating for a hermeneutic of reading praxes of these South Asian fiction, such as are found in the three volumes of *Her Mothers Ashes*, which recognize "patterns of inter-generational and intra-generational relations among [South Asian] women" (xii) in order to unpack the multiplex of "attitude(s) of the new generation of [South Asian daughters in North America] toward the role models of the older generation of [their mothers]" (xi).

Conflicting attitudes of diaspora South Asian daughters toward their mothers reveal tensions generated by the politics of personal liberties encouraged by Western education and lifestyle, and filial duties toward the residual yet ever receding South Asian culture trapped in a predominantly Euro-American cultural milieu. Hence, Pilarr Cuder-Dominguez et al. maintain the following: "schemes of honour and duty provoke most conflict in the stories. Honour and duty are demanded of the younger generations, especially the women, the traditional carriers of symbolic purity. Thus, the young women become often the territory of dispute, pressed by parents and young husbands to accept their traditional roles" (15). This is done despite the spirit of resistance programmatically activated in the daughters through higher Western education, which promotes combative discourse as a way of generating female agency within patriarchal systems contrary to South Asian feminist subterfuge silence for the same purpose (15).

Shauna Singh Baldwin's "The Cat Who Cried" stages this use of silence as a stratagem to negotiate through and disorient female-directed patriarchy in the homeplace. Mataji imagines her daughter-in-law to have been polluted by her Western higher education, and proceeds to then question her honour, which sets the stage for serious misunderstanding between them:

> Mataji was suspicious of me as soon as she heard that her youngest son wanted to marry a woman he had met studying in America. That I am Indian was merely an

> indication of his good sense. That my parents sent their daughter to study in America was an indication of a family tendency towards wasteful spending. Ever since that I was a bad influence on the son who was to have lived with her in that huge white bungalow on Aurangzeb Road in her old age. (38-39)

Mataji's distrust of her daughter-in-law is conditioned by her supercilious assumption that the latter's Western education has distorted and undermined her brahminical defined roles as a Hindu woman: the good mother and wife who upholds both her husband's and her own family's honour. Ania Loomba articulates poignantly: "Although the ideal woman here is constructed in opposition the specter of the memsahib ... together [with] older brahminical notions of female self-sacrifice and devotion with the Victorian ideal of the enlightened mother, devoted exclusively to the domestic sphere" (219). The possibility of Indian Hindu female agency, which Western education premises, is hence severely curtailed by patriarchal matriarchs acting as phallocratic cultural gendarmes. Mataji's hostility toward her daughter-in-law is further substantiated by Ania Loomba's reference to India's anticolonial discourse in which women who dared to question their subalterity within this brahminical structure are severely sanctioned verbally and socially (219). Consequently, Mataji's surveillance of her daughter-in-law is based on an aggregated role of mothers as gatekeepers, protectors, and custodians of Indian family sanctity through the control of Indian women's sexuality in relation to female engagements with the outside world. To Mataji, her Western educated daughter in-law cannot be trusted with the finances of the home—as she believes the daughter in-law will be uncontrollable—nor should such a woman be allowed also to work. Western education should not be a passport to female agency. Mataji uses this spurious argument to justify her son's opposition to his wife's desire to earn some income outside the home. She quips: "Beti, he is only thinking of you—going out to work with all those strange men" (41). To Mataji, the narrator's behaviour is tantamount to a dereliction of brahminical female roles, which indirectly undermines the illusory hold of power by mothers-in-law in their sons' homes. It is this power of control that the narrator, with her American education, contests, but she finds herself lacking the necessary courage to do so openly. Though boiling with righteous indignation when she insensitively gives away the narrator's family necklace, a gift from her mother, Mataji adopts her mother's advice that stipulates that the best form of resistance in such domestic situations is for the wife to retreat into silence and fake submission. As Cuder-Dominguez et al. stipulate in these stories "the lessons these [mothers] consider most suitable for their daughters are those of silence and submission, and the mothers themselves are the best models of [such] behavior" as modes of subversion (18). Nevertheless, the same mothers deliver contrary messages to their sons, encouraging them to be authoritative, toplofty, and tyrannical.

Subsequently, this seemingly antipathetic style of "self-projection" enables both mother and daughter to uphold their family honour insidiously under attack by Mataji and her son:

> "Yes, you going back. And you are going to be silent. No one will ever say you were raised to be troublesome. Do you want them to say that all your education only make you like some American feminist?"
>
> "How can you say that if you care for me?" I sobbed.
>
> "I say it because I care for you, little one ... But you will have to live with the family who have you now." (42)

The mother elucidates her choice of silence and public performance of submission in response to the daughter's attempt to peddle her Western feminist ideals: "Be careful when you use that word [feminist]. Men become afraid. If you want to survive, you must always let a man believe he has you under control. Silence is an excellent instrument, beti. Use it well" (42). Nonetheless, "there are limits to silence" especially when a woman's agency is imperiously abrogated. Gayatri Chakravorti Spivak in her provocative essay "Can the Subaltern Speak?" makes the case that in Euro-American capitalist and colonized spaces [here in South Asian patriarchal culture], the subaltern female does not have the political tools, cultural narratives, or the language with which to speak and be heard (90-104). In "The Cat Who Cried" the daughter/wife narrator echoes Spivak's position and proceeds to unveil and challenge the totalitarian cultural assumptions of Mataji believing she is the custodian of unblemished cultural ideals that are retrievable and transferable to daughters, even in diasporic and plural cultures: "The subaltern cannot speak. There is no virtue in global [South Asian] laundry lists with `woman' as pious item. Representations has not withered away. The female [writer as writer] has a circumscribed task which she must not disown with a flourish" or own with abandon (308). But as Benita Parry, in "Problems in Current Theories of Colonial Discourse" notes in his incisive critique of Spivak's position shows, even the mother's politics of silence is a form speaking. Strategic silence is resistance and does not emanate solely from "an absolute [challenge to the] power to the hegemonic discourse" as Spivak contemplates (39). In "The Cat Who Cried" Baldwin projects maternal—mother and mother-in-law—discomfort at cultural changes suggesting a female independence while simultaneously seeking to assert female subordination. The mother transfers her hopes for a liberatory feminist practice to her daughter through a mimetic act of reinstating the statue removed by Mataji and bringing it back to her daughter Sheila's room with no spoken words of complaint (44). In the process, her sarcastic response to Mataji's question whether a cat had meowed undermines the power of Mataji's surveillance: "Yes, Mataji. I was the cat who cried" (44).

Unlike the tripartite adult relationships in Baldwin's "The Cat Who Cried," Shani Mootoo's "Wake Up" reverses the linear matrilineality involved in mother-daughter stories. The daughter not the mother performs the role of psycho-emotional and social comfort. Unable to openly confront the husband's philandering, the emotionally fractured mother displays symptoms of co-dependency with little agency or desire for self-actuation. She then engages in secretive and self-destructive acts of drunkenness and smoking masquerading as acts of rebellion, which go unnoticed by the man: "She has been awake enough for worry to percolate and cause her to smoke. It calms her, to smoke. Or perhaps it is her quiet act of retaliation" (50-51). She is also confronted by the children who tell her that her degenerate "self-destructive, degrading means" are evidenced in the symptoms of physical deterioration

(51). Hence, the mother's body "shows skin swollen with worry and loneliness, her emotions too emaciated to feel anger" (50). To the children, these acts are inconsistent with her role as a South Asian wife and mother. As indicated above, the South Asian wife is expected to accept the acts of a cheating husband; as a mother, she should demonstrate emotional strength and composure, and not openly complain or show weakness to the children. However, the daughter's empathetic understanding enables her to see the mother's scandalous behavior as an assertion of "her own rebellion. Asserting that, at least, in her own eyes, she can maintain some modicum of power on these crazy nights when she feels less than a wife" (51). Definitely, the mother's actions are further disempowering and lack any agency.

The frantic behaviour of the mother is pivoted on a guilt complex embedded in the patriarchal ideal of Indian woman as the model of the perfect mother and wife that must have the strength and power to confront and overcome any problems in her marriage in relation to her husband's behaviour. Though she feels inadequate to the task of reassuring and protecting her mother (53), Angenie nonetheless maturely responds to the call of filial duty and transforms it into maternal responsibility. The mother commands and appeals: "Come. Come into her bedroom. To sit and offer wisdom, companionship, solace. Subordination and authority given to me to juggle in the same hand like double-edged swords" (51). The call is ambiguously both authoritarian and supplicatory: "Come. A strange demand at a time like this. It is not a request where the response might be a flower bud unfolding of itself to offer and give deliverance, but rather a command, a hand reaching into one's intestines and ripping out yard after yard, desperately searching for things it has not even defined" (51). Angenie simultaneously empathizes and repudiates the mother for her dereliction of duty while insisting on filial obedience in this tragicomedy of mother-daughter roles reversals. Consequently, Angenie's own adolescent desires and fears are disarticulated because her "mother needs [Angenie] to calm her, not encourage her fears with my own" (52). Angenie subsumes her own adolescent needs to take care of her mother's justified but inordinate fears. The mother destroys any admiration the daughter may have developed for her over the years, and further complicates for the little girl the confusion about her sociocultural location as a female. In this dream, there is a vivid and an allegorical representation of Angenie a little girl with her mother on a "leaking, tossing and tumbling" rowboat "in the midst of a grey-and-silver vicious storm" (52). The dream reflects the role reversal between the mother and daughter and exposes the dysfunctionality of Angenie's family: "The little girl in this boat ... calms and comforts and reassures her mother ... she takes off her shirt and wraps it around her mother's shoulders; she materializes a fire out of thin air to warm her poor frightened mother ... all the while taking pains to cajole the sinking morale of her mother in a voice controlled, calm and gentle" (52). This role reversal between mother and daughter in a stormy patriarchal world in which women are caught and in which the mother has no agency to protect the daughter, but instead depends on the psycho-emotional security, negatively impacts Angenie and generates an inferiority complex in her toward her sex/gender. The mother's psychoneurosis makes her impervious to her teenage daughter's needs, and she shows no gratitude to Angenie, who performs the role expected of her brother. Her monomania emanates from her feeling of betrayal having played the angel in the house as romanticized in heterosexual marriage and compulsory motherhood narratives. She now wants to kill that angel, but she neither has the tools nor courage to do so. As Virginia Woolf has argued in "Profession for Women" (456-60), this angel in the house mindset must be destroyed before women can have any say in their lives. Angenie, hence, converts her helpless rage into a blistering diatribe against her children and herself: "I can't go on like this any longer. I do everything for you all. I've devoted my life to you all. I have never neglected my responsibilities. I've been a damn good wife, and this is what I get in return" (Motoo 52). Her smothering anger develops into a jealous comparison with other wives who engage in extramarital sexual adventures, which if discovered would ruin their honour and that of their families: "I should have been a wife like all those other women, their husbands don't know where they are in the middle of the day. I only stay with your father because of you all, you know, not a damn thing has changed in these fifteen years since we got married" (52). In her self-pity and desolation, the mother attacks Angenie's pride in these words: "You're the eldest, Angenie, if only you were a boy, but I have to call on you, I am so lonely, I don't want to spend the rest of my life worrying where your father is, what am I going to do, look at my hands, they're shaking, look at my face, I am a wreck, I can't go on like this, I just wish I could die" (52). Angenie is shocked to realize that "even her mother prefers males to females, placing her love for her husband (and often for her sons as well) above her love for her daughter" (qtd. in Herman and Lewis 150). Angenie sees her mother's actions as "a rejection ... a betrayal ... Not only does her esteem for her mother suffer, but her own self-esteem is endangered by the thought that she might share her mother's inferior status" (150). Through her words and actions, the mother psychological abandons Angenie while professing her dependency on her which generates in Angenie, an impulse to replace her father in the matrimonial bed (Mootoo 56-57), which is subliminally revealed in an incestuous dream with the mother as the potential lover. Upon waking up however, she feels ashamed, angry, and disgusted with the mother. In the dream, Angenie's cry for the mother not to leave her reflects what Phyllis Chesler describes as a girl's desire "for the mother's love all to herself ... what the girl wants is nothing less than union with the Feminine Eternal, she cannot accept its loss or its ongoing absence in her life" (209). The feeling of maternal rejection in the dream is highlighted in Angenie's "demand with the power of an impetuous, desperate kiss that she not desert me" (56). The next morning, the mother withholds desired acts of bonding with Angenie and widens the gulf between them. The mother's withholding of affection from the daughter ironically triggers in Angenie a review of the inferior position of women in her culture, both in the home space and in the public arena: "Being a female [her] future looks grim, claustrophobic. I worry that I am expected ... to grow up to be just like her. The alternative to being just like her is to be just like him" (57). Subsequently, Angenie becomes embittered against the mother, and by association, her sex and what she sees as her future. In playing the role of the mother at her age, she somehow begins to understand the levels of stress that women must silently endure in her culture. She does not desire to become like her mother.

Angenie's fight to separate from her mother's fate is developed in Farida Karodia's "Crossmatch" (121-141) and Narsimhan's "Love, Long Distance" (147-156). These stories examine how choice of male partners for marriage leads to tensions between the cultural conservationists' attitudes of mothers versus the daughters' postfeminist and postcolonial liberatory understanding of women's roles. Set in Lenasia, a predominantly Indian diaspora suburb of Johannesburg, South Africa, Karodia's "Crossmatch" reveals British-educated Sushila Makanji on a collision course with her mother in relation to the choice of a marriage partner: "[Sushila] leaned back against the veranda wall, titling her face to the sun, imagining what it would be like to be forced into marrying someone she despised" (121). Like Angenie, Sushila's is dissatisfied with the subservient place of women in the Indian community in South Africa. Consequently, she is exasperated with her sister's life as a wife and mother: "Although Indira was making a valiant effort to disguise it, Sushi had sensed a sadness about her that she had not detected on her previous visit" (121). Indira's life seems unfulfilling as a wife and a mother, even though she obediently and docilely followed her female path. Sushila, as Judith Herman and Helen Lewis have presented, wants to escape what she perceives as "the oppressed condition of women" and hence create her own world that is "different from her mother['s]" and sister's through combative behavior defined by crudity, rebelliousness, and unsettling candidness (153). Like Angenie, Sushila rejects what labels as "quaint" maternal collusions with oppressive tendencies of patriarchy (128). However, Sushila's rebellion against her culture may be driving her into an English neo-patriarchy masquerading as equality in an entertainment industry where the profits do not go to the performers but to mainly male company CEOs and where there are sex, gender, ethnic, and race based inequalities in remuneration. If Sushi believes that in living with an Englishman she is socially and racially accepted as an equal, she does not fail to grasp the full impact of Indira's wry comment about the man's Englishness: "Yes, but this isn't just any man. It's an Englishman" (135). Indira's comment implicates the triple historical colonization of South Asian women—first, by the English male, second by the English female, and third, by the South Asian male. These multiple sites of the South Asian female's marginalization are further compounded in their Hindu or Muslim cultural locations. Moreover, it also hints at the liminal spaces for the construction of agency that Sushila's relationship with Kevin provides for Sushila, which is denied Indira. Of course, as Rosalind O'Hanlon has argued, no system of domination, be it patriarchy or foreign imperial enterprise, has ever been so corrosive as to completely erase or neutralize every possibility of resistance (191) despite Spivak's absolutist claim to the contrary in her essay (111). What is revealing of course at this point is Sushila's grudging awareness reflected in her nervous response to Indira's statement that Sushila's relationship is not with just any man but an English man—a superior male species that then by implication creates an illusion of social upward mobility reserved for only English girls. Sushila's discomfort at this envious accusation that she has chosen the colonizing English male over the colonizing Hindu male shows in how she grimaces wryly and turns to avoid confronting the issue. She is aware of how this could further hurt and complicate her already strained relationship with her mother because of her disdain toward her mother's ideals.

In addition, Sushila must also learn how to negotiate her Indianness through her adopted English girlishness, without exoticizing herself in her tripartite location: British, African, and Indian. Unlike the daughter in "Wake Up," who is deprived maternal protection, Sushila is unaware that her disrespectful behaviour ironically weakens her mother's position, as she will be held responsible for any infringement on the family honour. Incontestably, this point is evidenced as Mrs. Makanji blames herself for what she regards as Sushila's scandalous dress code: "We should never have let her stay in London. Just look at her. Who dresses like that, eh? ... Slacks are okay. I wear slacks too ... But what is that she's wearing? Those tight, tight pants? You can see the shape of everything. Has she no shame to be seen in public like that" (123). Sushila's believes her dress signifies her sexual liberation from restrictive Hindu cultural female dress code. Ironically, however, Sushila may be sucked into a false sexual liberation ideology promised by English dress code for girls, but which, nonetheless, is dictated by the male gaze that essentializes, oversexualizes, and commoditizes the female body.

Sushila's position is complicated further by her unwillingness to accept her mother as a smart and strong woman whose strategies of silence and appearance of subservience has worked favourably for her: "Sushi observed her mother from under lowered eyelids ... there was a certain elegance about her that Sushi admired. She also admired the way her father lavished attention on her mother. He was thoughtful of her" (124). Confirming this, Sushi's father wishes his favourite daughter would act cunningly as her mother. However, to achieve this, Sushila has to submit to the Indian cultural practices of maternal interventions in the choices of marriage partners for daughters: "Mr. Makanji had reminded his wife that they had not been successful before.... They had arranged three meetings, none of which had turned out well. Sushila had been rude and indifferent towards the boys and their families" (125). Sushila's rejects this cultural practice of helping choose husbands for daughters. This subsequently diminishes her mother's social standing, which is interpreted as a rejection of her mother. The mother panics and "feared that Sushi had grown apart from them and that it was too late to bridge the gap" (123). Later she laments: "We have lost her, Arun ... We have lost her. I can't bear the thought of her going back to London to work on that stage" (125). The mother's lamentation reflects her fear of being blamed for her Western educated daughter's deviation from the cultural norms defined for women in Indian society and that those deviations will be blamed on the mother. This family's relocation in South Africa and their Western education does not automatically translate into any changes in the performance of women's roles. The mother expects total obedience from the Sushila, which the latter finds difficult to accept. The tension between daughter and mother is exacerbated by Shushila's cultural alienation and her inability now to distinguish between the power of subversive submission and the powerlessness of combative masculine resistance. Shushila's mother and father both understand that in their context, choices must be made available to Indian daughters who may want to delay the traditional roles of wifehood and motherhood in order to pursue a career and become financially independent. The compromise also includes an understanding that those who chose marriage and motherhood, such as Indira, must not be denigrated by those who choose otherwise. Consequently, Sushila must rethink her overly, racistm and domineering Anglo-centric attitude to her sister, Indira, and her mother, who chose marriage and motherhood (134-35). Shushila must also come to terms with her own inferior position in the secret illicit sexual relationship with Kevin, which she cannot disclose to her parents.

If Karodia's "Crossmatch" shows only the potential tension in mother-daughter relationship arising from maternal overinvolvement in marital-partner choices for the daughter in Hindu families, Mahtab Narsimhan's "Love, Long Distance" stages the terrifying consequences of a daughter's self-selected husband, Zubair, in a Pakistani Canadian Muslim family setup. The opening conversation between mother and Razia, her daughter, reveals an exasperated daughter unwilling to accept what she sees as the mother's vexatious critique of her choice husband: "'You're lying ... I don't want to hear any more word against my husband.' 'Razia, you're my daughter, why would I lie to you? . . . The spare money I keep in the kitchen jar is gone. If you didn't take it Zubair did. It's a small amount, but yet ... why would he take it, without asking first?'" (147). The contentious relationship derives from Razia wanting to be the angel in the house and to sacrifice her otherwise supportive mother in order to placate a thieving and unscrupulous husband. Zubair assumes a taken for granted superior male position in the marriage, although he fails to perform prescribed roles as husband and provider in this Muslim homeplace. Imported from Pakistan through Internet dating, Zubair remains unemployed, and though enjoying the luxury reserved for a manorial lord, he refuses to look for work and ruthlessly exploits his position as the man in the house. Razia's mother is confronted by guilt; she feels somehow responsible for the presence of this spousal abuser masquerading as a husband to Razia (149). In their exasperations and guilt complexes, mother and daughter hurl accusatory projectiles against each other: "'Razia, I *know* you've gone through a lot to get married. This last few months have not been easy for any of us, but Allah knows we tried. We tried our *best* to find a good match for you'" (147, emphasis in original). Infuriated, Razia rejects this appeal for absolution from her mother and argues that by taking "matters into [her] own hands" (147), she succeeded where her mother had failed. The opening drama exposes the tension between mother and daughter because of Zubair, and reveals the dangers of falling into the trap of male defined social role of women in the Pakistani community, even in a non-Islamic Western European location. Tensions between mother and daughter drive Razia into the trap set by Zubair, who now exploits the situation for his own benefit. Undoubtedly, mother-daughter disagreements, as this story demonstrates, create spaces for men to further oppress women. In this story, mother and daughter both try to blame each other for Zubair's behaviour. They create guilt complexes in each other, and consequently lose focus on the common problem in their home. Nevertheless, Razia comes to secretly accept her mother's position. However, she cannot openly agree with her mother because she made the choice and wants so desperately to show the world that she is her own woman, who is a sexually desirable object to a man. Thus, she would rather live in shame than bring shame to her family with a divorce by Zubair. In her actions, she dramatically silences and subordinates both herself and her mother, and further disempowers them both.

Maternal silencing as a given potential for narrative agency is represented in Geeta Kothari's "Her Mother's Ashes." Lally, an after-school program worker, states upfront that she "has never considered herself a storyteller, a necessary skill for this job that fits her like her old school coat—several sizes too big, with the saleslady's assurance she'd grow into it" (178). Lally's inability to tell stories, she confesses, is traceable to her mother's concealment of the trauma of being rejected by her father because of her sex; the family's financial ruin following the partition of British India into India, Pakistan, Bangladesh, and Kashmir; and migration to the United States of America. Despite her claim of narrative incompetence, "Lally ... [re]imagines her mother, eighteen and frightened, holding onto her uncle's hand—as they board a train bound for Hoshiarpur" (179). The maternal silences generate narrative and imaginative spaces in which Lally (re)constructs a daughterly narrative of mother/motherland. As a child, anytime she tries to coax her mother to tell her about preindependent India, the mother always gave very brief sentences and refused to say more. The mother's most repeated phrase is "We lost everything. We had so much, and then, one day, we had nothing but the clothes we wore" (178-179). The inability of the mother to give more detailed narrative descriptions of what happened to the family and the country at the time of partition of British India simultaneously distresses the daughter and fires a desire for more: "Lally wanted to hear more, but even at ten she knew that if she asked for a happy ending, her mother would clamp her lips tight and walk away" (179). Not being able, therefore, to understand the mother's trauma, the daughter must fill the gaps and silences of the mother with bits she garners from her grandmother. The mother does not want to pass onto to the daughter the details of her painful memories. She has only the end of the story to give the daughter. The daughter wants her mother to share with her the maternal histories, both from a biological perspective and from a geopolitical nationalist one. Sharing the pain could draw mother and daughter into a closer relationship.

In conjunction with the children's curious interrogations, working as mnemonic catalysts for rememory, Lally revisits her mother's erratic narratives. Using improvisation to reconstruct her matrilineage from the haphazard scraps of painful memories and deep disturbing silences, she becomes the intentional biographer of that matrilineage. In her new role, Lally reimagines and redefines herself as the keeper, translator, and transferor of Indian national cultural history and family secrets. Her grandmother now sarcastically recollects how foolish Lally's grandfather had been when he rejected Lally's mother for being born a girl. This grandmotherly sardonic humour enables the exhumation of the skeletons of psycho-emotional wounds endured silently by both the grandmother and mother under Indian patriarchy. According to Lally's grandmother, when Lally's mother is born her birthdate is not registered. The grandmother concludes that there was so much confusion in the house that no one remembered to register this birth: "What she doesn't say, what she can't say, is that the disappointment of having a first-born-girl child was so keen, that her grandfather first asked the doctor if he was certain and they told him that maybe he should check again" (182). Underlying this forgetfulness, therefore, is the feeling of emasculation by the wife. This rejection of the mother from her infancy by a father traumatizes the little girl and creates in her a certain unwillingness to talk about her childhood in India. The grandmother's memory about this incident and others enables Lally to understand and relate to her mother's silences about her childhood. The snippets transmute into emotional and spiritual strands of reconnection when she returns to India to perform the last funeral rites of her dead mother. In India, she meets the extended family members and is able to further understand her mother's roots, which now become hers.

Having buried her mother back in India, Lally becomes her mother, being now the sole possessor of the mother's stories in diaspora North American location: "All she had were her mother's stories. What did they mean? Lally never hears her mother's voice" (180). That voice is a prophecy that "'One day we're going to lose all of this.' We lost everything. No home, no business, no nothing. My parents had to start all over. And that was it. She never said how she felt, and the harder Lally tried to remember, the less she knew" (180-81). The mother's brief story of loss and dislocation is replayed in Lally's life. She is culturally dysfunctional and spatially dislocated as an Indian girl, unable to perform properly as a South Asian daughter (180). Her ignorance of the Hindu rituals of mourning, coupled with her Americanized upbringing, causes her great discomfort with her Indian family back in New Delhi: "The way her two aunts cackled in Punjabi, the heavy, spicy smell of the food, the lingering scent of jasmine soap on her cousins' skin—it was uncomfortably familiar and unknown, both at the same time" (181). Lally's redemptive tears for a dead mother mingle with the muddied and unforgiving waters of the Ganges to offer moments of emotional reprieve and absolution. Evidently, therefore, Lally's trip to India is empowering though without any comfort, for even though "Lally understands that she has become that storyteller she thought she never was," it brings her no satisfaction. "Her mother's stories concealed more than they revealed, and that has been gnawing her all this time.... She should feel cleansed, refreshed; instead, a wave of nausea hits her and she has to bite her lip to hold herself still" (187). Lally's only security from this is that she "can finally see a face on the four-year-old forgotten under the seat of a bus. It is her own" (187). Lally's act of "retrieval, recording and re-reading" both her mother's and grandmother's stories enable her to root three generations of women in the new landscape of the USA (Parameswaran 3-8).

Uma Parameswaran's description of acts of storytelling by South Asian writers as acts of "retrieval, recording and re-reading of women's work" qualifies Meena Alexander's "By Lake Mendota" to be read through the theory of the "three Rs of feminist" maternal narratives (3). Dora secretly steals her mother's diary believing it conceals the untold details of her mother's life: "I opened her closet, pushed aside a packet of needles, a silver goblet. And there it was, under a pile of folded silk, a green-backed journal. So I stole her journal. Rather I took it away without telling her. Perhaps if I had asked her, she would have let me, who knows" (162). However, what she discovers are single-line phrases, shopping lists, spaced among blank pages. Such lines as "Went and sat with him by the water's edge" (164) and "Met in Union Square. The ground was wet" (165) have a cataleptic effect on the adult Dora. She enters a harrowing psychosomatic phantasmagoria where "a curios disturbance filled [her] ... as if sweet water from the depths of Lake Mendota had poured into [her], filling [her] up like a jug. And someone had taken the jug and shaken it so harshly the water turned brown as if churned" (164). In this hallucinatory terrain, contradictory feelings or omens are envisioned: "A girl stood over me, her hair tight in two braids. She was shaking me so hard I wept to be let go" (161). The dark girl, probably the ghost of the mother's traumatic childhood, seeks to prevent any transference of the consequences of traumas caused by unfulfilled dreams, emptiness, and bitterness onto her daughter. A dream that prefigures the vision at the lake is initiated by her unresolved anger against her mother for wanting to separate her from her Euro-American friends and away from the American culture of junk food and the carefree lifestyle of upper-middle-class children. She would rather go to a summer camp than go with her mother to India to visit the grandmother and get a taste of her other culture. Like the story of Lally, whose mother found it impossible to tell her the stories of her Indian past in "Her Mother's Ashes," Dora's mother finds it extremely difficult to write. The two stories reflect the difficulties immigrant mothers often have in communicating their past from their native countries of origin to their diasporic daughters. Such gulfs of silences often create tensions and misunderstanding, if not a type of negative curiosity in the daughters countered by a guarded secrecy from the mothers. Dora discovers this in her mother's case. Dora's curiosity overwhelms her, and she steals the mother's journal, hoping to find a treasure trough of autobiographical information. She is disappointed with the cryptic notes she finds, with no clues to interpretation. Thus, her disappointment turns into a nightmare that turns all the beautiful objects bought for the trip rotten, and they must be discarded—a metaphor of failed dreams that would unite the three generations of women with the motherland India.

Nonetheless, the journal hints at the mother's secret sexual liaisons, acts of subversion by a South Asian woman. The journal generates in Dora a critical examination of her own unromantic relationship with Eric, whom she thinks she loves, in these words: "mama and that man she thought she loved ... what is the difference between 'thought she loved' and 'loved'?—were too much inside me" (164). Haphazardly stitched together with broken threads of silences, the mother's battered memories are contemplated in the sacredness of ecological spaces: "the mirror of heaven ... what a lake is called" or "the sky in the middle of the earth" as her mother had often told her (162). In a way, the journal mirrors the mother's life: unvoiced in public but recorded as surreptitiously as "fall leaves slipping gold and red onto the clear water" (162).

Interestingly, the journal is the only place where the mother can articulate through uncoordinated phrases her broken thoughts, feelings, and experiences. She lacks the language of reconnecting with her mother across the oceans and, by association, reconnecting with her Indian cultural heritage she escaped from: "Writing came to her with difficulty ... It was almost as if a single syllable sent home would tear her apart. As if she had to stretch her own substance so fine, to pen it through the hazards of crossing ... Why couldn't she just write a few lines ... But she tried to explain it to me, draw me into her difficulties" (163). Her inability to write is mitigated somehow as she draws her daughter into her a healing narrative, where mother-daughter collaboration becomes a ritual transference of matrilineal heritage: "'Dora I can't write home to my own mother.'" And later, she requests of Dora: "Will you draw a picture, Dora, I can send your grandmother in India?" (163). Dora draws a "lady in a sari with a big black bag in one hand. In the other, she held onto a little girl who had two long braids. They were going up the steps of an airplane" with red steps and overhanging blue sky with sun and stars, which all "shone on that lady holding the little girl" (164). Dora's innocence permits her imagination to reduce a depiction of collective desire of three generations of women for bonding though reunification visits by Dora and her mother to India where Dora's grandmother lives. Dora's work, unlike her mother's, lacks the corrupting influences of nascent emotional scars, and, hence, it can encapsulate the intense strain on the emotional bonding between Dora's mother and her grandmother. Dora assumes the voice of her mother and tells her mother's, her grandmother's, and her story of desire. Celebrating this moment of collaborative articulation of desires and reconstructing daughter-mother-grandmother bonding reveals how South Asian daughters engage writing as an act of resurrection, recording, and reinterpreting their immigrant mothers' silences.

The narrative representations of mother-daughter relationships by South Asian daughters in *Her Mother's Ashes, Her Mother's Ashes II, and Her Mother's Ashes III* are testimonial celebrations of matrilineage, both in contexts of cultural questioning and maternal reclamations. In the narratives, the tensions, joys, silences, strengths, and weaknesses of the feminine subcultures of immigrant South Asian families are highlighted, performed, and validated in the liminal spaces allowed South Asian migrant communities in Canada's sociopolitic ideology of multiculturalism, the homogenizing cultural politics of the melting pot of the United States of America, the integrationist policy of Britain, and the neoapartheid system in South Africa. Their stories reflect the type of cultural hybridity Loomba denotes as informed by colonial and postcolonial constructs in which race, gender, and culture play pertinent roles. In these stories, the cultural hybridization enabled by migration and Western education, allows these daughters to exploit the "fault lines within these categories" embedded in the patriarchal and colonialists discourse praxes that define South Asian "women and gender as emblematic of [their] culture(s) and nation(s)" (223). These stories provide a new understanding of how diasporic locations provide safe spaces for South Asian women's narrative recuperations of their matrilineage outside and within both Western and South Asian gender constructs.

WORKS CITED

Alexander, Meena. "By Lake Mendota." *Her Mother's Ashes and other Stories by South Asian Women in Canada and the United States*, vol. 2, edited by Nurjehan Aziz, Mawenzi House, 1998, pp. 162-71.

Aziz, Nurjehan, editor. *Her Mother's Ashes and other Stories by South Asian Women in Canada and the United States*. Vol. 1. Mawenzi House, 1994.

Aziz, Nurjehan, editor. *Her Mother's Ashes and other Stories by South Asian Women in Canada and the United States*. Vol. 2. Mawenzi House, 1998.

Aziz, Nurjehan, editor. *Her Mother's Ashes and other Stories by South Asian Women in Canada and the United States*. Vol 3. Mawenzi House, 2009.

Baldwin, Shauna Singh. "The Cat Who Cried." *Her Mother's Ashes and other Stories by South Asian Women in Canada and the United States*, vol. 2, edited by Nurjehan Aziz, Mawenzi House, 1998, pp. 37-49.

Chesler, Phyllis. *Woman's Inhumanity to Woman*. Thunder's Mouth, 2001.

Cuder-Domínguez, Pilar, et al. *Transnational Poetics: Asian Canadian Women's Fiction of the 1990s*. Mawenzi House, 2011, pp. vii-xvi.

Cuder-Domínguez, Pilar, et al. *Transnational Poetics: Asian Canadian Women's Fiction of the 1990s*. Mawenzi House, 2011, pp. 3-43.

Deer, Glen. "Asian North America in Transit." *Canadian Literature*, vol. 163, winter 1999, pp. 5-15, www.canlit.ca/wp-content/uploads/2015/09/CL199-Full-Issue.pdf. Accessed 20 Aug., 2016.

Herman, Judith Lewis, and Helen Block Lewis. "Anger in the Mother-Daughter Relationship." *The Psychology of Today's Woman: New Psychoanalytic Visions*, edited by Toni Berna and Dorothy W. Cantor, Harvard University Press, 1986, pp. 139-63.

Karodia, Farida. "Crossmatch." *Her Mother's Ashes and other Stories by South Asian Women in Canada and the United States*, edited by Nurjehan Aziz, Mawenzi House, 1994, vol. I, pp. 121-41.

Kothari, Geeta. "Her Mother's Ashes." *Her Mother's Ashes and other Stories by South Asian Women in Canada and the United States*, edited by Nurjehan Aziz, Mawenzi House, 1994, vol. I, pp. 177-87.

Loomba, Ania. *Colonialism/Postcolonialism*. Routledge, 1998.

Mootoo, Shani. "Wake Up." *Her Mother's Ashes and other Stories by South Asian Women in Canada and the United States*, vol. 2, edited by Nurjehan Aziz, Mawenzi House, 1998, pp. 50-58.

Mukherjee, Arun Prahba. Introduction. *Her Mother's Ashes and other Stories by South Asian Women in Canada and the United States*, edited by Nurjehan Aziz, Mawenzi House, 1994, vol. I, pp. ix.-xiii.

Narsimhan, Mahtab. "Love, Long Distance." *Her Mother's Ashes and other Stories by South Asian Women in Canada and the United States*, vol. 3, edited by Nurjehan Aziz, Mawenzi House, 2009, pp. 147-56.

O'Hanlon, Rosalind. "Recovering the Subject Subaltern Studies and Histories of Resistance in Colonial South Asia." *Modern Asian Studies*, vol. 22, no. 1, 1988, pp. 189-224.

Parameswaran, Uma. "Names Resonant and Sweet—An Overview of South Asian Canadian Women's Writing." *The Other Woman: Women of Colour (Color) in Contemporary Canadian Literature*, edited by Makeda Silvera, Sister Vision, 1995, pp. 3-18.

Parry, Benita. "Problems in Current Theories of Colonial Discourse." *The Post-colonial Studies Reader*, edited by Bill Ashcroft et al., Routledge, 1995, pp. 36-44.

Rustomji, Roshni. "Porous Borders." *Her Mother's Ashes and other Stories by South Asian Women in Canada and the United States*, vol. 2, edited by Nurjehan Aziz, Mawenzi House, 1998, pp. 59-69.

Spivak, Chakravorti Gayatri. "Can the Subaltern Speak?" *Colonial Discourse and Post-Colonial Theory. A Reader*, edited by Patrick Williams and Laura Chrisman, Columbia University Press, 1994, pp. 66-111.

Ty, Eleanor. Preface. *The Politics of the Visible in Asian North American Narratives*, University of Toronto P, 2004, pp. ix-2
Woolf, Virginia. "Professions for Women." 1931. "The Death of the Moth." *The McGraw-Hill Reader: Issues across the Disciplines*, 11th ed., edited by Gilbert H. Muller, McGraw-Hill, 2011, pp. 456-60.

21. Lives of Mothers and Daughters in Brazil and Canada

The Mother's Artistic Influence as Seen by Four Women Writers

LIDIANE CUNHA

In the second half of the twentieth century, Brazilian and Canadian women writers produced a large number of novels and short stories in which the central characters are women pursuing a career in the arts. Through their personal and professional journeys, these fictional women often become aware of the influential role their mothers have in shaping their lives. By reminding us of the relationship between women artists and their female predecessors, Brazilian and Canadian writers validate Virginia Woolf's claim that "we think back through our mothers if we are women" (610). In the novels of two prominent Brazilian women writers—Clarice Lispector's *Near the Wild Heart* (1944) and Lya Luft's *The Island of the Dead* (1984)—and in the short fiction collections of two Canadian authors—Gabrielle Roy's *The Road Past Altamont* (1966) and Margaret Laurence's *A Bird in the House* (1970)—such a relationship affects many aspects of the protagonists' experience as a woman artist.[1] Specifically, the actions and limitations of their mothers and other female ancestors can either impede the protagonists' artistic development or encourage them to embrace their artistic ambitions.

In this intergenerational relationship, the nature of female predecessors' influence depends on the traditional discourses of motherhood that prevail in each of the two societies and how women experience those discourses. Patriarchy imposes similarly social and creative challenges on the lives of the protagonists' mothers, aunts, and grandmothers in the selected Brazilian and Canadian fiction. However, their particular reactions to those challenges produce distinct intergenerational dynamics in each one of these literary traditions. By comparing the role these female ancestors play on the protagonists' formative years and the complex relationships that the latter develops with the former, I argue that as a product of the particular female discourses experienced by former generations of Brazilian and Canadian women, the mother-daughter relationship impacts the protagonists' personal fulfilment and artistic potential differently in the selected fiction. In the first section of this chapter, I explain how two distinct discourses of femininity produced two unique female experiences in each society before the 1950s, and how such discourses shape the lives of the protagonists' female predecessors in the texts. In the second section, I show how the relationship that these earlier generations of women were able to develop with the young protagonists affects their lives and professional aspirations. The analysis of how women feel connected to or disconnected from one another is significant for two reasons. First, it reveals how powerful constructions of femininity can become across generations, and how they can shape the way women relate with their daughters and other female successors. Second, it shows that women can create powerful connections with their daughters and use these relationships as tools not only to support and inspire these younger generations but also to help them challenge discourses that restrict women's artistic potential.

FROM SILENCE TO COURAGE: THE MOTHER FIGURE IN THE LITERARY IMAGINARY IN BRAZIL AND CANADA

As Lispector, Luft, Roy, and Laurence inevitably juxtapose the imaginary and their historical realities, their protagonists' mothers, aunts, mothers-in-law, and grandmothers struggle with social and artistic limitations that resemble the barriers imposed on women who lived in the late nineteenth and early twentieth centuries in Brazil and Canada. I believe that the early generations of women portrayed in the texts capture two distinct scenarios: the silencing and marginalization of women in Brazilian society and the existence of opportunities that allowed women to play constructive female roles in Canada. These cultural realities shape the lives of the protagonists' female predecessors in unique ways in each of the two literary traditions.

The mothers who are part of the young protagonists' lives in the Brazilian novels experience female roles that resemble the conservatives' discourses of femininity reinforced in Brazilian society in the late nineteenth and early twentieth centuries. Embedded in religious narratives, the education system, and the artistic communities, such discourses effaced women from existing as speaking and artistic subjects and placed those who were considered rebellious in the margins of society. As an example, the Catholic Church idealized and perpetuated submissive maternal roles in Brazil and other Latin American countries through the cult of the Virgin Mary in the past.[2] Moreover, the education system and artistic community systematically discouraged women from participating in the intellectual and cultural productions as readers and writers in the nineteen century. For instance, wealthy families in Brazil widely accepted female illiteracy.[3] Finally, the discourse of femininity made available to the few female readers at the time continued to reinforce an inadequate image of femininity.[4] Still, Maria Bormann, Júlia Lopes, and a small group of women managed to establish a career as writers—hence, rebelling against the dominant discourse of femininity reinforced by the country's religion, education, and literary representations. Nevertheless, these nineteenth-century women writers confronted a biased literary market and readership that rejected their books and discredited their value.[5]

It is true that the development of the mass media, technological innovations, and other significant changes in the period around the First World War contributed to transforming the lives of young Brazilian women in the first half of the twentieth century. Aware of the transformations in female behaviours in North America and Europe, these young women became "more conspicuous" and started to participate in public events (Rachum 120). Brazilian women also gained more access to their cultural communities than their nineteenth-century ancestors had been allowed. However, despite the existence of prominent women artists, such as painter Tarsila do Amaral and novelist Rachel Queiroz, traditional discourses of femininity continued to restrict women's roles in society and, by extension, to ignore and undermine their creative potential in the first half of the twentieth century. For example, Brazilian women generally could not secure professional careers until the 1980s, and this reality was also true for many women writers whose works were largely ignored by their literary communities.[6]

In the selected novels by Lispector and Luft, oppressive discourses of femininity and motherhood similarly prevent their central characters' mothers from expressing themselves and playing strong female roles. In *Near the Wild Heart*, Lispector denounces the silence imposed on unconventional women who attempted to challenge these oppressive discourses in the first half of the twentieth century. When child Joana is introduced to the reader, her mother Elza has already been silenced through death. The protagonist learns about her deceased mother when she overhears a conversation between her father and a friend. Joana's father describes Elza as far from the conventional middle-class woman in Brazilian society: "She was slender, disdainful—you know what I mean, don't you? — intimidating ... so independent and embittered" (25). His description of Elza as "the devil" frightens Joana (25), but at the same time, the child knows that she has no real reason to fear her mother, who "was like a father" (26). By reimaging her mother as her father, Joana attempts to preserve the image of her deceased mother as an influential part of her life and by doing so, places her in the same position of power as a paternal figure. Nonetheless, Joana also learns through her father's stories that such a strong woman pays a high price for deviating from traditional female roles. As soon as Joana's father introduces Elza to his family, "it was as if [he] had brought in some contagious virus, a heretic" to their homes (26). When Joana's relatives perceive Elza so negatively, Lispector reminds us of the existence of strong and independent women who have been rejected for being non-feminine. Moreover, Elza is erased from the narrative just as the unconventional women of earlier generations were silenced by Brazilian society and ignored by their artistic communities.

In *The Island of the Dead*, Luft reduces maternal figures to a shadow or ghost in the narrative to expose the marginalization of women who have children prior to the central character's generation. Young Renata briefly mentions her parents as two people who "treated her as someone special, leading her to think innocently: I'm different from others. I am an artist" (12). Even though her mother initially encourages her to develop her talents, she does not interfere with Renata throughout her difficult adolescence, during which she was "a solitary girl, a quiet adolescent, not sad, but isolated by discipline and solitude" (10). Whereas Joana's mother is silenced from the beginning of Lispector's novel, the mother is part of Renata's life, but only as a ghost or shadow. As such, the mother does not actually have material existence for her daughter. This absence may also suggest that, whether Renata's mother is complicit with this system or feels unable to challenge it, the discourse of femininity reinforced by society constrains her life and agency. In contrast to Renata's mother, her mother-in-law, whom everyone calls Mother, is "a symbol of dedication" (39). She carries her heavy burdens and, without any complaints, takes care of her disabled daughter Ella. Mother is also "more of a mother to [her step-children] than had she, Renata, been to her own children" (45), thus serving as a counterpoint to the absence of maternal affection that Renata's mother stands for. Yet since Mother embodies the sacrificial image of the mother, she cannot defy patriarchal discourses of femininity.

By deliberately inhibiting these maternal figures' social and artistic potential, Lispector and Luft expose and question how society repressed Brazilian women's agency prior to the 1960s. More importantly, as I discuss in the second section, the social repression of women's creativity and personal development can also negatively impact their ability to establish a positive relationship with their daughters in the novels. The conservative discourses imposed on and often embraced by women indirectly turn them into negative models to whom their daughters cannot relate as they pursue unconventional female roles (as painters, musicians, and other artistic professions) in the context of Brazilian society. On the contrary, when women are exposed to meaningful discourses of femininity and choose to embrace it as mothers, they are more likely to understand and support their daughters' decisions to fulfil their artistic potentials. In turn, their daughters see in their mothers empowering female models to whom they can identify. As it is in the case of the mother-daughter relationship in the selected Canadian fiction, such an intergenerational connection helps mothers validate their daughters' artistic endeavours.

Prior to the 1950s, Canadian society similarly thrusted negative roles on women; it controlled their private roles as women and mothers and excluded them from professional careers in the public space. For instance, many nineteenth centuries women writers could not challenge patriarchal discourses of femininity, as well as the dominant views of race and class, that prevailed in England and Canada.[7] But in contrast to the discouraging situation of Brazilian women writers of the time, significant factors allowed a larger number of Canadian women to question their limited female identity and contribute to women's participation in public positions, especially to those of writers. First, the Catholic Church in French Canada indirectly led women to develop their teaching and writing skills, which encouraged them to play more active roles in society.[8] Second, the need to improve children's education in Canada promoted women's literacy and valued their professions as writers of juvenile literature—hence making it "increasingly acceptable and profitable for women in Britain and English-speaking North America to write for young readers" (Gerson, *Canadian* 74). Finally, the development of popular print and the establishment of cultural periodicals created opportunities for women to make a living as journalists and literary writers in Canada.[9] By showing that women could perform active roles as writers, painters, and journalists, Frances Brooke, Catharine Parr Traill, Susanna Moodie, among other female pioneers, contributed to the legitimization of artistic identities for women and even mothers. They became exemplary models for the upcoming generations of Canadian writers who claimed those forerunners as their "ancestral voices" (Smyth 15) and frequently acknowledged their existence in their own texts.[10]

In the early twentieth century, Canadian women continued to fight for empowering female roles in the home and professions in the public sphere. Significant economic changes encouraged women to pursue a profession, which, in turn, affected their roles as mothers. During the Second World War, for instance, "many Canadian mothers found themselves in the paid labour force for the first time in their lives, and, in a limited number of cases, their children were cared for in publicly funded, licensed child-care facilities" (Arnup 9). Furthermore, women did not passively receive the discourse of motherhood imposed by society and the government in Canada.[11] As women gained more access to public positions in the first half of the twentieth century, their literary careers also became more widely accepted in Canada than in Brazil.[12]

In Roy's *The Road Past Altamont*, the two mother figures who raise protagonist Christine symbolize the strength of generations of women who envisioned and practised active female roles in Canadian society prior to the 1950s. Portrayed as powerful women who nevertheless face the burden of raising a large number of children, Christine's grandmother and mother represent the typical ambivalence Roy felt towards the French-Canadian discourse of motherhood.[13] But instead of underlining their oppressive status, the writer actually celebrates both women's assertion and power, especially their creative power. One summer, Christine's grandmother (Mémère) makes a doll out of ordinary objects for the young protagonist. Enlivened by the discovery of "the infinite and ingenious resources of [Mémère's] imagination" and "creative talent" (9-10), Christine believes for many years afterward "that it could not possibly be a man who made the world" but "an old woman with extremely capable hands" (16). Sharing Mémère's creative talent, Christine's mother Eveline is an avid storyteller. She also confesses her other artistic dreams: "[she] might have been able to be ... a musician" (135). Moreover, as a "proud and powerful mother" (Lewis, *Literary* 86, 91), Eveline transgresses traditional maternal roles when she accepts that Christine accompanies their neighbour to a short trip to Lake Winnipeg. By doing so, Eveline allows the protagonist to explore the world outside the confines of her home, and indirectly teaches her an important lesson about the value of women's independence and creativity. During this trip, Christine learns that a free and creative mind needs moments of autonomy and, perhaps, solitude to be able to make profound reflections on the self and the world.

In *A Bird in the House*, although the protagonist Vanessa's mother Beth and her aunt Edna live in a constraining reality comparable to the environment that silences the female characters in the two Brazilian novels, both women manage to challenge traditional discourses of femininity. First, Laurence emphasizes Beth's free mind as she confesses the ambitions she once had to pursue a postsecondary education. When young, Beth "got the highest marks in the province in [her] last year of high school," but Grandfather Connor "didn't believe in education for women, then" (187). Complementing Beth's unconventional mind, Edna offers her niece a powerful and artistic model of femininity. There is no doubt that Edna is a woman ahead of her time. She has a romantic affair for many years, defies her father's discouragement of this relationship, and even leaves the house for a one-day trip with her suitor—all significant transgressions at that time. Moreover, her rebellious femininity is not her only impressive trait: Edna also plays the piano despite the fact that her father disapproves of her music and calls it "rubbish" (167).

Like the many generations of Canadian women who had previously questioned acceptable discourses of femininity and forged public identities prior to the 1950s, the mothers, aunts, and grandmothers Roy and Laurence portray in their short fiction collections defy the conventional female roles in their societies. As I explain in the next section, their characters' ability to challenge the social norms of being a woman also allows them to connect with the protagonists, fostering a mother-daughter relationship based on understanding and support.

FROM DISRUPTIONS TO CONNECTIONS: MOTHER-DAUGHTER DYNAMICS IN BRAZILIAN AND CANADIAN FICTION

Lacking a voice and a meaningful presence in their daughters' lives, the women portrayed in the two Brazilian novels cannot support their daughters' rebellion against rigid female roles, let alone their choices for a profession that has been often reserved for their male counterparts. In conservative societies, such as the social reality that is represented in the two novels, two destructive types of mother-daughter relationships negatively impact daughters' creative and personal developments. First, society can undermine any strong maternal figure in order to preclude a potentially powerful relationship between two generations of women. Second, mothers may accept conservative discourses of femininity and, as such, cannot understand or relate with their progressive daughters. In both situations, unable to find in their mothers the female model that legitimizes their social and professional transgressions, daughters face a more challenging road ahead in their liberation from the social enclaves that reduced their predecessors to silent and weak figures. Female empowerment "is extremely difficult," especially if "mothers ... are unavailable to their daughters" (Rich 245). In the specific context of women who want to pursue an artistic career, the existence of a strong maternal figure can already contribute to daughters' professional success. Otherwise, as Linda Huf explains, in the absence of "a mentor of her own sex who has also thrown in the kitchen towel ... the woman artist must become her own model or mother" and "give birth to herself" (153). This act of self-creation, however, is a challenging task, as women become aware of the danger of being forced upon their predecessors' powerless position.

In *Close to the Wild Heart*, Joana's father hopes that Joana does not inherit Elza's unconventional female qualities, stating that "even I prefer that this little one shouldn't take after her" (26). This is not the case. Elza continues to live as the kind of woman that the protagonist chooses to become and in the "freedom she often experienced" (39). However, Elza's influence gradually fades away. In the oppressive context of Brazilian society, Elza has to be not only silenced but also erased from her daughter's memory. Such a strong woman could become a role model that validates Joana's singular femininity, thus developing a potentially empowering connection between mother and daughter. Unfortunately, just as her family undermines Elza's powerful female personality, they similarly inhibit Joana from fully developing her female existence and creative self. When her father passes away, the child is left to the care of her aunt and uncle. The religious views of this conservative society drive Joana's family to consider the young protagonist as "a little demon," and even the town's priest is disturbed by Joana's behaviour (46). Since Joana challenges the ideal of femininity that the Virgin Mary stands for—pure and obedient—the child's singularity is condemned as satanic and, therefore, unacceptable. As a result, her aunt and uncle decide to send Joana away to a boarding school, whose strict discipline might "help tame her" (46). The narrator moves forward to the beginning of Joana's adulthood without describing her experience in the boarding school, which suggests that her family succeeds in silencing the child during this period. The destruction of the relationship between Elza and Joana and the social pressure she faces during her formative years contribute to the protagonist's confusion and stagnation at the end of the text. In fact, Lispector closes the narrative with an ambivalent ending, as Joana even considers suicide: "Ah, so she would die. Yes, she would die" (Lispector 178). But then decides to live on and "transcend [her]self in waves, oh, God, and may everything come and fall on [her]" (186). Although her conclusive monologue suggests that she chooses to embrace a powerful femininity, Joana is aware of the fact that she will continue being misunderstood and punished just like her mother Elza was.

Although society deliberately erases the image of a strong mother from her daughter's memory and, by extension, destroys a potentially powerful mother-daughter relationship in Lispector's novel, daughters cannot relate with their mothers for different reasons in Luft's text. Accepting conservative discourses of femininity, Renata's mother and mother-in-law cannot emotionally connect with their daughters or become the female models that could validate their personal and professional transgressions. Although her mother-in-law is initially portrayed as a dedicated mother, the narrative gradually constructs a different picture of motherhood through a series of flashbacks. In fact, Mother disapproves of her daughter Ella's affair with her stepbrother and refuses to offer the necessary support when the young woman mostly needs her. During an attempt to elope with her lover, Ella suffers a tragic accident that paralyzes her body and, gradually, her mental capacities. Unable to escape the confined space of her injured body, Ella constantly rings a bell and demands the attention that her mother previously did not offer her. Similarly, during her difficult adolescence, Renata cannot count on her mother who questions the protagonist's dedication to music and tells her that "no one has everything at the same time" (10). Renata builds a successful career as a pianist, but abandons her passion for the music in order to become a housewife and stay-at-home mother, two positions that she does not enjoy. Renata feels stagnated in unconventional female roles, just as Ella is trapped in her disabled body. The conflicts between these two mothers and daughters emphasize the pain that such a disruptive relationship can inflict upon mothers and daughters when society does not provide women with the necessary resources to liberate the next generations from sexual, social, and professional restrictions. Furthermore, the conservative female roles offered to the two mothers preclude Ella and Renata from finding an alternative in their own lives. Physically or mentally stagnated, both young women succumb to similar restrictions that they once attempted to reject in the role models embraced by their mothers.

In contrast to the negative relationships developed by mothers and daughters in the selected Brazilian novels, the previous generations of women depicted in the two Canadian short fiction collections can understand and support the protagonists' personal and professional ambitions and, by doing so, foster meaningful relationships with their daughters, nieces, and granddaughters. As Rich once noted, "a woman who can believe in herself, who is a fighter, and who continues to struggle to create liveable space around her, is demonstrating to her daughter that these possibilities exist" (247). In the two Canadian texts, Mémère, Eveline, Edna, and Beth teach Christine and Vanessa about the value of art and provide the resources needed to foster and fulfil their creative potential. More than just creating a supporting environment for the two protagonists, the women who nurture them also construct a female legacy. This artistic lineage can be a powerful intergenerational connection; it allows daughters to relate to their mothers and gives continuation to the artistic aspirations one generation was not able to pursue. As many Canadian women writers in the second half of the twentieth century have realized, "without continuity from mother to daughter, women remain detached from their origins and fragmented in their being" (qtd. in Forsyth 44). Instead of reinforcing the differences between the women artists of the time and their female ancestors, and the conflicts generated by those differences, Roy and Laurence propose a more constructive intergenerational relationship.

Young Christine gains the self-confidence she needs to set out on a journey to become a writer largely because Mémère and Eveline teach her about the power of artistic creation. As Christine perceives her grandmother's talent as divine power, she learns that artists are capable of bringing life and meaning to the world. Through her ability to tell stories, Eveline also mentors Christine's artistic self. After recounting a different version of a family story, Eveline explains that the past "changes precisely as we ourselves change" (123). She thus establishes an artistic bound with Christine, preparing the child to understand that words and memory modify our perception of what we experience in the past. As Christine identifies with her mother and grandmother, she realizes that imagination "was [her] family gift" (9). Imagination in fact becomes the foundations for an artistic legacy Christine inherits from her female predecessors. Such a legacy however needs to be secured, and this is primarily Eveline's role in her relationship with the protagonist. Although she has never fulfilled her artistic potential, Eveline does not threaten Christine's artistic liberation. Quite the contrary, believing that Christine "will do everything [Eveline] wished to do in [her] place and better than [she] could" (135), the mother supports her daughter's decision to pursue a literary career in France. Eveline thus connects with her daughter based on their similarities and, by doing so, reduces the gap existing between her and Christine. When she reveals the artistic potential that these three generations share, Roy suggests that a mother-daughter relationship that focuses on continuity, not difference, can incite in the daughters the confidence to believe that they too can become creative.

Vanessa benefits from a similarly constructive mother-daughter relationship in *A Bird in the House*. Like Christine, Vanessa leaves her hometown to obtain an education and fulfil the professional dreams that never became part of her female predecessors' reality. But she only does so because of the role her mother and aunt play in the protagonist's life. Claiming that she does not want her daughter "to stay here for ever" (187), Beth attempts to do anything to offer Vanessa an opportunity to go to university. Whereas Beth supports Vanessa's intellectual development, her aunt introduces the protagonist to the liberating power of art. When Edna plays the piano, Vanessa feels that the "notes would jitter and prance, strut defiantly, swagger from ceiling to floor and out the window, making [Vanessa's] feet want to follow them, away off somewhere, far away from home" (167). Identifying with her aunt's creative freedom, the aspiring writer has learned an important lesson: that "language, like music, can liberate" (Stovel 241). By the end of the narrative, however, Beth and Edna cannot liberate their selves. Yet they do not force her into a similarly constraining reality, which could create conflicts between the thwarted mother and aunt and the ambitious daughter. Instead, by offering Vanessa the tools to fully develop her intellectual and artistic potentials, both women foster an empowering mother-daughter relationship, one based on love, support, and their mutual interest—education and art.

CONCLUSION

Women writers have often expressed "an ongoing lament for the missing, silenced, absent mother and her mediating, nurturing presence, in social institutions and discourse, and in story" (Brandt and Harms14). Lispector and Luft similarly express their sorrow over the fact that their society has not only silenced their mothers and other female predecessors but also fuelled the frustration and anxiety of their daughters, thus destroying a potentially powerful connection between many generations of women. On the one hand, reduced to ghosts and weak female figures, the mothers present in the Brazilian texts do not even have the power to understand their daughters' need to liberate their selves. On the other hand, afraid of becoming their own silenced, absent, and missing mothers, Joana and Renata feel that they lack a relatable role model. As a result, these two generations cannot connect with each other and establish emotional and artistic bounds that could help the daughters to fully develop their artistic potentials. It is thus not surprising that lacking any supporting relationship and a strong role model, Joana, Renata, and the generation of women artists they symbolize, do not easily achieve their personal and professional goals. Nevertheless, we should not blame mothers for failing to understand their daughters' ambitions and encourage their journey to personal and artistic liberation. Even when women knowingly embrace traditional female roles and impose them on their daughters, their complicity and the lack of support as mothers must be analyzed within the historical context. In fact, many Brazilian women "could not be aware of both their [state of] dependence in the patriarchal order and their annihilation as a subject" (Cunha 108). One way to restore this disconnect between mother and daughter is by creating "a kind of strength which can only be one woman's gift to another, the bloodstream of our inheritance" (Rich 246). However, as long as such intergenerational connection is not possible, "women will still be wandering in the wilderness" (246). This is precisely where the two narratives leave Joana and Renata: robbed of unconventional and supporting maternal role models, they continue wandering in the wilderness. Lispector and Luft hence suggest that a disruptive relationship between mother and daughter can destroy the existence of a strong artistic lineage in women's lives.

The intercultural comparison in this book chapter forces us to recognize that the Canadian writers portray a social reality very different from the one that Brazilian female writers paint in their works. Roy and Laurence honour the valuable contribution made by the many courageous women who lived before the second half of the twentieth century. As these women fostered supporting relationship with the upcoming generations, they led to the latter's liberation from social and artistic restrictions. In this intergenerational connection, female predecessors and early generations of women artists contributed in their own ways to the perpetuation of a strong artistic legacy. Whereas Mémère, Eveline, Beth, and Edna inspired in their granddaughters, nieces, and daughters the ability to create art and later on prepare a liveable space for the development of their professional choices, Christine and Vanessa feel the need to realize the dreams their predecessors could not fulfil. As a result, as these two generations identify their shared desire to become independent and create art, they can relate to one other in a more constructive way than the two groups of women portrayed in Brazilian fiction.

The relationships between the protagonists and their mothers, grandmothers, and other female ancestors show the existence of a complex tension between the cultural systems that construct female roles and women's individual, often political, decisions to challenge those roles in their lives and those of their daughters. This conflict between society and the women artists who the protagonists symbolize begins with their mothers, who accept or challenge the traditional discourse of motherhood. They then pass on this conflict to their daughters who, in turn, struggle to reconcile the idea of femininity projected on their mothers and their own desire to contribute to their cultural heritage. Even though female existence and roles are often constructed by restrictive discourses and reinforced by powerful social codes, mothers can find some intrinsic power to actively participate in their daughters' liberation from such discourses and codes. The discourse of motherhood, for instance, "contains stories that need to be questioned, stories whose lack of questioning has harmful consequences in two areas: it hinders informed ethical evaluation of social policies affecting women, children, families, daycares, and schools; and it leads to alienation, frustration, co-optation, or unwitting diversion in many women's lives" (Hall 341-42). In the fiction by Roy and Laurence, women can redefine these stories by fostering supporting relationships with their daughters and thus transforming the lives of upcoming generations of women. In the works of Lispector and Luft, these changes are not fully realized across generations. Nevertheless, Lispector and Luft at least allow their female readers to become aware of the detrimental effects of traditional discourses of motherhood, perhaps motivating them to change the oppressive system in which their daughters live.

ENDNOTES

[1]All references to the Brazilian novels and French Canadian fiction are taken from the English translations.
[2]The Catholic Church's celebration of this maternal figure glorified motherhood and cultivated "women to be self-sacrificing moral guardians of the family" (Tiano 265). By doing so, the Catholic Church in Brazil restricted the idea of motherhood to women's reproductive functions and, as a result, rejected their potential contributions to the public sphere.
[3]Until the 1820s, when the first girls' school was founded in Rio de Janeiro, women's illiteracy was considered "a sign of nobility" and "an essential contribution to morality, for [it] prevented women from corresponding with their secret lovers" (Hallewell 160).

[4]Male "literature, plays, and newspaper articles" of the time, for example, "attempted to ridicule the [few] female doctors and insist[ed] that it would be impossible to ... take care of children and follow a career" (Duarte, "Feminismo" 206).

[5]Duarte observes that nineteenth century women writers were later "excluded from the canon by the [literary] history and critique," which "systematically eliminated women from belles-lettres." In fact, their works were barely mentioned in Brazilian literary criticism and anthologies until the 1980s, when feminist scholars finally uncovered the female writing published prior to the 20th century ("Arquivos" 65-66).

[6]The employment rates of women in Brazil rose "from 18 percent in 1960 to 33 percent in 1980" (Tiano 275). The literary anthologies of the time show that women were also excluded from literary careers: For example, Antônio Amora's 1960 anthology, *History of Brazilian Literature: 16th to 20th Century*, lists thirty-six writers who contributed to the modernist literary movements from the 1920s to the 1940s, but only two are women.

[7]Canadian women writers could not easily challenge the dominant view of gender, race, and class of the nineteenth century. As an example, in *The Canadian Settler's Guide,* Traill endorses the dominant view that maintains women within the confines of the home. She insists that women should be constantly occupied in domestic duties—even in cases of emergency, "it is better to be up and doing" (196). Brooke's *The History of Emily Montague*, Moodie's *Roughing It in the Bush*, and Traill's *The Backwoods of Canada* create romantic portraits of the First Nations inhabitants, reinforcing their status as victims. Their works also make references to the superior status of British upper-class families while undermining North American and European working-class immigrants.

[8]The Catholic Church in Canada used the image of Virgin Mary to defend women's obligation to become sacrificial mothers, but paradoxically, promoted women's roles as readers, educators, and writers. For example, the "Church emphasized mothers' duty to instruct their children, a responsibility that required reading aloud to them," thus leading to women's "early involvement in writing for children" (Gerson, *Canadian* 26-27).

[9]The periodicals of the nineteenth century "welcomed women's

writing" because "rates for literary products were based on the reputation rather than explicitly on gender" (Gerson, *Canadian* 25, 84). As a result, women gained a public space to write critically about their female conditions.

[10]Literary portraits of pioneer female figures can be found in Laurence's *The Diviners*, Carol Shields's *Swan: A Mystery*, *The Box Garden*, and *Stone Diaries*, Margaret Atwood's *The Journals of Susanna Moodie* and *Alias Grace*, and Alice Munro's short story "Meneseteung."

[11]When society "reinforced once again the centrality of full-time motherhood for Canadian women" in the postwar period, they "attempted to control and change the circumstances of their own lives" (Arnup 9, 12-13).

[12]Anne Dagg's 1986 study estimates that in "English Canada, from the beginnings to 1950, women have represented 40 per cent of the authors of books of fiction and 37 per cent of the authors of books of poetry" (qtd. in Gerson, "Anthologies" 57).

[13]Roy's late writings are often considered conservative because she emphasizes the image of Québécoise mother (Lewis, "Trois" 166). However, her fictional mothers are not traditional and naïve. Whereas Roy respected French Canadian women mothers and particularly recognized their hard work, her maternal characters "represent an attack against this maternal myth" because through her feminist consciousness, she questioned the "the dangers that are inherent in an obsessive maternal instinct" (Lewis, *Literary* 77).

WORKS CITED

Amora, Antonio Soares, editor. *História da literatura brasileira: Séculos XVI-XX*. Saraiva, 1960.

Arnup, Katherine. *Education for Motherhood: Advice for Mothers in Twentieth-Century Canada*. University of Toronto Press, 1994.

Brandt, Di, and Heidi Harms. *Wild Mother Dancing: Maternal Narrative in Canadian Literature*. University of Manitoba Press, 1993.

Cunha, Helena Parente. "A mulher partida: A busca do verdadeiro rosto na miragem do espelho." *Entre resistir e identificar-se: Para uma teoria da prática da narrativa brasileira de autoria feminina*, edited by Peggy Sharpe, Mulheres, 1997, pp. 105-38.

Duarte, Constancia Lima. "Arquivos de mulheres e mulheres anarquivadas." *Estudos de literatura brasileira contemporânea*, vol. 30, 2007, pp. 63-70.

Duarte, Constancia Lima. "Feminismo e literatura: Discurso e história." *O Eixo e a roda*, vol. 9, no. 10, 2003/2004, pp. 195-219.

Forsyth, Louise H. "The Radical Transformation of the Mother-Daughter Relationship in Some Women Writers of Quebec." *Frontiers*, vol. 6, no.1/2, 1981, pp. 44-49.

Gerson, Carole. "Anthologies and the Canon of Early Canadian Women Writers." McMullen, pp. 55-76.

Gerson, Carole. *Canadian Women in Print 1750-1918*. Wilfrid Laurier University Press, 2010.

Hall, Pamela Courtenay. "Mothering Mythology in the Late Twentieth Century: Science, Gender Love, and Celebratory Narrative." *Canadian Woman Studies: An Introductory Reader*, edited by Nuzhat Amin et al, Inanna, 1999, pp. 337-45.

Hallewell, Laurence. *O livro no Brasil: Sua história*. University of São Paulo Press, 2005.

Huf, Linda. *A Portrait of the Artist as a Young Woman: The Writer as Heroine in American Literature*. F. Ungar, 1983.

Laurence, Margaret. *A Bird in the House: Stories*. 1970. McClelland and Stewart, 1974.

Lispector, Clarice. *Near the Wild Heart*. Translated by Giovanni Pontiero, New Directions, 1990.

Lewis, Paula Gilbert. *The Literary Vision of Gabrielle Roy: An Analysis of Her Works*. Summa, 1984.

Lewis, Paula Gilbert. "Trois générations de femmes: Le reflet mère-fille dans quelques nouvelles de Gabrielle Roy." *Voix et Images*, vol.10, no. 3, 1985, pp. 165-76.

Luft, Lya. *The Island of the Dead*. Translated by Carmen C. McClendon and Betty J. Craige, University of Georgia Press, 1986.

McMullen, Lorraine, editor. *Re(dis)covering Our Foremothers: Nineteenth-Century Canadian Women Writers*. University of Ottawa Press, 1990.

Rachum, Ilan. "Woman Suffrage, and National Politics in Brazil: 1922-1937." *Luso-Brazilian Review*, vol. 14, no. 1, 1977, pp. 118-34.

Roy, Gabrielle. *The Road Past Altamont*. Translated by Joyce Marshall, New Canadian Library, 1976.

Rich, Adrienne. *Of Woman Born: Motherhood as Experience and Institution*. Norton, 1976.

Smyth, Donna E. "Thinking Back through Our Mothers: Tradition in Canadian Women's Writing." McMullen, pp. 14-21.

Stovel, Nora Foster. *Divining Margaret Laurence: A Study of her Complete Writings*. McGill-Queen's University Press, 2008.

Tiano, Susan. "The Role of Women" *Understanding Contemporary Latin America*, edited by Richard S. Hillman, Lynne Rienner, 2005, pp. 263-96.

Traill, Catharine Parr. *The Canadian Settler's Guide*. Toronto Times, 1857.

Woolf, Virginia. *A Room of One's Own*. 1929. *Selected Works of Virginia Woolf*. Wordsworth, 2005, pp. 561-634

21.
"Their Mother Was Waiting for Her"

Mother-Daughters Relations and Irish Identity in Deirdre Madden's *One by One in the Darkness*

CHARLOTTE BEYER

In this essay, I explore the portrayal of mother-daughter relations and Irish identity in Deirdre Madden's 1996 novel *One by One in the Darkness.*[1] Set in Northern Ireland in the 1970s and 1990s before the Good Friday Peace Agreement, the novel depicts the Quinn family's shared history through the stories and reflections of three adult sisters and their mother, and the conflicted history of Northern Ireland forming the background. Through the interwoven narratives of the mother, Emily, and her daughters Helen, Cate and Sally, Madden's novel investigates their experiences in a Northern Irish society marred by conflicts and divisions, their father's traumatic murder because of sectarian violence,[2] and the impact of these external pressures on women. By analyzing Madden's representation of mothers and daughters, I examine how *One by One in the Darkness* foregrounds the richness and importance of female relationships through its portrayal of the complexities of these relationships[3] and by exploring the implicit impact of the symbolism of Mother Ireland on maternal experience.[4]

Madden's representation and depiction of mother-daughter relationships is especially significant because portrayals of these relations have largely been absent from mainstream cultural discourses, per critics. In Irish literary and cultural contexts, the topic of mother-daughter relations remains a neglected topic, as Anne Fogarty explains: "The cathexis of mother and daughter is ... an unwritten story in Ireland because it is largely uncharted, hidden in the obscure domain of women's fiction" (85). However, Fogarty further suggests that "the many plotlines that form the narratives of the female portrayal of relationships between mothers and daughters can, however, be recovered from the rich but silenced archive of contemporary Irish women's writing and opened up for scrutiny and evaluation" (85). The mother-daughter theme has been important in unlocking the complexity of Irish women's writing, according to Heather Ingman, who suggests that: "in the context of familial relationships, it was the mother-daughter relationship that struck a new note in [the literature of] the period and from this date onwards challenged the centrality of the father-son relationship in the Irish canon" (*A History* 206). Ingman's commentary specifically pertains to the short story form; however, her observations are also relevant to the present discussion of Madden's depiction of female relationships.

Madden uses narrative structure to specifically place Irish mother-daughter stories at the centre of the family picture of *One by One in the Darkness*. Although haunted by family trauma, the females in the Quinn family in *One by One in the Darkness* remain connected. This interconnectedness is emphasized by setting the narrative in the present during one week in the 1990s, but featuring extended sections of flashbacks sequences into the family's past, which depict the daughters' childhoods and the mother's youth. These continuities are highlighted in the book using recurring motifs which illustrate emotional and mental connections between females across generations. Madden's emphasis on familial relationships among women is central to the novel, and reflects a wider preoccupation in contemporary women's writing with sisterhood and mother-daughter relations (Palmer 112). This topic has previously been trivialized in Irish literature, as Patricia Coughlan argues, creating: "a need for persistent intervention in the canon to redress the occlusion, omission and marginalisation of women writers by those male-focused metanarratives which still dominate perceptions of Irish literary tradition" (1). Through the central theme of mother-daughter relations in *One by One in the Darkness*, Madden constructs an alternative narrative centred on women's experiences.

MATERNAL PERSPECTIVES IN *ONE BY ONE IN THE DARKNESS*

One by One in the Darkness explores the themes of motherhood and mother-daughter relations through implicitly alluding to the symbolic importance of the figure of Mother Ireland and depicting the oppressive aspects of Irish maternity before and during the 1970s. Fogarty suggests that the stereotypical imagery of maternity associated with the historical figure of Mother Ireland remains a problematic influence in contemporary times: "The images of Ireland as a hapless abandoned maiden, a homeless crone, an exacting, tutelating spirit who needs to be propitiated, and as a melancholic mother who demands unceasing sacrifice and devotion from her children ... continue to inflect the ways in which femininity is construed in the country today" (87). Also, commenting on the figure of Mother Ireland, Linda Clarke explains that "Some commentators have argued that Ireland depicted as Mother has been so effective that it is entrenched in the idea of woman in stereotypical roles" (1). However, Madden's novel suggests that these oppressive aspects related to Irish motherhood are changing because of cultural and social developments initiated by feminist struggle and resulting cultural awareness, as seen through the perspective of female characters often consigned to the margins of that history. According to Rebecca Pelan, this shift, "has been facilitated by the second wave of the women's movement, which created a framework for women's voices to be heard and through which literature (re)gained its place as a key site for the articulation of the key issues that directly affect women" (xi). *One by One in the Darkness* provides both structural as well as thematic emphasis to its analysis of motherhood through its allusions to symbolic representations of Irish maternity embodied in the figure of Mother Ireland. Through its textual representations of Irish identity and maternity, Madden's novel explores the consequences of "hav[ing] the identity of [Ireland] embodied in the feminine Ideal of Mother" (Clarke 1), and the significance of this for Irish female roles and identities. A 1991 television documentary *Mother Ireland* explores the significance of the image and myth of Mother Ireland, and states the figure "emerged as a powerful symbol of nationalism in the eighteenth century, and it lingers today as a social, cultural, and political reality." Referring to the postcolonial dimensions of Irishness and femininity, Bernadette Devlin stresses in the 'Mother Island' documentary that "If you look at aggressive countries, imperialist countries, they tend to be male countries ... people who have a long history of oppression I think tend to think of their community and their country as motherland ... that is an acceptance of the analogy of oppression and the oppression of women."

In *One by One in the Darkness*, the allusion to Mother Ireland and the maternal realm also includes the symbolic and gender-political ramifications of the identification of women with colonialism. Madden's novel uses the religious and cultural tensions of Northern Irish life to contextualize her narrative representations of the changing nature of motherhood and maternal experiences, and to pose critical questions of the continued influence and impact of religion on motherhood and female sexuality. *One by One in the Darkness* introduces the theme of motherhood very early in the novel by highlighting the problematic aspects of maternity in a contemporary Irish context by raising the issue of single motherhood. In the opening pages, Cate, the middle Quinn sister, reflects on her pregnancy and unmarried status as she prepares for an imminent journey back to visit her mother and sisters in Northern Ireland and to tell them her news. Through Cate's concerns about her pregnancy outside marriage within a family of Northern Irish conservative Catholic attitudes, the novel deromanticizes notions of pregnancy and motherhood by presenting them outside a traditional family unit and portraying the ambivalence toward motherhood and the ambivalences of maternal experience. Cate's pregnancy and the familial conflicts it triggers reflect Fogarty's point that "tensions between conservatism and feminism, traditionalism and modernity may be traced in the many mother-daughter plots that occur in recent Irish women's fiction" (88). Several central images and scenes in the book encapsulate the intensity and emotional investment of the mother-daughter bond. One of these scenes revolves around emotional symbiosis and physical intimacy. Cate recalls her mental response to witnessing a mother with her young daughter sitting entwined on an underground train, the mother caressing the daughter's face (148). Cate's reflections on the scene reveal her ambivalence regarding "too much" maternal closeness and hint at her unresolved feelings towards her own pregnancy.

The theme of food and female nurturing serves an important and complex function in the portrayal of mothers and daughters in Madden's novel,[5] a theme connected to Irish history through its resonances to the Famine. A scene in the book's opening pages revolves around the ritual of homecoming and the sharing of food. As Cate arrives home, she sees her mother "was waiting for her by the parlour window, as had always been her way" (7). These wordless rituals and patterns are depicted as central to maintaining and sustaining mother-daughter relations, and serve the function of releasing affect in characters and eliciting the reader's response, as seen by Cate's body language and emotional response to her mother's constancy in standing by the window show: "Cate hugged her and cried, afraid that she would forget her resolution and blurt out her news all at once" (7). Similarly, the important communal act of eating together and sharing a family meal establishes a sense of relationship and continuity in the mother-daughter and family relationships: "Cate always loved the first meal with her family when she came home.... It reminded her of the visceral, uncomprehending emotional closeness that had bound them together over dinners of baked beans and fish fingers eaten at the same table when they were small children" (8).

The significance of such shared experiences of female bonding is reflected in the simplicity and beauty of the scene, which is emphasized through the visual clarity of the imagery and the sensuous descriptive language. The symbolically poignant setting of the kitchen is further foregrounded through its reassuring appearance of timelessness amid the social-political uncertainties of the time. As Helen reflects, "because nothing had changed there was something timeless about the kitchen" (21), which she likes, and makes the locus, in Rebecca Long's words, "the perfect location in which to engage in the act of remembering" (14). As well as providing the focal point for idealized memorialization of the past, the kitchen is also the locus for present-day mother-daughter disagreements and familial conflicts as well as their potential resolution, as is seen in Emily's insistence that she and Sally leave the conservatory and go to the kitchen to discuss Cate's pregnancy. Focusing on this domestic space between mothers and daughters, Madden's novel both celebrates and problematizes the emotional and symbolic significance of shared meals as nurturing personal experiences and through allusion to collective Irish culture and the history of famine. Nurturing is a central activity associated with maternal figures as Deborah Lupton explains: "From a psychoanalytic perspective, the emotions and desires associated with food are inextricably intertwined with individuals' relationships with their mothers" (44).[6] Importantly, however, in Ireland, issues of food are also historically linked to the Famine. Caused by the failure of the potato crop in the mid-nineteenth century and the lack of action by the English government to help the Irish, the Famine killed around one million people (Bloy). This historical trauma has marked the Irish cultural and historical imagination, and the preoccupation with food in Madden's novel implicitly alludes to that traumatic history. As well as echoing a collective history of surviving suffering, representations of food preparation, shared meals, and the domestic sphere contribute to elevating the everyday and celebrating female experiences of caring and nurturing. The kitchen setting is the central symbolic locus for the novel's most complex intense and painful events and confrontations, reflecting the importance of this complex domestic space in Irish women's writing.

The focus on Emily, the mother figure in *One by One in the Darkness*, is crucial to the examination of Irish maternal experiences and perspectives. Through Emily's character, the novel portrays the lived experiences of the ideological and symbolic construction of Irish motherhood. Her narrative depicts the predicament of growing up female in rural Northern Ireland in the early- to mid-twentieth century, a time when traditional Irish views on procreation and women's domestic roles prevailed. Emily's story is strategically introduced toward the book's middle—a narrative strategy that produces the effect of gradual peeling away narrative and historical layers. The novel gives the reader insight into Emily's childhood and young womanhood prior to marriage and maternity. This dimension helps to present her character as not merely locked into a maternal role in relation to her daughters; instead, it provides space within the narrative to depict her early life in its fullness prior to having children so that the complexity of her story is narrated and understood by the reader. Emily's childhood is traumatized by the tragic death of her father and later by the distant relationship with her mother:

> Her spirit was broken by the time she was twelve, but spirits, whether those of a child or a society, never break cleanly, and the people who did not understand this were shocked when the dull, quiet girl, so eager to please, suddenly displayed a violent temper. (114)

Through her harsh demeanour, Emily's mother was instrumental in breaking her daughter's spirit by showing so little regard for her feelings and forcing her to suppress a healthy emotional response to grief. This portrayal shows the painful effects of emotional repression and the role mothers can play in perpetuating this damage. Reflecting on her political ignorance regarding the Troubles, Emily is forced to acknowledge that her lack of knowledge is rooted in repression—"her sense of personal dispossession had been so intense that it would perhaps have been asking too much of her when she was a young girl to unravel the strands of her own unhappiness" (115). In contrast, Emily's relationship with her own daughters, particularly Sally, the youngest, is characterized by loyalty, constancy, and emotional warmth. Their mutual dependence is evident as Sally reflects the following: "the last thing their mother ever wanted for Sally was for her to be autonomous and independent. It suited her perfectly to have her youngest daughter as a companion, whose will and whose nature she had formed to fit with her own needs" (140). Importantly, the potentially damaging effects of this interdependency are also conveyed: "when Sally felt she lacked privacy in her life, or that her mother was selfish in her behaviour towards her, those thoughts were immediately joined by a searing guilt for allowing herself to entertain such ideas" (146). Helen, Emily's oldest daughter, reflects that her mother as a young woman living away from home while working as a teacher experienced "a special time, a time when she'd been happy" (76), but had to leave the job after she married. This requirement for Emily to give up her work rendered her "doubly colonised" (Ingman, *Irish Women's Fiction* 216) and resulted in further maternal estrangement. Emily's own reflections on this self-effacement and negation of her professional ambition and self-determination reflect her resignation, illustrating historical and cultural change and the impact on women's expectations and experience (117). Examining Madden's representation of Emily and her relationship with her own mother, Ingman argues further that she "is only prevented from making the same mistakes with her own daughters by her husband Charlie" (*Irish Women's Fiction* 216). Emily's bitter and unresolved relationship with her own mother serves as a warning of the consequences of poor communication and lack of empathy, and demonstrates how these may result in missed opportunities and failed relations. Emily's resentment of the perceived imperfections of her husband and children is counterbalanced by a nightmarish vision she has of her family and herself travelling on a life raft toward an abyss—an image she realizes she needs to learn from to transform her responses to and expectations of others by taking responsibility for her own happiness.

The novel's many references to Emily's love of flowers and plants underline the symbolic maternal inheritance shared by the daughter Cate, Emily, her mother, and Granny Kate through evoking their response to flowers and colours. For Emily, flowers are an antidote to her pain at loss and bereavement. Flowers represent renewed health, alternative spaces of growth, and the continuity of female connection in defiance of the pain and deaths caused by the political and religious violence and conflict surrounding her. Flowers serve to distract Emily from the memories of her husband's murder: "Her daughters teased her about her mania, but she only smiled. She knew they understood" (106). Whereas Long associates Emily's intense feelings for flowers with the memorialisation of her husband's death (9-10), I agree with Bridget Hogan who notes the mythic significance of the flower motif.[7] The Greek Demeter-Persephone myth is frequently alluded to within contemporary women's writing, including Irish women's literature. The work of growing and caring for flowers and plants engages Emily in a cyclical temporal experience that specifically echoes the Demeter-Persephone myth through its suggestion of an alternative life-affirming dimension to linear clock time: "it hooked her into the circle of the seasons, and time would otherwise have been a horrible straight line, a straight, merciless journey at speed towards death" (206). The cyclical return of the seasons evoked by plants and flowers relates to this myth's defiance of absence while affirming the emotional and psychological continuity of female connection, encapsulated by the phrase "their mother was waiting for her."

DAUGHTERS AND SISTERS

As a counter-representation to the stereotypical image of maternity associated with the figure of Mother Ireland, *One by One in the Darkness* presents the close mental and physical connection between mothers, daughters, sisters, and their ever-evolving lifelong relationships with one another. Rather than representing mother-daughter relations and bonds between sisters in an idealized manner, Madden's novel portrays these bonds in a manner that highlights their complexity, echoing other Irish fictions exploring this theme. Fogarty points out that "Painful rapprochements and intractable tensions continue to be the fulcrum of Irish fictions that focus on the complex ambiguities of the mother-daughter relationship" (114). The female characters in *One by One in the Darkness* experience disagreements and tensions in their relationship while sharing a sense of sisterly solidarity and responsibility to nurture and help one another. Despite their disagreements, their mental connection remains unbroken. This bond is illustrated through Cate's recollection of how she and her sisters and mother simply say, '"it's me"' (8) when speaking on the phone; they do not need to introduce themselves formally by name. This instant and intuitive identification of female kin illustrates the power of sisterhood and family bonds. Madden depicts these relationships by retelling the characters' personal histories, depicted through flashbacks, overlapping accounts, and the intricate and at times circuitous routes of memory and personal histories. Long comments on the way the novel employs memory to suggest the partial and subjective nature of experience, and states that the "timeless space" of shared childhood memories is compromised by human fallibility (7). This ambiguous memory space is evoked when Cate summarizes the sisters' relationship as she gazes at a photo in Helen's flat depicting the three sisters as children sitting together. Cate concludes that sisterhood is inspired by loyalty and acceptance of difference: "with your sisters, what you had 'in common' was each other" (88). *One by One in the Darkness* establishes connections among females through the deft employment of such narrative techniques as memory sequences and flashbacks, which allow the sisters' past experiences and childhood perceptions to be represented as an organic part of the textual fabric. This technique in the novel is also examined by Long, who comments on the link between history and selfhood: "Identity in the narrative is intimately connected with the idea, memory and experience of that past" (2).

The novel portrays the differences between the three sisters by foregrounding their contrasting personalities and the differing social positions they each occupy, as a way of emphasizing the heterogeneity or difference between and among females, a strategy also highlighted by Long who asserts that "Their responses to these crises are as distinct and separate as their personalities" (2). Helen, the oldest sister, is portrayed not only as contained and serious in her pursuit of justice but also as a reliable ally for her sisters in their hours of need. Helen's sisterly role is confirmed by the flashback to her early schooldays and recollection of a childhood story: "The story Helen had liked was about Annie Oakley, who had shot quail to feed her little brothers and sisters because they had had no grown-ups to look after them" (32). Helen's responsible character and determination, her self-definition and how she manages her home, deliberately oppose conventional expectations regarding feminine homemaking. Her bedroom is described as a private space, not arranged to invite patriarchal approval; her living room has a "chilly atmosphere, and the rest of the house a "clinical neatness" (45). Similarly, her everyday clothing does not involve dressing for male approval but is instead practical and comfortable (45). Although Helen is passionate about justice and consumed by her work as a solicitor, her emotional core nevertheless remains closely connected to her sisters and mother. This is evident in Helen's feelings of solidarity toward Cate, and her determination to protect Cate from their mother's initial condemnation of Cate's unmarried pregnancy and prevent further family arguments on the issue rather than abandon Cate to deal with these issues alone (54-5).

The novel contrasts Helen's professional gravitas and political engagement with Cate, who lives in London pursuing a successful career and defines herself in opposition to rural working-class images of Irish femininity. Cate's character is full of contradictions, which accentuates the sisters' differing personalities. On the one hand, Cate is critical of other females and reflects on what she would change for improvement, from the furnishings and wall colours in Helen's living room (87) to other women, hypothetically, "assessing their hair, their make-up, professionally, but not unkindly. She liked to think" (87). On the other hand, Cate is seen as an embodiment of "kindness, luxury and generosity" by her mother Emily (108). Cate's aspiration to appear urban and sophisticated is reflected in her name change from Kate to Cate. The name change allows her to attempt a masking or erasure of her Irishness in the English metropolitan context. Long suggests that Cate's change of her name is "fuelled by a desire to belong to a community outside of her family circle" (12). However, the external markers of the illusion that Cate creates of affluence and self-assurance, through expensive clothes and accessories, are contradicted by her inner insecurity over her unmarried pregnancy and her fears about how her mother will receive the news. Cate's pregnancy reveals her conflicted feelings at the prospect of motherhood (90) and her fear of the conflicts it may trigger, as her situation as a single mother is less straightforward at the family home. Cate's professional career and affluence render her a successful social climber, yet within an Irish context still emphasizing the traditional, she remains vulnerable and in need of her sisters' and mother's protection. The contradictions of Cate's character highlight the continued pressures brought to bear on Irish women, individually and collectively, by religious and social conventions.

One by One in the Darkness establishes connections and continuities between mothers and daughters within domestic spaces. Cate's character is a central focal point for many of these investigations. Through her rich imaginative life, Cate remains in emotional contact with her sisters and mother as visualizes them asleep in their homes: "she lay now for more than an hour thinking about her family. She liked to imagine them still asleep, each of the three women lying in the warm darkness of her own room"

(1). Echoing her mother's relationship to flowers discussed previously, Cate's character and fascination with flowers is a vital focus for the establishment of intergenerational connections between females. Cate remembers her grandmother's yellow roses as she gazes at the yellow roses that she has put on the table of her own London apartment. The tactile quality of the rose petals, and the vibrant warm colour they exude, poignantly establish narrative and matrilineal links between Cate, the granddaughter who lives in London, and Grandmother Kate and her Irish garden with the yellow roses. Such motifs underpin the novel's examination of the mother-daughter relationship through intergenerational continuity.[8]

Evoking the Demeter-Persephone myth of enduring mother-daughter love discussed earlier, these representations conjure a feminine realm of fertility, creativity, and wisdom, which implicitly challenges the death and destruction caused by sectarian conflicts among males and patriarchal authority, and emphasizes the importance of female continuity and relationships across the generations. However, Cate's character also forms the focal point for many of the novel's representations of mother-daughter conflicts. Nonetheless, as Fogarty explains, such mother-daughter conflicts can also become the very measure by which female identities are reconstituted: "The very turbulence of the mother-daughter bond becomes paradoxically the means by which feminine identity with all its painful intergenerational entanglements can be reimagined" (89). Commenting on historical representations of motherhood, Paulina Palmer writes: "A number of novels, chiefly ones written in the 1970s, foreground the oppressive aspects of motherhood. They depict women's reproductive capacities as making them vulnerable to male control, and describe childbirth and the raising of children as painful, burdensome experiences" (95). The women's conflicts furthermore echo the troubled Northern Irish society in which the novel is set and the continuation of sectarian violence it represents.

The youngest sister, Sally, plays the most direct role in helping Emily to accept Cate's pregnancy. Protected by her mother during childhood, Sally has remained at the family home teaching in the local school. However, she shows her inner strength when she draws on her knowledge of Emily's estrangement from her own mother. Sally confronts Emily, and helps her to face up to and accept the reality of Cate's situation, preventing a history of maternal estrangement from repeating itself. Confronting their mother with the realization that Cate could have had an abortion in London without anyone's knowledge, Sally makes Emily realize that this baby is already a part of their family and must be welcomed; its existence cannot and should not be denied (123). Sally is determined to heal her family's fractures and, through that, ameliorate the negative effects of Emily's distant and cold relationship with her own mother. However, Sally is also aware of the negative dimensions of her role in the family dynamics, but she hides her resentment: "The long years of trying to please everyone had taken their toll. Concealing her true feelings if she knew they might cause pain or displeasure ... had become so natural to her that she now found it impossible to do otherwise" (135). Sally's reflection on her situation echoes Fogarty's point regarding Irish mother-daughter plots, which, she argues, portray "Daughterly dereliction and melancholia, and maternal neediness, oppression and longing [as] the twin but warring energies" (Fogarty 89). Through the portrayal of Sally's reflections and behaviour, Madden's novel demonstrates the emotional depth and complexity of female family relationships.

One by One in the Darkness suggests that the differences between the sisters represent their attempts to position themselves in differing ways in relation to the ideological and religious messages instilled in them at school: "Work hard, girls, because you have more to give society than you can perhaps realise. We need our Catholic doctors and nurses and university lecturers; our Catholic lawyers and civil servants" (60). This mixed educational message suggests the possibility of a self-determined future for young females with professional careers aspirations, as alternatives to the traditional domestic and maternal roles constructed by religious and social conventions. However, the message, and its emphasis on religion, also points to the enduring conflicts surrounding Catholicism in Northern Ireland and the negative influence of conservative discourses surrounding femininity and maternity. Although Fogarty's observation that "The figure of the mother also becomes associated with the trauma of a past that can neither be buried nor resolved" (86) is accurate to some extent, *One by One in the Darkness* emphasizes female difference through the nuanced complexities of the sisters and uses female solidarity across the generations as a counter-discourse to the violent male-dominated society underpinned by religious tradition and political strife. Madden's novel suggests that the representation of these conflicts is essential to avoiding an idealized portrayal of motherhood and mother-daughter relations (Fogarty 113). The depiction of the three sisters and their mother enjoying the "warm, half-spoken intimacy" (177) of their evening together at the end of the novel strengthens this interpretation. The characters' sharing of stories and memories consolidates mother-daughter bonds and draws attention to the problems caused by painful family legacies and the stigma of unmarried motherhood in a strict Northern Irish Catholic religious setting.

CONCLUSION: THE "HALF-SPOKEN INTIMACY" OF MOTHER-DAUGHTER RELATIONS

My reading of Madden's representations of the mother-daughter relationship in *One by One in the Darkness* has focused on the depiction of the domestic and emotional lives of the novel's female characters. The book addresses gender-political issues relating to the construction of Irish identity and gives voice to specifically female experiences of sisterhood. Madden's narrative focus emphasizes Palmer's point about contemporary women's writing: "Mother-daughter involvements and their ambiguous pains and pleasures are ... a focus of immense interest" (112) and "this makes a welcome contrast to the neglect they have suffered in the past" (112). Pelan has commented on the problem of marginalized female experiences and perspectives and how these issues have affected Northern Irish women's writing and feminism: "it has always been more difficult in Northern Ireland than in the Irish Republic to discuss women's lives, their politics, or their cultural practices as distinct from the broader politics of Northern Ireland" (53). Commenting on Madden's novel, Long states that "In their own individual and intimately personal ways, each of the central characters ... experiences a crisis of identity and of self-representation"

(2). Ingman's assessment reflects this view: "The four women's dreams and visions, expressing more than they can articulate in language, register a subconscious protest against the constraints of the political circumstances in which they are trapped" (*Irish Women's Fiction* 217). Examining the issue of identity in Madden's work, Margarita-Saà states the following: "Loneliness, death, politics, the family, religion and art are themes that Deirdre Madden has tried to come to terms with in her work, and her characters have to wrestle with such transcendental issues" (50). Through positing a crisis of a personal and familial nature centred on the issue of motherhood, Madden's novel draws attention to the multiple meanings of individual and collective conflict. In Madden's novel, despite their close mental and physical connection, each of the Quinn sisters must make separate life choices that involve reassessing their relationship to one another and their mother; they must confront the ambivalent maternal legacy associated with the symbolic figure of Mother Ireland. Through its nuanced structure of interwoven narrative strands, *One by One in the Darkness* explores a conflicted contemporary Northern Irish society, but insists on the centrality and continuity of female familial bonds in the face of sectarian violence through the novel's central vision of the mother-daughter relationship.

ENDNOTES

[1]The quotation in the title of this essay is from Madden 7.
[2]My references to Irishness and Irish identity in this essay are inclusive. When referring to the specific region that forms the setting in Madden's novel, I use the term "Northern Irish," whereas "Irish" is the term I use to discuss identity more generally.
[3]Ingman also examines this topic in *Irish Women's Fiction* 215.
[4]Fogarty also discusses the figure of Mother Ireland in relation to a number of Irish women writers' work, including Madden.
[5]I also discuss food and the mother-daughter relationship in Beyer, "Dolls and Dead Babies."
[6]Furthermore, food in Irish women's writing frequently has negative or problematic connotations when portrayed in light of the mother-daughter relationship, according to Chang (55).

[7]Hogan, however, does not specify *One by One in the Darkness* as a representation of the Demeter-Persephone myth.
[8]I have also discussed intergenerational relations between females in Beyer "'My Mama Had a Story.'"

WORKS CITED

Beyer, Charlotte. "Dolls and Dead Babies: Victorian Motherhood in May Sinclair's *Life and Death of Harriett Frean*." *May Sinclair: Re-Thinking Bodies and Minds*, edited by Rebecca Bowler and Claire Drewery, Edinburgh University Press, 2016, pp. 156-76.

Beyer, Charlotte. "'My Mama Had a Story': Mothers and Intergenerational Relations in Andrea Levy's Fiction." *Reading/Speaking/Writing the Mother Text: Essays on Caribbean Women's Writing*, edited by Cristina Herrera and Paula Sanmartin, Demeter Press, 2016, pp. 121-42.

Bloy, Marjie. "The Irish Famine: 1845-9." *The Victorian Web: Literature, History and Culture in the Age of Victoria*, www.victorianweb.org/history/famine.html. Accessed 29 Sept.2015.

Chang, Ann-Wan-li. "Daughters on Hunger Strike: The Irish Mother-Daughter Resistance Plot in the Stories of Edna O'Brien, Mary Lavin, Éilís Ní Dhuibhne and Mary Leland." *Estudios Irlandeses*, no.3, 2008, pp. 54-64.

Clarke, Linda. "Mother Ireland. . . The Myth." Paper given at Literature & Psychoanalysis in Dialogue, 9 November 2013. ICLO-NLS—Irish Circle of the Lacanian Orientation, www.iclo-nls.org/wp-content/uploads/Pdf/Mother%20Ireland%20%E2%80%A6The%20, *Myth*.pdf. Accessed 29 Sept. 2015.

Crilly, Anne, director. *Mother Ireland*. Produced by Crilly Anne et al. Channel 4, 1991. www.youtube.com/watch?v=3glM5PYoB7s. Accessed 30 Sept. 2015.

Coughlan, Patricia. "Introduction." *Irish Literature: Feminist Perspectives*, edited by Patricia Coughlan and Tina O'Toole, Carysfort Press, 2008, pp. 1-17.

Estévez-Saà, Margarita. "Deirdre Madden's Portrait of the Woman Artist in Fiction: Beyond Ireland and the Self." *Nordic Irish Studies*, no. 10, 2011, pp. 49-62.

Fogarty, Anne. "'The Horror of the Unlived Life': Mother-Daughter

Relationships in Contemporary Irish Women's Fiction." *Writing Mothers and Daughters: Renegotiating the Mother in Western European Narratives by Women*, edited by Adalgisa Giorgio, Berghahn Books, 2002, pp. 85-118.

Hogan, Bridget. "Is the Mother Re-Visioned in Contemporary Irish Women's Literary Fiction?" Dissertation, University of Limerick, 2013, ulir.ul.ie/handle/10344/3256. Accessed 29 Sept. 2015.

Ingman, Heather. *Irish Women's Fiction: From Edgeworth to Enright*. Irish Academic Press, 2013.

Ingman, Heather. *A History of the Irish Short Story*. Cambridge University Press, 2011.

Long, Rebecca. "'Around the Sky': The Memory of Trauma in Deirdre Madden's *One by One in the Darkness*." *Limina: A Journal of Historical and Cultural Studies*, vol. 20, no.1, June 2014, pp. 1-16.

Lupton, Deborah. *Food, the Body and the Self*. Sage, 1996.

Madden, Deirdre. *One by One in the Darkness*. Faber & Faber, 2013.

Palmer, Paulina. *Contemporary Women's Fiction: Narrative Practice and Feminist Theory*. Harvester Wheatsheaf, 1989.

Pelan, Rebecca. *Two Irelands: Literary Feminisms North and South*. Syracuse University Press, 2005.

About the Contributors

Charlotte Beyer is senior lecturer in English Studies at the University of Gloucestershire. She is currently co-editing two books for Demeter Press, *Mothers Without Their Children* and *Travellin' Mama: Mothers, Mothering, and Travel.* Charlotte's forthcoming crime fiction publications include *Teaching Crime Fiction*, which she is editing for Palgrave, and the 2017 special issue on contemporary crime fiction, which she is editing for the journal *American, British and Canadian Studies.* She is on the Steering Committee for the Crime Studies Network and on the editorial board for *American, British and Canadian Studies* and *Feminist Encounters.*

Mary Bronstein is an educator, filmmaker, rogue feminist scholar and mother based in Brooklyn. Recent works include feminist analyses of *The Babysitters Club* series (Lexington) and *The Lonely Doll* series (McFarland), original philosophical theory on mothers and daughters (Demeter) and original theory on the connection between children's toys and rape culture (Demeter). Her film work includes the award-winning and internationally shown *Yeast* (2008). In 2015, Mary founded Urban Girl Scouts, a radical feminist scouting program for young city girls, and in 2016 she co-founded Kid Code, a progressive sex and menstruation education program for both girls and boys.

Cheryl Chaffin is a muse (to herself and perhaps to others), a parent, a lover, and sometimes (when circumstances demand) a fighter. She teaches composition, literature, and creative writing at Cabrillo College in Santa Cruz, California. She has published essays, poetry, and academic articles. Currently, she is completing a memoir about writing and writers. Her favourite thing is to travel and, after that, to take long hikes, sleep in, and fold laundry. Seriously, she likes to do domestic things with her hands—cook, garden, clean. She has ardently returned to daily meditation and reading *The New York Times* since the 2016 election.

Lidiane Cunha holds a PhD in comparative literature from the University of Alberta. She is currently a research associate at Concordia University's Simone de Beauvoir Institute and a Visiting Professor at the Department of English at the University of Ottawa. Her dissertation examined twentieth-century Canadian and Brazilian fiction centred on the lives of women artists and their experience as mothers. Cunha's research interest includes the literary representation of women artists, and mothers; the feminist debate on maternal experience and practice; and the discourses of motherhood in Canada and Brazil.

Charlotte Henay is a mother, teacher, writer, academic, and storyteller of multiracial ancestry. She has a background in critical race theory, education administration, and teaching. She has been an administrator and consultant in First Nations, mainstream, and international education contexts. She is currently a PhD candidate at York University in Comparative Perspectives and Cultural Boundaries. She works to counter extinction myths through storywork, Indigenous methodologies, and remembering. Charlotte writes about cultural memory, and grandmothers' gardens, as an activist for Afro-Indigenous futurities.

Cristina Herrera holds a PhD in English from Claremont Graduate University and is associate professor of Chicano and Latin American studies at California State University, Fresno. She is author of the 2014 study, *Contemporary Chicana Literature: (Re) Writing the Maternal Script* and has published in journals such as *Chicana/Latina Studies*, *Journal of Caribbean Literatures*, and *Food, Culture & Society*, among others.

Laurie Kruk teaches at Nipissing University. She has *published The Voice is the Story: Conversations with Canadian Writers of Short Fiction* (Mosaic, 2003) and *Double-Voicing the Canadian Short Story* (Ottawa University Press, 2016). She is also the author of three poetry collections: *Theories of the World* (1992), *Loving the Alien* (2006) and *My Mother Did Not Tell Stories* (2012).

Dannabang Kuwabong is a professor in the English Department, University of Puerto Rico, Rio Piedras Campus, San Juan. His work has appeared in several journals, including the *Journal of the Motherhood Initiative for Research and Community*; *Canadian Woman Studies les cahiers des la femme*; *ARIEL: A Review of Internal English Literature*; *La Torre*; *Sargasso*, and *The Caribbean Writer*. He is the co-author of *Myth Performance in the African Diaspora: Ritual, Theater, Dance* (2014) and author of four anthologies of poetry: *Visions of Venom* (1995); *Echoes from Dusty Rivers* (1999); *Caribbean Blues & Love's Genealogy* (2008); *Voices from Kibuli Country* (2013).

Janet MacLennan is a professor of communication studies in the Department of English (Humanities) of the University of Puerto Rico Río Piedras. She has published in a variety of communication books and journals on a range of communication-related topics. Her current focus is on human beings as storytelling beings, particularly in the context of the medical humanities. And so she enjoys bringing this narrative perspective to her co-editing of *Mothers and Daughters* and *Travellin' Mama*, both with Demeter.

Renee Norman, PhD, is a prize-winning poet, writer, and retired educator. She received the Canadian Association for Curriculum Studies Distinguished Dissertation Award for *House of Mirrors*, published in 2001 (Peter Lang). Her poetry book, *True Confessions*, (Inanna) was awarded the Helen and Stan Vine Canadian Jewish Book Award for poetry in 2006. She is also the author of two other books of poetry: *Backhand through the Mother* and *Martha in the Mirror* (Inanna). A fourth co-authored book of poetry, *Hearing Echoes* (Inanna), co-authored with Carl Leggo, was published in 2016. Previously, she worked as a classroom teacher, university professor, and school board consultant. She is the mother of three daughters.

Priya Parrotta Natarajan is a writer and singer committed to fostering empathy, curiosity, and responsibility across geopolitical divides in the interest of our shared, brilliant planet. She is the author of *The Politics of Coex istence in the Atlantic World*, which brings light to what is arguably the Caribbean's greatest gift to the world: centuries of experience in living together. Her current project is titled "Music & the Earth."

Donna Sharkey holds a PhD in international education. She was a professor at the State University of New York with research interests in education, gender, violence, and resilience. Currently, she is writing creative nonfiction. She is the mother of two daughters, Renata, her youngest, and Alessandra, who died one year ago.

Alma Simounet-Bey has been a professor of English and linguistics at the Department of English of the College of Humanities, University of Puerto Rico, Río Piedras Campus since 1968. At present, she is the director of the department. She carries out research in ethnolinguistics, bilingualism, language, and identity, and discourse analysis.

Dorsía Smith Silva is an associate professor of English at the University of Puerto Rico, Río Piedras. She is the co-editor of *Caribbean without Borders: Caribbean Literature, Language, and Culture* (2008), *Critical Perspectives on Caribbean Literature and Culture* (2010), and *Critical and Feminist Perspectives on Caribbean Mothering* (2013), and editor of *Latina/Chicana Mothering* (2011). She is currently co-editing two books: *Travelin' Mama: Mothers, Mothering and Travel* and *Mothers, Mothering, and Globalization*. In addition, she has published articles in the *Journal of Caribbean Literature*, *Journal of the Association for Research on Mothering*, and *Sargasso*, and her poetry has appeared in *POUI: Cave Hill Journal of Creative Writing*.

Batya Weinbaum teaches English, folklore, and world, women's and American literature at American Public University, where she has worked since 2013 online, as well as Western Literature at Life University in Marietta, GA. She got her doctorate at University of Massachusetts at Amherst in the Department of English. *Islands of Women and Amazons: Representations and Realities,* her fieldwork cultural studies dissertation about Isla Mujeres, Mexico, was originally published by University of Texas Press. A new, expanded second edition has just become available on Smashwords She offers writing workshops on Isla every January and edits the journal Femspec, an interdisciplinary cross-over journal dedicated to the challenge of gender through speculative means now in its twentieth years. She has won awards and prizes for her fiction, poetry, lifetime accomplishments and teaching. Her most recent art show was at the Center of the Arts, in Floyd, VA. She has published in numerous journals and anthologies, as well as several critical and creative books.